I0050532

HOW IT WORK$
AND WHY IT DOE$N'T

HOW IT WORK$
AND WHY IT DOE$N'T

In 2008, Gunther Grant became a publicly traded company.

The next 16 years has been compressed into these 308 pages as to what could have easily been 2,500 pages or more spanning a lifetime of issues and situations that happened between many of the events I've written about in this guide. If SERIOUS changes were not made, this guide would never have been written and I would have ended up falling to the same fate many CEO's have succumbed to.

I call this a guide because it is written to guide the reader, not entertain them and may warrant follow-up guides and books.

Most business, financial or stock trading books tell you what you need to do to succeed and if that were true, we would all be millionaires. Proof all that mumbo jumbo does not work.

Copyright © 2025 by Grant Newsteder All rights reserved.

No part of this publication may be reproduced, distributed, or transmitted in any form or by any means, including photocopying, recording, or other electronic or mechanical methods, without the prior written permission of the publisher, except as permitted by U.S. copyright law. For permission requests, contact Grant Newsteder.

ISBN Paperback: 979-8-9986244-0-7

This book is dedicated to the

100,000,000+ investors who lose in total about

$300,000,000

Every trading day on penny stocks

And to the million$ spent each day by people paying fees believing they will get some sort of funding, grant, loan, angel or venture capital investment that never materializes.

For the idea person, business owner or investor, this may be the best $34.99 you ever spend in your entire life!

Before you start a business or even consider looking for capital to fund your ideas or to expand an existing business, this guide will show you why most fail.

Before you or someone you know *"again"* spends and loses any part of the $300,000,000 lost to investors *each day* on those so-called EXCITING penny stocks, invest in this guide. It will show how to avoid mounting losses and why that always keeps happening.

If you are reading this page, having taken interest, you have just made a huge life decision for the better! Most of what you read in this book will never be forgotten and also constantly be remembered your entire life as you move from an idea person to a business owner to an investor or CEO of a public company.

If you or anyone you know believes starting a business, taking their company public or investing in those so-called HOT penny stocks will make you or them rich...guess again.

Read page 7

If you want to take your company public or someone you know invests in penny stocks, read this first.

Millions of investors buy billions of dollars worth of shares in 1,000's of hot PUMPED **penny stock** tickers. *That is a fact.*

Companies "*SAY*" they need the money to put their exciting plan into action and you can easily see $20,000,000+ in shares sold on many of those individual penny stock tickers. *(The pump)*

But the *financial data* shows many tickers have **NONE of the MONEY** investor's thought went to the company when they invested.

WHY? Because most shares investors buy from brokers do **NOT** come from the company and the money **NEVER GOES** to the company. That means you are **NOT** investing in the company. *Another fact.*

So when is investors **MONEY** going to get to the company to make the HOT new plan work so the share price rises and it benefits shareholders? **NEVER!**

If the shares investors buy from their brokers do not come from the company, where did the shares come from?

3rd party "debt investors" who are in on the scheme will pay some of the public company debt in exchange for shares at a *fraction* of the market price. Those shares are **NO longer owned** by the company and are resold to brokers CHEAP to deliver to investors accounts.

Because the schemes plan was for the company to only sell billions of shares cheap, the broker's that *oversold* shares short at the higher price, *purchase* the **USED non-company** owned shares from the 3rd party debt investors for a fraction of what brokers sold the shares for.

Brokers deliver the oversold shares to investors for much less than what investors paid so **NO investor** can sell at a profit. *(The lock out)*

The *float rises and the share price falls* as the endless amount of shorted 3rd party debt shares are diluted into the market. *(The dump)*

Everyone makes money except the investors that lose all their money that never even went to the company they invested in. This is the reality of how this works and why it doesn't. *Or is it?*

This guide will explain what you will have to deal with if you decide to start a business, be a publicly traded company *(Like I became)* or if you invest in penny stocks known as the pink sheets or OTC Markets.

Most will find this guide informative and some may take offense, but the fact is, this is the way it is and it's not what you may have anticipated or believe even exists in the marketplace, but it does.

If you want to start a business, be prepared to lose all your money and if you own a small semi-successful business that wants to expand, be careful when looking for a financial partner. And anyone seeing your potential may end up your competitor or try to destroy what you accomplished by pretending they want to help you.

Most will want you to fail and some will try and weasel their way into your operations to cause damage and if they fail, they slither back for another chance only to try and destroy you again. Don't trust anyone!

They say to err is human, to forgive divine? Bullshit! Its, fool me once shame on you, fool me twice shame on me.

Turn your back on those you forgive and when you're not looking they will stick the knife in again and mumble, *"this time will finish him off"*

Every morning when you wake up you will only be able to count on one hand's 5 fingers the people you trust and 3 of them will be, *"Me" "Myself" and "I,"* and the other 2 you better make damn sure you know who they are. I am not angry, I am pissed and that means I am taking action, not revenge, fixing, not giving up, forgetting not forgiving, correcting things my own way and ignoring everyone else.

Many professionals say people need to listen to others in order to make changes for the better and by not doing so, you will fail.

I tried that many times only to find they made things worse. What I did learn from all those so-called professionals is: Most have NO clue what they are doing and if they did, why is it they have not succeeded?

A guy in NJ used to make videos on how to win the lottery and he made millions selling the tapes. I bought one and his opening statement was: The reason why he never won the lottery using his own method is because he does not believe in gambling. *HOW CONVENIENT.*

If you can get past the hurdles in this guide, you will emerge smarter and seasoned as to how this works and why it doesn't.

I'm going to show and warn you what **NOT** to do and what to avoid so you don't end up beaten, bruised, broke, in jail or the morgue.

If you become a publicly traded company like I did, schemers will try to acquire your public stock ticker. If you reject them, they will work to destroy your share price and company by any means possible.

Schemers lie to investors they can make the shares rally up and make things better if they all pressure the CEO to quit and turn over the company to the scheme. If that happens, the investors will end up having their shares cancelled with no compensation, as the scheme is reverse merged to a new diluted Pump and Dump stock ticker.

You will need to become numb to fear and threats of violence; Laugh at social media when schemers post insults towards your family and friends to get you to react irrationally to distract you so you give up from the negative pressure of being an emotional punching bag.

Lizards (You will read about them as well) will do and say whatever they can to get hold of your company and it will all be lies and insults.

When you walk out of your house, you will wonder if your hair is a mess and look half dressed at 6am going to 7-11 just to get milk for breakfast knowing someone may be watching so they can post your image on line with the caption, THE SLOB LOSER CROOK CEO.

You will be introduced to 1,000's of people who all want to be your new best friend who all pretend to want to help you (not financially) with one goal...to take or destroy what you have.

And they all have the knife hidden up their sleeves.

When you are done reading this, you will remember it forever and often encounter events you read about and how to avoid them.

If you want to start a business or if you invest in those hot topic penny stocks or you want to take your company public, it will be you against everyone and you won't know what is real or what is fake, what is true and what are lies. And you will not know whom to trust. **You may end up not even being able to trust yourself.**

LEARN SOME TERMINOLOGY BEFORE MOVING AHEAD

- *Pump and Dump (P&D):* is used to describe various public companies that pump news so they can dump shares that always decline in price and dilute the shares in the market.
- *Pumper:* Someone that is hired to pump and excite investors
- *Scheme:* is anything associated with questionable activity. A pump and dumps scheme, a financial lending scheme etc.
- *Schemers:* Individuals that are the ones running the scheme.
- *Asked price:* the price you have to pay to buy shares in a company from your broker.
- *Bid price:* the price your broker pays you if you want to sell.
- *Spread:* is the commissions made by the market makers equal to the difference between the bid and asked price. Bid $.01 asked $.015, market makers make the spread $.005.
- *Market Maker(s) (MM's)* set the price of shares based on how many sell and how many are bought. The more sold on the bid the lower the share price, the more that are bought on the asked, the higher the share price (But beware of deceit)
- *Liquidity:* means lots of shares are trading
- *Dilution:* means lots of shares are being added to the float
- *Float:* the number of shares that are available to trade.
- *BOD*: (Board of Directors)
- *99%:* Naive investors who buy into scheme scam stocks
- *Stock Ticker:* the letters associated with a public company. My publicly traded company "Gunther Grant" ticker is *GNGR*.
- *Public Vehicle:* the ticker only (Not the company)
- *Forward stock split:* when a company multiplies their shares
- *Reverse stock split:* when a company reduces their shares
- *Debt Investor*: a private individual who buys shares from the company cheap. Once purchased, they are no longer owned by the company. *(Read page 7 again)*
- *Shell or blank check Co:* A public company that has NOTHING
- *SPAC*-Special Purpose Acquisition Company, Same as a *shell*
- *Short squeeze:* When brokers that oversold shorted shares are forced to buy them back for more then they sold them for.
- *Naked shorted shares:* Shares sold to investors that don't exist but can trade as if they do exist. AKA, Phantom Shares.

CHAPTER PAGE

ANYONE CAN BE THE BEST AT SOMETHING

Someone has to be the best waiter, doctor, pilot, and chess player and be the best CEO. Some can be the best at investing while most are not and some are also the best stock scammer, scam lender or market manipulator. Good or bad, someone has to be the best at something.

Many believe being the best at something will allow that to translate into becoming a financial success, that's true and false and depends on many factors including what path you take and how you execute your plan and more importantly will you get funding or investors.

If a medical doctor sells shares and tells people if they invest in **MD-Doctor, Inc** the share value will rise when they perform profitable surgery, will not work with lenders or investors.

If the same doctor invents a device to help with a surgical procedure that can save lives and the Dr. takes that company public and tells investors the company could sell 100,000 of the devices for $2,000 for sales of $200,000,000, they would easily be able to sell shares of stock because people would not be investing in the doctor but in the shares they anticipate would rise in value based on that inventions sales.

To become a huge success you don't have to be a doctor or even educated to stumble onto an idea that can be so well received in the marketplace that creates wealth beyond your dreams. Age 9 or 90, there is still time, not as much as we think but don't give up yet!

Harland Sanders of Kentucky Fried Chicken did not make millions until he was 74 years old and Judge Judy first aired on TV when she was 54.

Richard Branson quit school at age 16, Henry Ford had no education and even the Wright Brothers never went to high school just to name a few. Non-professional visionaries that created and innovated, that became *wealthier than most educated professionals.*

When I took the risk in life with only my GED and made it to CEO of a publically traded company, proves it is possible but does not happen overnight or even happens on the first try when starting out in business. *Changes must be made.*

It is the uneducated risk takers that faced failure or great success. Those that failed had to go back to the daily blue collar grind while those that did not fail ended up in the pages of FORBES magazine of world's richest people. You do **NOT** need an education or college degree to succeed. Anyone at any age can achieve great success.

Investors also want to be the best at investing like a financial wizard and make millions buying cheap penny stocks on the OTC (Pink sheets) and you don't need a college degree or a GED. Most who believe using stock charts, tips and news releases when investing will give them an investment edge to success are 100% **WRONG!**

If all that were true, everyone would be a millionaire.

Same with reading all the data about starting a business or being public, words vs. reality are worlds apart.

Looks good on paper, failure in reality.

If you want to start a business or take your business to the next level and become publicly traded or you invest in penny stocks, make sure you have a back up plan that includes having to make serious changes along the way and also be prepared to lose all your money.

This guide will show you what to expect from the business environment, capital markets and as a CEO or investor. This guide will also warn and redirect you to avoid the FAKE DETOUR signs set up in your path that lead you right over the cliff.

Do not panic react when you think you have nothing left but chance. That is when the status quo kicks your ass to the curb.

Also keep in mind, I have severe Dyslexia so you may find grammatical errors but I had this guide edited as best as possible.

If you know someone who is great at something that wants to achieve success in business or as a public company, or who invests in penny stocks, this guide will save them lots of money and a world of hurt before they decide to do either.

BUSINESS OWNER OR INVESTOR

As an entrepreneur

You may have already figured how to incorporate and set up a home-based business. And like many business owners the dream of taking your company public. If you need help, email me.

And of course friends and family are saying what a great idea! But I hate to tell you they are just being nice and will be the last people to ever invest in your idea (Well maybe a little) so don't let others false excitement and support lead you to costly and confrontational decisions.

Prepare for the real data not the BS you read on the Internet. And do **NOT** give any of those so-called professionals or lenders your money (Especially up-front fees) thinking they can help. *They cannot!*

As an investor

If you invest in penny stocks on the OTC markets (the pink sheets), aren't you frustrated every time you buy a specific ticker that almost immediately it drops in price and keeps falling day after day?

Are you one of most who sees all or mostly **RED** in their accounts wondering and frustrated why the HELL won't even ONE of those damn tickers rise in value? This guide will also explain why and how that *always* happens. *(Read page 7 again)*

It may depress the hell out of you and also open your eyes.

If you do manage to take your company public like I did, or you invest in these penny stock schemes, the shares in your company or the shares in your trading account will likely always end up in the **RED.**

If you do own a small successful business, that success on a small scale can also lead to costly decisions that fail to achieve the same success in larger markets. If you are making money on a small scale, hold onto that success before making the jump to big business.

If you are one of the millions who think they have the winning idea and believe it will be a huge success if it becomes a reality, most others will not think the same way and ignore your pleas for capital.

SMALL TO BIG BUSINESS TRANSITION

You can have the best product that's been proven on a small scale, but to move that to the mainstream will be a process that can end up in total failure. You can be the BEST at something and still fail.

A small business like custom made wallets that sell for $25 that cost $5 to make; the belief is that since you sold 100 wallets for $2,500 at craft fairs you can sell 1,000,000 nationally for $25,000,000. Seems logical but you need $5,000,000 to fund production.

And getting national sales requires supplies and payment terms before you get paid and that is IF your wallets all sell out. Usually the dream is to get into BIG BOX stores but that is not as easy as selling at a booth at your local craft fair. And where do you get $5,000,000?

Everyone dreams of selling to the big box stores. You see the entrepreneurs on Shark Tank saying that is the goal. I *DID* achieve that goal with one store at a time growth while others want the entire chain of stores, only to realize they cannot deliver.

When you see Shark Tank contestants ask for $100,000 to get into all COSTCO locations, the reality is they need million$. And what you proved is a winner with small-scale sales may not succeed in the national market place. So, you need $5,000,000 and no one will invest. And if you prove you can succeed over 10 years slowly, smaller investors won't want to wait that long and still won't invest.

If I recall, a woman made handcrafted potholders she sold successfully at local craft shows and made a deal with Sam's Club that if they don't sell she will take them back.

That is called "guarantee the sale". That means if they don't sell, you will not get paid and have to take back the inventory.

She (Like others) was so sure her successes on a small craft show scale would translate to national sales that she mortgaged her house and cashed in her retirement savings to produce the potholders.

After a month with no sales, they were all returned to her and she blamed Sam's for her losing her house and savings.

Her logic was since they sold well at craft shows, they would also sell nationally so it can't possibly be her fault they did not sell.

High priced craft show impulse items cannot compete with cheap foreign machine made potholders. Craft show YES, big box NO!

It's like being the small town high school football hero and tossed into the NFL where they are quickly annihilated.

Business owner or investor, be careful wanting too much too fast. My products in the big box stores (further on in this guide) were because we took no chances with too much too soon and focused on one store at a time and also because we could not get funding to expand faster.

Notice I said we WERE? (I'll get to that) and why change is GOOD!

People become desperate to achieve financial goals and in most cases they are older and do not want to wait 10 years to see results. Most will panic wanting too much too fast and Investors know going from small to big business FAST rarely ever works.

Many believe their idea is so great, investors will throw money their way and most spend years trying to find capital (with no luck) so more time wasted when they would have been more productive starting small.

When investors are told the plan also involves taking the company public, they know that rarely, if ever, works out that way. Many investors or investment groups have seen how taking a company public offers NO benefit to investors or shareholders.

Most investors know the issues facing companies that do manage to go public that are not aware of the struggles after being public that more often than not, destroys the very business that went public.

And reduces any chance of investors getting back their investment.

Telling people you would like to take your company or idea public in order to raise capital is actually a deterrent to investors who know much of what you will soon read about.

Let's move ahead with what most start-ups dream of.

Becoming a publicly traded company.

SO YOU WANT TO BE PUBLICLY TRADING

Everyone sees what being public can do for a company or the benefits of investing in them. Most of the wealth attributed to the world's richest people is because they are publicly traded and own shares in their company. If TESLA, Amazon, Microsoft, Facebook, Berkshire Hathaway and many other companies were not publicly traded, those CEO's personal wealth would be far less and drop them from the list of world's richest people.

It's ALL about the shares of stock and at what price.

You could be worth billions on paper with cash net worth of only $1,000,000. *It's all about the stock*. If you were not public you would drop from being a billionaire to a measly millionaire.

For example, a CEO of a private company that does $2,000,000 in sales before costs, labor and overhead who takes a $100,000 annual salary could have a personal net worth of $1,000,000.

Taking that company public with a share price of just $1.00, that same CEO that issued themselves 500,000,000 shares would have a new worth of $500 million. Wealth on paper they call it.

If that CEO sells company shares to raise capital to expand to $20,000,000 in sales and the stock jumps to $20 per share, that CEO would be worth $10 billion (on paper) and be listed in FORBES richest people. Seems all too easy, so close yet so far.

Most companies stay clear of being public for many reasons but you can see how *shares, not cash, make wealth. Remember that!*

You can make mega bucks going public or make mega bucks investing in those start-ups, but that is not as common or as easy as some think.

Those who say it is so EASY, comes with a price.

If you plan on taking your company pubic like I did, you will be up against competing questionable pump and dump companies that use false or questionable exciting hyped data they know investors want to hear that render your company invisible to the investment community.

And invisible you will be.

To see how this works, (before it doesn't):

Let's start with being a publicly traded company because many who own businesses want to become public and investors can't buy public shares unless the company is public first.

If you Google, "Why take your company public" this is what you find.

*To raise capital and **potentially** broaden opportunities for future access to capital. To increase liquidity for a company's stock, which **may** allow owners and employees to sell stock more easily. To **possibly** acquire other businesses with the public company's stock.*

Potentially, may and possibly** means you **WON'T!

Whoever wrote that is a lawyer or service that says they can help so they can bill you $70,000 then another $250,000 to take your company public so they can screw you and buy the public vehicle later on for $5,000 and convert it to a pump and dump scheme. If you take your company public like I did, you end up with **2 parts** that remain separate from each other.

(Part 1) Is a private company that is **not public**.

(Part 2) Is the public entity (Stock ticker) also known as **the vehicle.**

To be publicly trading and issued a stock ticker, you have to first file with regulators and show your private company is valid and operational with no SEC issues and is not a shell or INTENT scheme.

There are approximately 32,000,000 small and 21,000,000 large businesses in the USA and many of them had planned to go public but never made it. With only approximately 12,500 OTC listed tickers, you can see how the millions of people who dream of being public never make it past the dream, and many who do go public end up in a nightmare.

Some have raised money from family, friends, neighbors, or money they have saved and everyone will be excited to know you may be public and they have gotten in on the ground floor of a great opportunity not knowing the truth of what will happen soon after being public.

What happens is, the valid operational company that was approved to be public is not exciting to investors and after being public and obtaining a ticker, the CEO soon finds out...

NO ONE will want your stock. Meaning No capital, not being able to sell shares and not being able to use shares to acquire assets. NOTHING! And I mean a big FAT ZERO except a falling share price.

The jump from being a private company into being a publicly traded company is not as difficult as it may seem. In fact, it's quite easy to do! If you do the filings yourself and understand what needs to be done, you can be publicly traded quickly.

The fine line between being an idea person or a successful private company to being publicly traded is a line easily crossed but once you cross that line, the other side is not what you think it was going to be but far worse than you ever imagined.

Legitimacy is gone, morals are not welcome, rules don't matter, regulations are avoided and laws are for suckers.

The success for your public company will depend on many factors that differ greatly from the ones you had as a private company. You will be morally and legally tested to your very limits.

You may believe being public means you just have to sell shares for millions of dollars for expansion and to become a major public company like others have done, **NOPE! Ain't gonna happen.**

It is important to **ALSO** remember, **any shares bought** on the open market, the money does NOT go to you or your company. Since the company and CEO cannot sell shares directly, the only ones who benefit would be initial insiders who had them deposited during the public launch and even then the stock will likely drop below profitability.

You get none of the money when shares are sold and no one wants restricted company shares all while brokers short your stock.

If you take the same path I did and are so sure or you are told your idea or existing operational business will get crowd funding, venture capital, angel or institutional investors to help finance and expand your business, know one thing.

ANGEL, VENTURE AND INSTITUTIONAL INVESTORS ARE A MYTH

Most investors I met are Warren Buffett investor wannabes who have little or no capital. I found that Angel and Venture Capitalists have egos far bigger than their empty wallets.

Before I took my *profitable* company public, we needed $4,000,000 to finance $14,000,000 in purchase orders to expand on our established sales. The $250,000 we raised was far less than what was needed to pay for the production but it was more than enough to go public.

Since all data says, take your company public and you can access capital to expand, I decided to file to become a publicly traded company. Once public we would sell $4,000,000 in securities and have the capital we needed for the $14,000,000 order. *YEAH SURE!*

The investors and financial wannabes we met over the years tell you they can help as they blow smoke in your face from their fake $2 COHIBA cigar so they can feel superior and will never invest in your idea or company no matter how legit because *they have no money.*

I call them millionaires without money!

I found that most investors want to be like a Shark Tank millionaire but they don't have the money or intelligence to make it happen so they say NO to investing so people see them as smart, savvy and shrewd when, in fact, they have no money. And most I met are not that smart either. *Smart-asses yes, intelligent, not so much.*

Unlike a plan or goal that requires capital after being public to make it operational, my company had the facility, employees, equipment, sales and purchase orders already in hand *before becoming a public company.* We went public to expand further proving validity, having a factory, sales and proven results means *NOTHING! Even when being public. A big fat ZERO!*

Three men from a small investment group came to see our production in operation for our wholesale club location orders to prove we can fill more orders with their investment. While watching us, one of the investors said to the other.

"What fun to watch this dog and pony show" then they laughed.

Like we were a joke or they just did not have any money that I found was almost always the case so remember this:

If investor's (or lender's) mouths are moving, they are lying.

If you pay a service to have a business plan written who say they will also send it to investors to get you funded, use it to line your kitty litter box because that is all it will have use for.

And if you did meet one with even a little capital, they will want 90% of your company, vote you out and liquidate the assets. Many (including banks) will ask if you have equity in your home and use that as business collateral and when the plan fails, they take your home.

After what I went through, I combined the groups of Angel Investors, venture capitalists and Institutional Investors into one phrase.

"All Angel and venture capitalists should be institutionalized"

Most CEO's will search and find 100's of fancy ads that say they can get you funded only this time you have to **pay them a fee first. Don't!**

Investor websites, investor lists, access to capital etc. These are all the things scammers know you need to hear to get you to pay them a fee.

Scam lenders know you will **NEVER EVER** get funded on your own and they know you will have no option but to **panic** and just say why not try it once with false hope and no results. The scammers who say if you pay thousands in fees you will get funded with millions is similar to the pump and dump stocks that say invest very little and you will also make millions. **See how similar?**

One scam lender told me he has an investor who **only** invests in confection companies. When I said we no longer do confections we now do jewelry, he said, **"your in luck."** that same investor also loves Jewelry! A scam lender will lie and say anything to excite you to get you to pay the fees. **AMAZING!**

One scam lender said he had a $4,000,000 investor on the other phone (what a miracle! They had exactly the $4 million we needed) and all I had to do was **give him my credit card** so he can charge me $5,000 and than forward the call to me.

I said, how about you forward the call and if they invest $4,000,000 I'll give you $250,000, not $5,000.

They always say NO WAY! They don't work for FREE and I reply I don't pay money for nothing either. That's if you consider transferring a phone call actual work and because the person on hold is in on the scam and would still say no, and you're out $5,000.

So forget about loans, investors, crowd funding, Banks, Venture Capitalists, Angel Investors, institutional investors or anyone saying pay them money and they will get you funded. *They WON'T!*

I tried a web-based capital raise program and the ONLY ones that contacted me were 100s of marketing scams saying if I pay them a fee (I did NOT), they will get investors for me. *Another scam, no results.*

What I did find amusing is when I found investors who wanted 90% of my company for their investment; they said they are taking a huge risk on what will surely fail so they need to have more equity in the company to use as a tax write-off when it does fail.

When I agree, I tell them they *must also agree* to sell me back 80% (they get to keep 10%) for 4 times their investment since they are so sure we will fail. They always reply, "NO WAY" because what if the company becomes a huge success.

Predatory investors know if you're profitable and operational, the risk is greatly reduced but they still say it's a failure to get you to give up more of your business for their crappy little investment. And they will NEVER agree to sell you back any shares knowing it will likely succeed and they end up controlling the company.

If you become a public company, your company valuation is reliant on outside investors who buy penny stocks. The problem is, they won't know you even exist and even if they find your company, its not attractive or exciting so they will pass and the share price will suffer.

I call those sub penny investors… *The 99%* that make up the majority of those who buy cheap shares in publicly traded companies that offer outrageous claims of quick wealth and huge returns based on hype and intent, also known as pump and dump stocks.

WHO ARE THE NAIVE 99%

I use 99% to represent naive investors who buy Pump and Dump stocks that are cheap and high-risk hot topic schemes. The 99% BELIEVE they will turn a $100 investment into $1,000,000 and eventually cost average and keep buying more shares as the price declines.

The 10's of millions of the 99% spend and lose on average, $300,000,000 per day on those pump and dumps stocks. PER DAY!

The 99% rely on websites and hot tips and rarely look at actual data. The 99% do NOT buy stocks when the price goes UP; they buy more as the price goes DOWN and eventually lose all their money.

Most of the 99% are in that mental state of "shoulda, coulda, woulda." It's easy to look back at a winning stock like AMAZON at $2 per share that went to $3,400 and keep saying they should have invested but that's not helping them in any way.

Because the 99% have very little money to invest, the scammers say QUICK buy this stock (Cheap) before they **become** the next AMAZON implying the shares may go from $.01 to $3,400 in just a few months, not 20 years like Amazon's shares.

The 99% go into Lotto mode and figure it's not a huge risk "it's only $100 to buy 10,000 shares so may as well try" all while the shares continue to decline and the 99% keep buying more. If the shares DID do what the scheme claims as being just like Amazon, $3,400 x 10,000 shares would be worth **$34 MILLION DOLLARS!** Per $100 investment!

The 99% are mostly blue-collar workers or those who are too young and naive about investing or they are older and with no real savings or retirement capital. They can't risk much; just little bits each month set aside. Money that won't help their retirement needs and also won't hurt their hand-to-mouth living situation. It's a low cost gamble that never works but they feel they have to try.

The fact is, on average **$300 MILLION PER DAY** is spent by the 99% on stocks that cost between $.01 and $.000001 that never recover.

The issue is they can't stop investing for fear the ONE hot Pump and Dump will go from $.0001 to $5 and they make $5,000,000 on a $100 investment and make back ALL their losses and also a HUGE profit. If that were true, every one of the 99% would be a millionaire.

As for the so-called liquidity and dilution and why many say that's a good and bad thing, most still have no clue how this all works.

Why do the 99% want to have a large liquid position in a declining priced stock when the liquidity is achieved with lots of diluted shares added to the float that always drop in price and never rise up?

It seems the 99% ONLY want liquidity on billions of shares and a constant decline in share price so they can buy more shares for less and never be able to sell them at a profit. And they avoid a low float valid company stock that can also be liquid with a rising share price and be able to sell shares at a profit.

What the hell is wrong with the 99%?

When those P&D stocks tank, the angry chat room posts that follow when the phones and emails go unanswered, are posted publicly because there is no way to contact the CEO or anyone else associated with the company. Notice the pumpers are all gone as well? You can find them on other chat rooms pumping a new ticker.

I have seen the 99% go ballistic as they continue to lose more and more money on schemes that never do what they say. Some of the 99% also panic and try and find ways to make money by literally losing their minds. The more they lose, the crazier they become.

One investor told me they wanted to give me $10,000 cash (A bribe) but they wanted a board member position and be paid $80,000 annually plus a $25,000 sign-on bonus, offering no working help to GNGR. So he gives me $10,000, I hand him back $25,000 and an $80,000 a year salary and he does nothing! CRAZY PERSON!

A man came into my store and introduced himself as a major shareholder in my company (I did not know him). I spoke with him, showed him around the operations and products we make and plans moving forward. He started to tell me why everything I did was wrong and that he needs to come in and make changes and be put on payroll as a consultant.

I soon realized this guy was nuts. One of his ideas was to create the world's largest "how many jellybeans in a jar" contest that would bring attention to our business and offer a grand prize of $1,000,000 to the winner. Then he said that I tell him the answer in secrecy so he wins the $1,000,000 and he gives me back $500,000 under the table so we each make personally $500,000.

I thought he was kidding at first, but he wasn't. His idea was as nutty as someone telling me they will help me rob my own house and they get to keep half of what we steal.

When I did ask him what he invested he said $200. I was pissed and took $200 from the cash register and gave it to him and said GET THE FUCK OUT OF MY STORE. 4 hours wasted, half my day. The next day he came back saying he was wrong, he invested $400 hoping I'd give him another $200 from the cash register? Not a chance. **Lunatic!**

Most of the 99% Retail LOTTO investors really need to stay CLEAR of the stock market and seek therapy. Even when a company does perform and their investment goes up, they are never satisfied.

When investors buy $500 worth of shares at $.01 (50,000 shares) and the company does a 1/1,000 reverse split, you would own 50 shares valued at $10 per share (same $500) then **if** the company performs well, unlike most reverse splits, the shares rise UP to $200, you turned $500 into $10,000. Better than losing $500, RIGHT?

The reason that pisses off investors is they BELIEVE if the company did not do the reverse split the shares would have still risen to $200 making the pre-split 50,000 shares worth $10,000,000. They actually believe that and accuse the company of ripping them off $9,990,000. Like I said the 99% are never happy, EVER!

Investors are rarely pissed about their investment because most investments are $100 (more or less). They are pissed off about the DREAM returns of $10,000,000 they already had spent in their imagination. They accuse the CEO of screwing them out of $10,000,000 because they can't play pretend with just $100.

I guess it's why people who play lotto **never** say they hope they win $100,000 with 4 numbers and be happy about that, it's the jackpot or nothing. The 99% Pump and Dump investors think the same.

It's why some will spend $200 on a lotto that has a half a billion-dollar jackpot and spend only a few bucks when the jackpot is only $20,000,000. WHAT! $20,000,000 is not enough to risk $200?

The 99% usually won't invest in a $.01 wallet company stock knowing the stock can go to $.25 because it's not the LOTTO JACKPOT. Pump and Dump schemes know this and offer what most penny stock investors want, Low price shares and lotto jackpot dreams.

Lotto pays out a big cash prize if there is **one** winner and with each additional winner the jackpot is reduced and shared between winners. Pump and Dump companies are *worse*, they promise *everyone* a huge lotto jackpot win with questionable intent PR news and paid pumpers with the promise *EVERY investor will hit the jackpot* on a small investment, not just **one** winner like a lottery.

How can ANY rational intelligent investor actually believe if 1,000's are buying the same shares that they *all* will benefit a jackpot win like only ONE lotto winner does? And REMEMBER! None of the money investor's pay for shares goes to the company so they CAN'T make the company plan a reality. *Read page 7 AGAIN!*

So where does $300,000,000 per day come from and where does it go to? The OTC data looks like this.

Try and keep up with me if you can (these are approximate)

- There are about 12,500 OTC stock (tickers) listed on the OTC

- About $3 billion dollars are spent each day on OTC stock trades

- About 10 billion shares are traded each day on the OTC

About 90% (9 billion out of the 10 billion) shares traded each day are from 100 (More or less) of the 12,500 listed tickers under a penny.

Those 9 billion low priced shares equate to about $300 million out of the $3 billion sold each day. The following examples clearly show, as a fact, that P&D investors are responsible for over 90% of all shares traded each day on shares priced below $.01 and proves

The 99% retail investors want lots of shares cheap

Here are just **5 out of 12,500 listed tickers** that total over 1 billion shares. That's over **(10%) of the 10 billion sold in one day.** The total dollar amount for these 5 tickers is only $176,174 on shares priced between $.0005 and $.000001 (average share price, $.00014)

	PRICE	% CHANGE	$ VOL	SHARE VOL
MC	0.0001	0.00	44,401	419,710,928
LT	0.0005	+66.67	87,192	186,369,077
3S	0.00025	-16.67	29,839	145,072,247
T	0.000001	0.00	142	141,654,248
OA	0.0001	0.00	14,600	136,500,028

These are some of the tickers the 99% buy into with the hopes their $100 invested at $.0001 (1 million shares) can move to $1 and make them millions. **Never seen it happen YET!**

Notice most of the tickers % price change is at 0.00% or negative. That proves that no matter how many shares trade (Liquidity), retailers can never make money because the price never goes up and is kept that way by the brokers and debt diluters.

The lower the price, the more shares the 99% can buy that keeps the $300,000,000 flowing into those schemes EVERY DAY!

And a huge part of the problem is the 99% do not search out companies to invest in, they almost always follow a new HOT pumper or get some news release sent to their email that introduces them to some new scheme hot topic gold mine or marijuana stock.

So unless you change your wallet company to some NEW HOT scheme, there is a good chance no investors will find your ticker and even if they do, they will not invest if its boring wallets.

Schemers know taking over an existing ticker/vehicle and reverse merging it into a hot new scheme is what will attract the 99%. Lizards will troll the markets and the OTC to look for public companies with active tickers to try and buy them out or con the CEO out of their vehicle. Lizards know they CAN'T make money with out the vehicle and they know they would be denied a ticker filing to be public as a scheme.

THE ANGRY LIZARDS

After speaking with agency regulators and other CEO's about my options and to get some advice, they all mentioned the term LIZARDS who are field operatives used to find tickers to covert to Pump and Dump schemes for their bosses so I'll use that term Lizards here.

No matter what you do as a public company, the only ones who will pay attention to your company are *scam lenders and the lizards*. We spoke to 100's of hired scouts *(Lizards)* who seek out an OTC company to convert to a scheme Pump and Dump who want the public company vehicle *(part 2)* not the actual company (Part 1).

The lizards are only paid when they make a deal because they are independent people not legally linked with the TOP people who run the scheme. This allows the lizards to threaten curse and try and use lies and illegal tactics to get you to sell the public vehicle just so they can make a few bucks while the TOP people have clean hands.

The lizards are the desperate ones, if they don't find a ticker they don't eat. The real money people live in $50,000,000 homes with $20,000,000 yachts in the Caribbean. If the lizards can't make a deal, they panic while the top people are living the good life regardless.

The reason lizards get frustrated with someone that owns a valid public company *(Like mine, GNGR)* that does not want to participate or sell the public vehicle is: lizards are not used to being rejected.

Regulations make it harder for companies to file to go public and tickers like GNGR become harder to find when there are only 12,500 tickers listed with only a small percentage that are well structured and legitimate like GNGR is.

If GNGR was acquired, they can file that the GNGR ticker has NO past reverse merges, NO ticker changes and NO stock dilution or reverse stock splits. And GNGR is *not a shell or blank check company.*

With no issues, lizards can use *GNGR's GREAT vehicle* to quickly get a new ticker fast and reverse merge into a new Pump and Dump and avoid having to file to be public knowing they would be denied.

When I tell lizards that my shareholders have to benefit by any deal, they usually ignore that request because they do not want to take any existing holders to the Pump and Dump and they try and replace my request with the mention of money (money they don't have).

Again: Lizards want the **PART 2** (Our public vehicle and ticker only) so they can merge their scam company (Part 1) into the (Part 2) vehicle so they don't have to file to be public, knowing they would be denied.

All lizards will use the same words and phrases over and over like a broken record. They don't change their tactic, which just shows they are so sucked into the status quo. They think everyone has to play the same status quo game. *I did not! Here are two examples…*

Here is the communications with two lizards who did not know each other and how similar they are. Remember the term *"**UMBRELLA**."*

Also BEWARE when you read or hear these in communications.

- Lawyers advising you to go public on a *horrible idea or any idea.*
- What's up **BRO** or *Hey BUD* or *Hey DUDE.*
- **MY PEOPLE** (Let me talk to "MY PEOPLE" or "MY PARTNERS")
- We just want to buy your **public vehicle (Part 2)**
- We will file to be a **NASDAQ** listed stock
- Our company is **worth BILLIONS**
- **Better hurry** before we buy someone else's Public vehicle.
- **We have $100,000,000 in capital**, it's always $100,000,000!
- **Then they curse and cry when you say NO!**
Here are emails from a Russian lizard and an Ex-Cop lizard.

The Russian, after I said GNGR shareholders have to benefit also:
*"Sounds good. I am not planning to sell shares because the products we are putting under "**UMBRELLA**" of your public company is highly scalable and the **revenue unlimited**. Let me talk to **my people**.*

Notice he says he's not going to sell his shares as if he already owns them. Broke lizards are so sure the CEO will make a deal, they get excited they will be getting some badly needed cash. And, he also says the revenue is UNLIMITED but needs the stock to make it happen. That means sell shares because they have NO other revenue.

*"Yes, I spoke with **my people** and that was the main question actually. We wanted to know how much money do you want to recover from your public company and then let us run the company as our own enterprise and you take **your successful company private** and run it as your own personal business? What we are concerned about is that we need to make **some strategic decisions** and don't want to be constantly dependent on **you to approve our decisions."***

Strategic decisions means Pump and Dump. Just for the fact I communicated with him, he figured he found a willing CEO and was relieved he may soon have his cut of the scheme money so he is able to pay his mortgage and car payments. And to get this close to a deal then have it rejected he also realized, finding another ticker won't be that easy, and he figures GNGR would just give in like most other CEO's do. Desperate lizards count the cash before getting it just like the 99% investors or those who play lotto.

His deal was HORRIBLE for GNGR and my shareholders and when I rejected his offer, he went crazy and started cursing and rambling like a crazy person, and so did the Ex-Cop lizard.

I am sure it's frustration because they rarely are rejected so they resort to temper tantrums. That may work with a stressed out mother who finally caves into getting her kicking and screaming kid a happy meal but how on earth do they think that same adolescence tactic will work when trying to acquire a public company?

After dozens of insults why are they still trying to make a deal with me if GNGR is such a HORRIBLE company so they say? And why would ANY public company entertain an offer from someone who writes the following? You think that they would just move onto another public company since they (Both) have **$100,000,000** as they claim.

Why not file to be public themselves like I did? They can't, FINRA won't let them. They need an existing public company so they don't expose their true motives that would deny them a ticker. If they both have those so-called **Billion Dollar** companies, they could EASILY file and be public. The reason they can't? There is NO COMPANY!

The Russian: After I POLITELY declined his offer.

"Anybody can make your stupid jewelry that requires the skill of a caveman so you will never have a competitive advantage. You can keep flying in the sky with your crazy idea that you would be able to fool the market and investors."

The Russian again: If they're worth billions and have $100,000,000 why do they need us?

*"In terms of my technology, if that was so simple to make them we would have 1000 Facebook App clones or Snapchat App clones and the market would not value these companies into billions of dollars. So software products with intellectual property and internal knowhow **like mine are worth billions right now**. So listening to your nonsense about my apps when you have zero knowledge on how they are built, marketed and make money for my company is just laughable."*

The Russian: again after ignoring him.

*"I gave you a chance. You blew it. Now keep digging in your **worthless company** trying to fool investors - it will never ever happen. Bu-Bye!"*

The Russian: Continuing to insult us after we ignored him.

"By the way, your website looks like shit that was put together by a kindergartener. Any investor that would go there would laugh and think you're a joke, but since you are ... all the pieces fit the puzzle. lol. Bu-Bye now.'

The Russian: Yet again after I stopped all communication.

*"Why are you such an idiot? You still don't want me and **my people** to get involved. I raised millions. **Do you want to get back negotiating?"***

After all his crazy emails he wants me to NEGOTIATE?

The Russian: When I questioned about HIS people.

"My people don't trust you especially after you miserably failed with all your attempts to raise the price of the shares for the past 10 years. The beauty of the stock market is that you can BS all you want. I am sitting on $100,000,000 committed to do a deal with a company like yours. The fact that you own 97% of worthless shit doesn't make you a millionaire. I am in the process of closing a deal with another OTC company."

My reply was polite, "***Good luck with your other OTC ventures.***"

Since there are not many honest and valid companies like GNGR, they may not be having an easy task finding another ticker with the same structure so they keep coming back with Insults then let's make a deal. I'm sure **HIS people** will also read this guide and see how CRAZY he was and re-educate him in the art of proper negotiations.

The Russian: Again!

*"**My people** have 5 ventures with millions invested in them. We want to spread our risk **across several OTC companies**. Your and other OTC companies with tiny market caps cannot absorb all our capital at once. That's why I am talking to you and others."*

He states we cannot absorb their capital? Does he think if he handed me a check for $10,000,000, I would say OH NO NO NO I can't take that much money? **REALLY!** Plus they have NO capital.

ALSO! To be public, you only need ONE OTC vehicle and saying they want to spread the risk over many and also saying they want to put their technology under the umbrella of **our company** is the tell tale signs he was leading GNGR and other OTC's into an **UMBRELLA.**

Recently I got yet another offer to buy GNGR's public vehicle from an Ex-Cop (The patsy) to cover **HIS PEOPLE'S** identity just like the Russian. **The UMBRELLA chapter is next.**

Just like the Russian, it starts out good and fair with ME always saying the shareholders must benefit AND APPROVE any deal in a buy out or reverse merger. But they seem to forget that is part of the deal. I posted this offer to show the similarities.

I have to mention that the Ex-Cop my not realize what he was getting into and may have drank the Kool-Aid from **HIS PEOPLE,** not realizing he would have been the patsy CEO while the schemers behind the scenes use him to do the dirty work. Then, he takes the fall when they vanish with all the money. *An Ex-Cop in jail… YIKES!*

I am also 100% sure that they figured him being an Ex-Detective would also give more validity to the pump and dump as investors see the CEO was law enforcement to gain investors trust.

This was proven time and time again on many Pump and Dump schemes. Washed up sports figures, retired music industry icons, ex military and many others that would have given some credibility to the Pump and Dump scheme to help contribute to the debt dilution so they can sell more shares on hyped false claims. A Pump and Dump even used Rudy Ruettiger, the famous Notre Dame football player and inspiration for the move RUDY. ***This data is publicly available.***

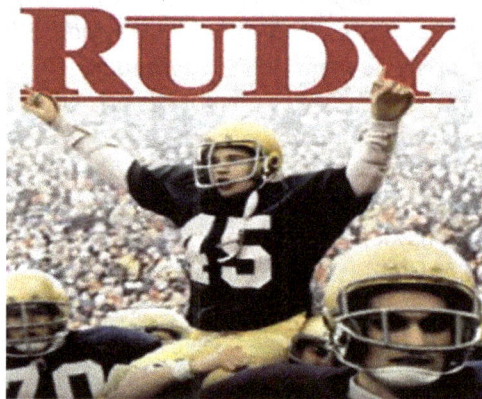

RUDY became one of the most Iconic sports films in history and then, decades later, the man the film was based on gets indicted by the SEC for a Pump and Dump scheme that netted almost $11M in profits for a sports drink attempting to capitalize on the legend's fame.

According to the SEC's complaint, Ruettiger was the principal founder and namesake of a company called Rudy Beverage Inc. He moved the company's operations to Las Vegas, where Ruettiger lived.

Ruettiger remained CEO. During this time, the company struggled financially with few customers, few assets, and no profits.

The SEC alleges that Ruettiger and an associate brought in an experienced penny stock promoter to orchestrate a public distribution of company stock in late 2007. Ruettiger gave the penny stock promoter sufficient control to turn Rudy Beverage into a publicly traded company.

The promoter became the primary organizer of the resulting Pump and Dump scheme according to the SEC's complaint. The marketing team identified a shell corporation for use in what's known as a reverse merger, which occurs when a private company acquires a public company (the part 2 vehicle) to become publicly traded.

The promoter aligned with a consultant to execute the merger and the company's transfer agent to issue purportedly unrestricted stock. On Feb. 11, 2008, they changed the name to "Rudy Nutrition."

Ruettiger authorized his signature to be placed electronically on an SEC filing, and Rudy Nutrition began to be quoted on the Pink Sheets on Feb. 21, 2008, under the ticker symbol RUNU.

The attorney associated with the scheme was a disbarred lawyer that arranged for three billion RUNU shares to be issued to entities, which sold almost one billion shares to unsuspecting investors in the public market during the scheme. *Sad story for one of my favorite movies.*

When the Ex-Cop tells me EXACTLTY what the Russian and others are told what to say and I decline, the Ex-Cop also went off on his cursing babbling rant. I can't imagine both the Ex-Cop and the Russian were told to curse and scream and is part of the *MARKETING METHOD?*

I know what the Ex-Cop told me was not from his vocabulary; *he's not that smart* or seasoned enough in this aspect of the market space to know 1,000's of lizards say the exact same thing. *Word for word, curse for curse, same outdated playbook.*

When I asked about *HIS lawyer* (Who I probably know) he replied (And either lied or truly is clueless how this works).

*The Ex-Cop replied: The lawyer, "I don't know his name" my friend, who is a lawyer, knows well and spoke with is one who is currently bringing a company public (Which my friend invested in a few years ago, (I should have jumped in too) on the NY stock exchange. It's **PROBABLY** going to be valued at close to **A $Billion.** This is a real deal large company with revenue in the **hundreds of millions of dollars.** This is real deal lawyer not a hack scam lawyer or law firm.*

The problem is, he states the lawyer is not a hack scam and says **he does not know who the SEC lawyer is**, (shouldn't he know WHO his lawyer is?) and also he states **Probably** be valued at **$1 billion and $100,000,000+ in revenue** just like the Russians said, "**A billion dollar company, with $100,000,000**" Same outdated playbook.

If they are making $100,000,000+, why go public to use shares to raise capital? **Because "THERE IS NO COMPANY OR CASH," that's why.** The Ex-cop was duped into setting up a scheme as the patsy and was probably told he would make MILLIONS but would end up with $0.

Lizards know GNGR's vehicle does not suck or they wouldn't want it so badly. It only sucks when THEY don't own it.

This proves when a VALID HONEST CEO and A VALID HONEST public vehicle remain together, schemers say they both SUCK but when they want just the vehicle, the vehicle is great and I can keep my great company private and separate from the vehicle. YOU SEE how this works? **Together we both suck, separated we're both great.**

This Ex-Cop knew he would screw all GNGR holders and "DO, IN REALITY" what he accused me of doing that never happened. After I rejected him comes the incoherent babble, **same as the Russian.**

The Ex-Cop wrote me after I declined his crappy offer:
Unfortunately, when I first inquired about buying you out we had an SEC lawyer look at the deal and he said it was not a good idea. You do not want to know what his valuation of GNGR was.

Like I am supposed to use his (Mystery) lawyers invalid measurement of my Company's value? **REALLY!**

And why say that after I said NO? They should have used their **lawyer data** and never even contacted me, **CORRECT?** The Ex-Cop wrote the following tantrums and like the Russian, **All because I said NO DEAL!**

The Ex-Cop wrote
You are truly a mentally disturbed person. I believed that you were simply inept, now I know who you really are, a conniving fraudster.
Where is the proof? Show the SEC and everyone the proof.

The Ex-Cop again: *I have to hand it to you Grant; you've kept up with this shell game for over 15 years.* **15 years proves we're legit and not a "here today, gone tomorrow" Pump and Dump. We should have had a 15th anniversary party!**

Again: *Perjury is serious in civil lawsuits.* **WTF is he talking about?**

Again: *YOU know you're a scammer and I am speaking the truth.* **From a dirty cop who lies, he wants ME to take his word that I am a scammer? Again show the proof, everyone is still waiting!**

The Ex-Cop again: *You should know that we are exploring numerous other similar options so you should decide if you're interested sooner rather than later.* **Same as the Russian, BETTER HURRY!**

He further wrote:
So to be clear, is that a stipulation to sell your shares? That shareholders who you deem must agree to your sale of stock. That's not what you initially advised me **(I told him 8 times)** *I'm not sure if* <u>**my people**</u> *will move forward. We're looking for a clean no contingencies deal of the* **public company vehicle only.**

To PROVE my point, when he ignored me insisting that his plan has to have my shareholders approval, he lied and said I never mentioned it. Here are the emails in order, first to last after he offered to buy GNGR.

Me:
I will send a letter to GNGR insiders **to inform them so they are on board** *and agree. They don't legally need to know but I have been fair and honest with them for years so it's* **best they approve your offer.**

Me again:
You would need to email the insiders who own GNGR share certificates and they would have to **sign an agreement saying they agree to your terms** *and agree to move to the new entity based on your offer to them.* **ALSO!** *The Ex Cop* **IS AN INSIDE,** *pre public initial investor.*

The Ex- Cop lizard replied:
I don't understand why we would have to do **anything** *with the share holders"* **That means, screw ALL GNGR holders! Dirty rotten Cop.**

Me again;
*I want **GNGR holders to agree to the terms you offer them**. I won't just sell the vehicle without them agreeing. How would you feel if I sold GNGR to another person and **you** ended up with NO shares on a reverse merger? Not too much to ask for since you're **SO legit!***

*If I sold the vehicle to someone else similar to his terms not taking the shareholders to the new entity, he would be screaming I screwed him and all GNGR shareholders. **PROOF he is trying to do just that.***

Me again;
*GNGR shareholders need to approve your offer and also **agree to hold me harmless as part of your offer to them.***

That's when the Ex-Cop wrote:
*So to be clear is that a stipulation to sell your shares? That share holders who you deem must agree to your sale of stock. That's not what you initially advised me. **(How much clearer could I have been?)***

*I told him 4 times before and 4 times after his post above and he still can't comprehend the communication? **So he lies and can't read? Or is he just stupid? I got the impression he is all three.***

Me again: *Right, present the offer to GNGR shareholders. **(No reply)***

Me again: *I can't sell GNGR without their ok. **(No reply)***

Me again: *Are you taking GNGR holders to the new company? If not I can't make any deal knowing they have zero chance. **(Again no reply)***

Me again: *Are you taking GNGR holders to the new vehicle? **(Hello, you there?)***

After my 8 concerns about GNGR shareholders he said I never mentioned (Yes I have all the emails as proof).

The Ex-Cop wrote: *"I can't imagine any sane person wanting to do any business with you. Good Luck Chocolate Man".*

So he's a liar, can't read AND just called himself Insane.

You see how this works? The lizards want what GNGR has, a great public vehicle, then when I say no, we both SUCK and they don't want it anyway. Why not just move on, why stick around then curse and kick and cry? Why even make contact with me initially if we SUCK?

Because they ONLY say we suck when I say NO DEAL and they have NO MONEY! Zip, zero, nada, bupkis.

Here is why they want the vehicle so you all see how EASY it is to understand.

Compare a P&D ticker and a Gun. Both are weapons used to rob people by taking investors money or committing armed robbery.

Now think about a crook that wants a gun but can't buy one at the gun store because they would be denied the permit.

Pump and Dump schemes do NOT file the way GNGR did with FINRA or do S1 registration elections is like the crook that can't buy a legal gun from a store. Pump and Dump schemes would be denied a ticker from FINRA with no valid operations and the bad actors needed to file are likely banned or want to remain anonymous.

The schemes use a lizard to look for a vehicle that already exists that does not require complex compliance that bypasses many SEC and FINRA regulations same as a crook paying a neighbor to go into the gun store to buy the gun legally so the crook can use it to rob people.

Using a gun to rob people they get very little money and if caught, go to jail. Using a pubic vehicle allows them to legally rob 1,000's at the same time and make million$ and not go to jail, rarely but some do.

They try and obtain, by any means, what exists out of the registration process to use it for no good to make money. This is how the patsy CEO (Like RUDY) ends up in trouble. Or if the gun is found, is linked back to the neighbor, not the robber.

Here is the PROOF I am 100% correct AGAIN!

Why keep pressing to get my company vehicle if they can go public the way GNGR did, since me and my vehicle both suck? Why offer me $100,000 or $500,000 for our vehicle if they can just file an S1 since they have $100's of million$? *Because they can't and they are broke.*

Just to mention, they also say **they can't** pay up front for the vehicle, only AFTER I give it to them, WHY? Because they have no money and based on their communication, you can bet they will never pay.

Because those who want the vehicle (For free) only want the vehicle for ONE REASON! To bypass regulations so they can rob investors on some scheme debt diluted Pump and Dump in secrecy knowing full well their business model is non-existent and they would be denied a new ticker filing to be public, and because they have **"NO MONEY."**

Proof they have no money: They (Both) said they have $100,000,000 but **need the public vehicle to make money.**

When I asked, neither the Russian nor the Ex-Cop ever showed any proof or legitimate operations they claim are worth BILLION$ with sales of $100,000,000 or more. Just show me the proof before I agree to a deal and they say they can't, its Top Secret. **SHHHHHHHHH!**

Pump and Dump Companies worth billions, that don't exist.

The billions are ideas on PAPER and there is no $100,000,000 either. PAPER has more value than legitimacy so paper ideas and paper shares are all they offer investors and in return the schemers will receive Billions in real paper currency.

The reason they say **NO** to getting GNGR holders to agree to the merger is they know they would be held legally liable and face a class action lawsuit for canceling their shares for no reason.

They want GNGR to be the one to face investors and the SEC who say: YOU SOLD THE COMPANY from under the shareholders. And I won't do that. And the other reasons they **don't** take the shareholders with them is:

They want ALL the money and they know investors will sue someone; they just want it to be ME after they vanish with the vehicle and cash, leaving me with the mess they create.

If someone is poor for a long time they get used to it and adapt like I had to do, but lizards make millions, then lose it, usually a few times over a decade or more. When they have it they spend it all, when they lose it, they panic.

When they do locate a vehicle hoping to make a deal to get some cash but are denied, that has to be aggravating. That is why they curse and cry, it's just a defense mechanism that further pushes back any possible deal and the fact they cannot control their desperation.

What BILLION-dollar company uses those cursing illiterate lizards to represent them in a multi million-dollar public company merger deal? NONE, because there is no company.

Lizards are so use to the status quo; they are unable to mentally handle any change. Most CEO's accept the offer because most CEO's are just as desperate as the lizards*. I am not one of those CEO's.*

I knew a man (Lizard) in Texas who was the lower level recipient of Pump and Dump money and he put a deposit down on a $5,000,000 house and bought fancy cars. After 5 years he must have known his money was running out so he aggressively went after OTC tickers thinking he would find a new victim quickly. His stress level must have been at "10."

I found that those lizards go through the OTC Markets alphabet of tickers and call every one. That is why I get calls every few months. I even joked about this to one caller and said, "YOU BACK TO LETTER G tickers again," and he laughed and said, "YUP!"

I rejected the Texas guy and he said, "YOU FOOL you're going to have money in your pocket, CASH MONEY." I say thank you but no and like the others, he cursed and cried.

Another guy who tried to scam me into a death spiral deal had a $2,500,000 home and when I last searched him he moved to a beat up small house mainly because he could not get a deal to cover his overhead. He, too, mysteriously passed away. NOT from Covid.

I am sure, schemers who have built a lifestyle based on living for the moment and have to pay next months bills, is just the way it is. Living day to day is the plan and the more people live like that, the more desperate they become to be able to sustain that lifestyle, even if it only lasts a few months or a few years. The desperate end up panicking and do and say whatever they need to get a deal done.

Curse, Insult, you're an idiot, you suck, But "Hey BUD! LETS TALK!"

Another lizard that tried to con me lived in a $3,000,000 exclusive home because he did a Pump and Dump scheme. I'm guessing he could not pay the mortgage or upkeep and forgot he had to pay taxes on that revenue or he just decided not to pay the IRS.

2 years later, I found out he had to move into a 2-bedroom condo that was priced at $175,000 and the $3M house was foreclosed.

Lizards know when trying to lure a CEO that $10,000,000 is not much and saying $1 billion is too farfetched so they round it off to $100,000,000 hoping that will excite CEO's. It's always $100,000,000 cash on hand and their billion-dollar company. Both don't exist.

So how do lizards get paid? They are issued bank ATM cards and in order to have those cards have money added to the account, the lizards have to make deals and get a Pump and Dump set up or they don't get money added to the ATM account (from a foreign bank).

Imagine a person with 5 ATM cards that did a deal and were able to take out $400 from each card per day ($2,000) for 3 years (Total $2,190,000), then one day, the account is $0 forcing them to get another deal FAST or lose their assets. That's why lizards panic.

If they don't get a deal, they can't pay the mortgage or pay for the PORSCHE so they either lose it all or go find another OTC ticker. They never save money; they spend it all and are unable to hide their desperation. *That is why they curse and cry when I say NO DEAL!*

In a few cases the field lizard looking for a ticker will try to impress me even more (because he's unable to make the deal) they will say, "you need to speak to the boss" *(His People)* I'll call him MR. X. They say let me get him on the phone.

I hear a distant overseas ring and a man answers and I get introduced and tell him my plans and what I'm doing, OBVIOUSLY with GREAT RESPECT (unlike the way the lizards speak to me), and with equal respect, Mr. X ends up saying: thank you and tells the lizard that Grant is not interested and he's doing good things for his company and his shareholders and to leave GNGR alone.

Now keep in mind, those BOSSES in the Islands have ALL the money so if no deal gets done, they still have the cash and lifestyle while the lizards are desperate to get some quick cash.

What is funny is maybe 10 different lizards that called me tried to impress me by calling the same Mr. X in the Islands and when we talked yet again he says "IS THIS GRANT AGAIN?"

I said, "YES they are just going though the OTC alphabet and they are back at tickers staring with G again," and he laughed. He then "ordered" the lizards, LEAVE GRANT ALONE!

Then Mr. X said (after talking to him 10 times) why don't you fly to Florida and we'll have a plane take you to our island and we'll hang out. I may take him up on that. I am sure I will chat with him again eventually, He's actually a nice guy and making money by way of market regulations that allow billion$ to be made *legally.*

What is MORE worrisome is knowing many scammers are linked to terrorists and US adversaries like China that are taking advantage of our debt stock system to steal BILLIONS from US citizens for their anti-USA causes. USA sucker investors paying for terrorists. NICE!

And I know how to STOP IT!

The desperate lizards in the field is so rampant, it's hard to find ANYONE that is honest and legitimate. Every day, every hour it's some hustle on a grand level or just some scam lender who needs back rent or grocery money trying to bill the CEO $5,000 thinking they will be fooled into getting $4,000,000 investment capital.

Another scammer yelled at me when I told him instead of me paying $10,000 up front for a $2,500,000 investment, he can have $500,000 instead. I made him a sweet deal since he's *SO LEGIT!*

I said to him since *"HE is processing the money transaction,"* when *YOU* get the $2,500,000, issue GNGR $2,000,000 and you keep $500,000. $500,000 instead of $10,000! I was being very generous.

He replied: You're a fucking moron. "Like I'm supposed to "TRUST YOU" to pay me $500,000 after you're funded? You will probably screw me and not even pay the $10,000."

43

I would not have issued him back $500,000, I told him to **keep** $500,000 from the $2,500,000 **HE processes,** proof he's a crook. Plus, if he were telling the truth about the $2.5 million and being a crook, he would have kept it all.

Only a CROOK talks like that. They don't trust anyone because they don't trust themselves and there is no $2,500,000 either.

Every schemer wants your money. Not just a little, but all of it. Money they say is the root of all evil but that is not true; Money is life and survival, food and medical, rent and clothes, a car and gas.

The people who say that money is evil are those whose brains have been so infected by money to the point they have to scam others for the rest of their lives just to survive each day.

The desperate ones are the lizards that want to live like a billionaire but can't seem to make it to millionaire without losing all their assets, then have to struggle in a cycle of trying to form another scheme.

When I tried to make deals showing how we CAN sell 1,000,000 GNGR rings for $99 to make $99 million, they ignore that knowing it can. The reason is, they just want to sell debt-diluted shares fast for $99 million and have no operational costs or overhead or work for it. Selling debt shares is FREE MONEY and no WORK that is rampant in the market place and continues to happen every day!

My logic is, if you work a 10-hour day to sell debt shares to make $10,000 and in the same 10-hour day my casting's can generate $50,000 why not take the higher road?

Because it takes time to set up a facility and takes actual work. Scheme pump and dumps get cash FAST with little effort.

It's almost impossible to get friends and family to invest $1,000,000 in a valid private operational business but it's EASY to raise $50,000,000 from the 99% on a non-existent **EXCITING** public company pump and dump scheme.

The proof that the money will never stop flowing is because retail investors will never stop buying into scheme pump and dump tickers.

Lizards become desperate because: *Tickers are getting harder to find, Investors are not. So what about the UMBRELLA?*

44

THE UMBRELLA

If you don't agree to sell the vehicle, the umbrella is a scammer's contingency plan so only they can sell shares with the promise of a long-term association while you get to keep your company and OTC ticker. Since they don't have the vehicle to add debt or control the ticker, they seek to acquire **ALL free trading shares** held by company associates with the promise to reinvest millions back into the company. It's money they promise later on that will never be paid.

Like the Russian said, they let our company acquire some false technology or scheme plan idea (What they would have used if they did acquire the vehicle) then they pump the shares at 50 cents and sell the 100,000,000 free trading shares we gave them for $50,000,000. When they are all sold, the stock tanks and they walk away with clean hands and no association with our company.

Umbrella means they **USE** the public company and CEO as if the company did the dilution and Pump and Dump when that was not the case. They make $50 million and the company makes $0 and the company ends up facing scrutiny and possible SEC enforcement actions. The umbrella is a relatively new term we have been told about as part of a plan from dozens of groups trying to get hold of our public company or acquire all free trading shares to do an umbrella.

The UMBRELLA plan is to create scam websites that the CEO knows nothing about and sent to investors (who don't look at real data). The schemers have their broker associates dump the shares and walk away with $50,000,000. **NICE!**

When the scheme is over and the stock tanks, the websites are shut down and the victim CEO that knew nothing about the scheme is left to take the angry calls. If you take your company public, DO NOT issue massive amounts of FREE trading shares ESPECIALLY when they say they will pay you after they make money. **You'll get ZERO!**

Many CEO's figure the UMBRELLA tactic is a way to get the share price up but the rise in share price soon ends when others involved dump all the FREE trading shares. Sure, you are PROMISED capital on the backend, but by now, you all have to know any promise is a lie.

45

In the end, the company looks like a fraud Pump and Dump scam. The stock rises to $.50 or more, then soon after, drops back to $.0001 with no real investor support other than those who paid $.50 who accuse the CEO of taking the money when that was not the case.

The UMBRELLA, in a way, allows the blame to fall on the company not those selling the shares on the umbrella plan. That is probably the real reason they start insulting and cursing the CEO when a deal is not accepted even on the UMBRELLA. They are pissed they are denied from making $50,000,000 and the lizard finders fee.

Then, they tell me when they raise $50,000,000, they will issue back to GNGR $10,000,000 as part of the agreement.

More lies to trick CEOs. Since they claim to have $100,000,000 cash on hand, why do they need to sell the shares for $50,000,000?

I said to the Russian, here is a better deal. You give GNGR $2,000,000 **up-front** from your $100,000,000 and not $10,000,000 on the back end *(Saving them $8,000,000).* Seems fair, RIGHT?

He (And others) said they legally are not allowed to pay up-front when, in fact, there is no law that says they can't.

It's because there is no $100,000,000.

When these schemes do finally get hold of a public vehicle, the lizards don't make as much money as the main players in the scheme and rarely ever save the money.

The lizards spend it like the world is going to end next month. But as tickers become harder to find, the money also is harder to make so when the lizards cash well runs dry, panic sets in to find another vehicle and create another Pump and Dump *FAST!*

I have been told many times that my company is not exciting or a HOT topic and also as CEO I am not flaunting wealth to others to get them to buy just shares. I tell them I do not sell shares for money, I sell products and they still say GNGR is boring and no one wants to invest in a company that is not impressing others with a wealthy CEO who is already rich and shows success.

ROLLS ROYCE vs. THE BUICK

Here is a perfect example; if a Pump and Dump CEO has a Rolls Royce, investors say he must be successful and his company doing very well and investors throw the CEO their money when the car was purchased using previous investors money.

The new pump has to show that NO investor has more than the CEO, creating a higher level of success or wealth attributed to the CEO that investors also want to achieve.

No one wants to invest in a company where the CEO picks up investors at the airport in a Nissan Sentra, investors see that as a sign the CEO is a failure and an investment risk.

As CEO *(Me)* owns a Buick *ROADMASTER, "**1996 gold collectors edition 350 LT1 corvette engine, dual exhausts 320HP 335 Ft Lbs. Torque, Dynaride, heated leather seats. 1996 MSRP $28,500.**" HA!*

If a Buick means my company is failing and it's because I don't have a nicer car, is that why investors passed on my company? Maybe I should have bought a Rolls Royce instead of reinvesting to expand the company and then they would throw me their money?

Investors like to live vicariously through a successful CEO based on what the CEO owns and promotes as wealth, when the fact is they got that wealth from the investors. That is why the legit conservative moral CEO will not be seen as a good risk and the stock price suffers.

You have a BUICK and a successful expanding business? You're not getting one penny.

You have a Rolls Royce and no operations and bullshit ideas? Let me get my checkbook?

The P&D schemers know full well a change to the look and dynamic to promote success though the CEO's ability to show wealth, money and assets is KEY to getting investors.

Maybe a Rolls Royce is truly the answer and changing to a Pump and Dump stock that will never benefit investors even though they think it will. Maybe it's the only option left for many desperate CEOs.

NOT THIS CEO! And I love my Buick.

Amazingly, Investors never see the company, only the Rolls Royce. Maybe the gold mines and marijuana fields are in the trunk?

They sure has HELL can't fit them in the Corporate HQ, P.O. Box.

Here is a great example. One scammer in Australia told investors he was the anonymous buyer of a $250,000,000 master painting and raised some investment capital, then used investor's money to buy fancy cars and rent a yacht to throw wild parties. And more people invested not because he had proof of results, but because he showed them he had wealth.

Major investment groups threw $100's of millions to him and eventually the true owner of the painting in Asia came forward to say that he owned the painting, not the Australian scammer.

When the smoke cleared, it was all a scam ruse to allow him to live a lavish lifestyle and eventually he ended up in jail having duped some of the biggest well-known investment groups.

What is interesting is he convinced some new suckers to invest in him that allowed him to show up to court in a $400,000 Rolls Royce when he was sentenced to jail. **NICE!**

Pump and Dump schemes offer the same visual lavish lifestyle that investors want. The fact is, intent means it won't happen.

I went to a stock promotion event in Florida and the schemers had 4 exotic cars out front to get investors excited. A simple Google search of the license plates and they all came up registered to an exotic Car RENTAL service.

The event was for attendees to get friends and family to buy the shares and we will all get shares for FREE based on 10% of what we have others buy. This way they use suckers to promote lies to friends and family so the scheme is not linked to illegal marketing.

PUMP AND DUMP DATA

This chapter is about stock tickers known as **Pump and Dumps (P&D)** that cause the 99% investors to lose about **$300,000,000** on any given trading day on shares that are almost always under a penny and most of them are in double and trip zeros, or even lower.

A Pump and Dump schemes only assets are a website, the ticker and the 99%. A scheme creates a corporation (on paper) for a new gold mine that does not exist except for the name they incorporated.

Since Pump and Dumps use INTENT on a non-existent company to sell shares, they would never be approved to be publicly trading and not be able to debt dilute shares to investors. In most cases, bad actors have been banned from being part of any public company due to previous SEC enforcement actions for securities violations.

A pump and dump scheme being set up knows an honest valid publicly trading vehicles shares will be of no interest to anyone so they wait for the CEO to panic and then they move in to try and take over your public vehicle.

That is when the Schemers rush in to acquire an existing vehicle (Ticker) so they can cancel all your shares and file to have a ticker change with no approval needed from regulators and they implant a patsy CEO.

Then the schemers can apply ANY intent, non-existent plan that is exciting just to sell shares to the 99% investors. Adding a GOLD MINE subsidiary to the ticker seems to work. But it's a gold mine **that doesn't exist!** And the shares in the gold mine are only $.01 with the claim they can hit $8.00 and move up to NASDAQ.

The logic with retail investors is, wallets at $.10 per share have no way to show how they will make $500 million like some pump and dump $.01 gold mine stock that says they **COULD** mine $500 million or more from their alleged gold mine. **Could meant won't.**

The 99% read the HOT new gold mine plan about the $500 million and how it will affect the share price. What the 99% don't realize is the only link between intent and truth of what does not exist is a fancy website. Since nothing exists, the shares link to what does not exist.

If you REALLY think about it, you're paying money for an image of a ticker in your stock account. That is all that exists for that investment because there is no company or products.

If you DON'T buy a stock ticker and write the ticker on your computer screen with a Sharpie magic marker, that has the same value as the ticker you see on the screen that is in your stock account. The difference is you paid for one image and not the other. Unless you have to buy the Sharpie marker setting you back $1.50 plus tax.

If you made 1000 copies on your printer that said GOLD MINE Ticker WXYZ 5,000,000 shares at $.0001 and sold them to people for $500 for each sheet of paper, you make $500,000.

That's similar to what investors are buying when they buy a Pump and Dump ticker from their broker. The difference is, the broker's shares are not even made of paper, they are just an image of a ticker.

How crazy buying a sheet of paper for $500 when it's just as crazy buying a $500 ticker image from your broker in a company that is also based on paper ideas? Both are exactly the same.

Investors are actually better off buying the sheets of paper for $500 because at least they will have something to write their grocery list on, or make a paper airplane?

Better yet, make them more useful and print them on toilet paper.

So what is real in all this? NOTHING! Except when investors lose money, and, of course, the Sharpie magic marker.

When shares go over a penny, most of the 99% retail buyers vanish and my data in this guide PROVES IT! That is why those hot pumped tickers keep the share prices on a *constant decline*. The more they drop in price under a penny, the more of the 99% investors jump in to buy them!

This example shows the progression of one of 1,000's of pump and dump tickers added to the OTC to replace old tickers that fold, and the cycle continues*. I use the word shares as reference to tickers.*

At $.0035, a company sold billions of shares totaling over $30,000,000 in *just one day!* They drop the price to $.0001 and sell more to cost average investors (The 99%) and lure new suckers.

Then after they make more money, they debt dilute more shares and drop the price again and let it lay there until people just get tired and move to another HOT ticker before they miss another train leaving the station.

Initially $100 got you 30,000 shares. Now $100 gets you 100,000,000 shares. The 99% end up spending $200 on the top and bottom end and end up with 100,030,000 averaged to $.000002 per share

DURING THE PUMP AND DUMP

SYMBOL	PRICE	% CHANGE	$ VOLUME	SHARE VOL
XXXX	0.0035	-12.50	$ 30,797,586	8,790,062,783

AFTER THE PUMP AND DUMP

XXXX
XXXX Management Corp

0.000001
No Inside bid / 0.0001 (1x1)

At $.000001, the 99% that cost averaged down to $.000002 cannot sell and would still be at a loss, plus the added brokers commissions, and trying to sell them at $.000002? Good luck!

Initially 100,000,000 shares cost $350,000 and now 100,000,000 shares can be bought for $100 and the new 99% that jump in believe they can go back to a penny believing they can make $1,000,000 on a $100 investment. And if they lose the $100, it's not a big deal.

Remember, the ones running the P&D scheme never want to be on filings or paperwork so they need a patsy CEO or President to take the fall and face the SEC. By not being charged and not banned from being part of another stock public ticker, the schemers in the shadows who hide behind a patsy CEO can keep creating more and more pump and dumps with no worries.

I met a person years ago that ran a P&D scheme who found a homeless person and bought them a suit from the thrift store and made them the CEO knowing he would sign anything he was asked to sign and since he was destitute he agreed or didn't even care.

After the P&D is over and the shares are all sold and investors moved on, they eventually reverse merge into a new entity with a new ticker and the old ticker is cancelled and no longer trading and the process starts all over again. And the homeless man returned to the streets with little to no money. I guess he gets to keep the suit.

On a fresh new HOT topic **P&D**, Brokers sell shares for $2 to some of the 99% when the new ticker is active and the float is only 10,000,000. The same 99% are told when the low share float are all sold, the shares will move up to $10.00 and the company will file to be listed on NASDAQ.

What investors don't know is brokers are selling 100,000,000 or more shorted shares at $2 because the brokers know soon the debt diluters will issue them the over sold shares cheap and the float will rise and the stock price will fall. ***Read page 7 again***

Making money is the result everyone wants when investing in a public company. But when a few people win many have to lose and those who make the money is decided long before investors are even introduced to any given company and the new ticker.

The winners who make the CASH are not to be confused with the share value even if the shares are worth more than what you paid. Remember, you only make a profit if you sell shares at a profit. If you paid $1,000 for shares, you are out $1,000 until they are sold for more than you paid which rarely happens on **(P&D)** stocks.

GREEN in a stock trading account is worthless compared to GREEN in your wallet even though most see only RED in their accounts.

The goal of the Pump and Dump is to get the 99% to fork over their cash and hand it to them for worthless shares. The 99% believe they are on some investment list of smart qualified capitalists, but the reality is the 99% are the P&D's sucker piggy bank and also, many brokers know this and are in on it.

A scheme will pay pumpers to post exciting news on chat rooms saying the share price will soon go from $.01 to $8.00 so you better hurry before you miss the boat. Or before they are up-listed to NASDAQ! *"Yeah sure."*

So why don't those mystery tipsters keep quiet and buy all the shares and keep all the profits for themselves? And how do they always seem to know about hot stocks before you?

Because they are not investors, they are paid to get you to buy the **USED** worthless shares. Their job is to excite you so you can't risk missing out on another new hot ticker.

No one finds these HOT STOCKS by themselves. It's all about the hot chat room tip, the secret email or phone call.

If investors did look at actual company data, they may not invest but they seem to always keep buying into those questionable tickers. Like it's a gambling addiction.

Chat room tipsters don't own shares in the company they pump. They say they own lots of shares and holding, but they don't even own ONE share because they know the shares are worthless.

The game of the P&D stock is to get to investors fast with some hot news, sell shares higher then dilute and sell billions of shares cheaper and cheaper before the scheme is exposed as non-existent.

And remember, the COMPANY does not get investors money!

If the 99% stopped investing billions each month on pumped stocks, the companies listed on the OTC would likely drop from 12,500 down to 5,000 maybe less. With no pump money coming in and no shares being sold, they would fold simply because they only survive by selling shares. But the sub-penny investors will never stop buying. *Never.*

The 99% are like lottery ticket players. Spend a little with dreams of making a lot, and if you don't play, you can't win. And when you don't win, it was only a little loss and you will make it up on the next bet.

The 99% end up having to keep buying into more and more tickers because a winner is so rare and if you miss one and it hits, it will be years before you find another one (If even ever).

Those who run the Pump and Dump schemes know this and make sure the 99% keep investing over and over saying if you don't invest, you will not be part of the success when one does hit.

If 100,000 investors each invest $400 in any given P&D stock, it's $40,000,000 that ends up in the hands of only a few who set up the P&D scheme. When the 99% lose $400 they figure they will make it back on the next hot stock and the cycle continues.

Like a concert, you pay $200 to see a band with 25,000 other fans. You're each out $200 but the band makes Million$. And Taylor Swift is KILLING IT.

Investing in a Pump and Dump stock is like a concert; You're out the money and end up leaving with only a memory.

One problem with buying P&D tickers is millions of investors are doing the same, and if they each own a small percentage of the same tickers and **IF** the price rises (But never does) the brokers just get more shares from the debt holders, not the bid.

So diversifying your P&D portfolio will end up being a portfolio of RED highlighted tickers and prices. You may see green for a short time but you will likely be unable to sell the shares at a profit.

The logic is simple but never works. If you buy 1,000,000 shares for $.0001 ($100) and you do that with 20 P&D tickers, you are into those 20 stocks $2,000 and if only ONE of them rises to even $.10 cents, that one ticker's 1,000,000 shares are worth $100,000 so you made $98,000 profit. In all my years, I have never seen this happen.

Since you need millions of investors so that only a few schemers can make millions of dollars, the 99% retail investors are the ones that always lose in the market, $300,000,000 PER DAY!

Debt-diluted shares are sold for less and less to prevent any rise in share price to STOP the 99% from making a profit. The more investors make the less the scheme makes. Knowing this, why would any P&D ticker even want to work to make products or sales and have the share price rise UP when they ALWAYS make more money selling diluted shares even if the shares price declines? And they will keep adding more shares to the float as long as people want to buy them.

When P&D investors are introduced to a new HOT STOCK, it's never a small shoe repair store that is going public. You will never read a post saying: "Quick get into this shoe repair store stock before they start repairing shoes and the stock explodes to the Moon!" *BORING!*

And on that note, NO ONE will invest in a Wallet company either.

Whenever a social event happens or a new technology is created like Artificial Intelligence (AI) or whatever the masses are talking about that is trending on a national or global level that is exciting news, that is when you see those P&D stocks magically enter the same space as those topics. Next up, Artificial Intelligence and Mushroom farms.

When gold prices hit record highs, many P&D tickers emerged as a new gold mine stock with some still pumping that hot topic today.

The higher gold prices go, the more gold mine tickers will enter the market. If gold prices drop and horseshit becomes valuable, the gold mine tickers would quickly shut down and emerge as a new horse manure company.

Data shows some tickers were a **solar panel** stock that changed to a **gold mine** stock that changed into a **marijuana** stock that again changed to a **Lithium Car Battery** stock and soon to be an **AI** or **mushroom farm** stock. A new corporation name change combined with a new website and ticker and it's business as usual.

Some aggressive schemes will associate a well-known person to their Pump and Dump structure like I mentioned a lithium mine stock says Elon Musk *could* eventually buy them out and some say they *could* be the next AMAZON. *COULD means WON'T!*

In the data on many tickers, you will find that a failed public company that operated as a successful restaurant supplier was reversed into a marijuana or gold mine scheme because that is what sells shares.

My favorite P&D terms are, they are going to enter this space with **disruptive potential** and we have started our **vertical integration.**

A P&D will issue news they FILED to be on NASDAQ and investors tell others they ARE going to NASDAQ when the company said no such thing. Filing and being denied is normally what happens.

When things eventually go south, some Investors start venting to other investors as if that will help. Soon they turn on the CEO who by then is long gone or sent back to the homeless shelter. Watching groups of investors on chat rooms post to the CEO what to file and how to file or even what to do to make the company better is, sad to say, not reaching their intended target.

When the stock drops, the CEO is accused of being a scam crook and if by some chance the stock goes back up, they congratulate the CEO as a financial hero.

Investors don't care if the CEO is a crook as long as the stock price goes UP! But crooks are not in this market to care what investors think or how much they lose.

Crooks take and never give. Investors give, and never get! TA DA!

Pump and Dumps are created to sell shares ONLY and not give a damn about investor's losses or opinions. Yet investors, for some reason, think something has happened due to the lack of actions by the CEO so they are going to set the CEO on the right path and tell the CEO what to do to make it better? ***YEAH SURE.***

The two things that most investors are interested in is, ***Pumped hot news and lots of shares cheap that keep falling in price*** so they can keep buying and cost average the share price to $.00001. Buy high and keep buying more for less? ***Good Lord!***

Sub penny investors seek out what they know is near impossible when they buy 5,000,000 shares at $.0001 for only $500. They HOPE it rises to $1 so they make $5,000,000 so they invest less over more cheap tickers hoping one will hit it big. The schemers know this and accommodate those investors. ***SO NICE OF THEM!***

You rarely ever see a Pump and Dump share price end up above a penny. But some do exist. Most Companies with very high share volumes are priced between $.0005 to even $.000001 per share and they sell billions of shares each day that never rise back up.

Often investors who see a P&D start to wind down, will STILL buy even more shares cheaper and say they just want to break even and get out of the stock but even that is a near impossibility.

To attract the 99%, Pump and Dump tickers advertise what does not exist or is even real and in most cases, impossible to achieve.

Cell phone carriers advertise on TV (Verizon, AT&T and others) as to why their cellular coverage is better than the other cellular carriers, but at least they offer real products and are operational (same as GNGR). Pump and Dumps have **no operations or products.** It's always intent, ifs and maybes, just to sell shares.

If you were using Verizon or AT&T and a new company said to pay and switch over to their new SUPERDUPER cellular network even though it's not even operational and never will be, would you switch? Hell no! So why buy shares in a company with no operations that will never become active?

You have to know by now that most tickers get none of the investor's money. If you do invest, you have to also know you will lose your investment knowing they cannot achieve their goal with **NO MONEY.**

STOP telling others you invested in a COMPANY when you did no such thing. Owning a ticker in your stock trade account means you likely own that small % of NOTHING!

Since most Pump and Dump companies have no intention (Even though they say they intend to) of becoming operational, they can pretty much say whatever they want as intent that excites investors to open their checkbooks. The more exciting and more impossible the intent plan, the more money the Pump and Dump makes.

This allows some of the most outrageous intent ideas like the meteor mining idea to land a craft on a moving meteor that drills into the meteor for gold and then comes back to earth. You can find MORE gold at yard sales for less cost.

The recent NASA craft that came back to earth with one CUP of space material from a comet, cost $100,000,000 and 7 years to complete the mission. So mining one cup of GOLD valued at maybe $200,000 at a cost of $100,000,000? Do the math. ***Or better yet INVEST! Kidding***

Since there are more people who invest in companies than there are public companies, most people who work for a living want to be part of something that may pay millions on a small investment.

Some investors (but not many) buy shares in start up's while most gravitate to the OTC Markets (Pink sheet) companies with shares selling for a penny or less. Some may buy a few shares in high priced blue chip stocks just to say they own part of the company but not enough to help with the cost of living or retirement needs.

Most cannot do what Jeff Bezos, Elon Musk or even what I managed to do, but not to worry, you can own shares in those companies just like the CEO. That makes you a part of the family.

What holds most investors back is their budget and the time it takes to realize profits so they look for cheap shares that are on the OTC with the belief the company will be a financial windfall fast and they are able to get in very cheap.

Getting in Fast and cheap is very EASY.

Getting in Fast, Cheap and make a PROFIT? Don't hold your breath.

Next comes the all too familiar " I will sue the crook CEO for fraud."

The 99% that keep losing will post many times they are going to sue the company and CEO but never do. The only way to even attempt to sue them is with a class action, but lawyers know you won't win so they won't take the case contingent on a win to get paid.

Most of the 99% investors spend maybe only $500 or less, so even if you did win a lawsuit, it would cost you $10,000 to recover $500. PLUS there will be no person or address to send or serve the suit to.

A $10,000 legal investment to win back $500 is as dumb as buying the pumped diluted stock in the first place. TA DA!

This is why pumped companies won't sell to one person $10,000,000 in stock but instead focus on small dreamer gamblers who each invest $500 more or less. You would sue if you invested $10,000,000 (Or send a hit squad) but not if you invested $500.

And it is much easier to get 20,000 people to part with $500 each than one person to part with $10,000,000. Investors with big dollars look at details that smaller investors do not.

If someone does invest $10 million into a Pumped scam stock, I want that person's phone number because I have a very old bridge in Brooklyn to sell to them. :)

Investors posting they will have the CEO arrested is not going to happen. Even though they think they have right on their side, they do not have the law on their side.

And remember, the planted patsy CEO of a Pump and Dump makes pennies on the dollar from those who invested. Your BROKERS made more than the company and CEO so call them for a refund.

When investors lose $500 on 10 or more tickers, they get angrier when they lose $100 on another one because they are mad it keeps happening. Plus they once again believed that the NEW $100 investment would recover the past $5,000 they lost. *Never does.*

The longer it takes to recover all their losses, the more they keep buying into more P&D schemes and the more they get frustrated because they continue to lose money stressing to find one winner that never happens. And if they stop, what if the one they decided against hits it big time, so they have to keep doing it.

Investors are mentally locked in a round room and are told the key to get out is in the corner.

Pump and Dumps know investors won't stop, so why should they?

Many investors actually post on chat rooms, threatening the CEO to refund everyone their money. *Really!* Tell the CEO to refund everyone the money? The CEO did not take the money, only a very small percent.

Who wants to work or spend years in school to become a *doctor* to be able to save $2,000,000 for your retirement when you can make $50,000,000 in 6 months not even with a high school diploma! All you need is a failed or willing public company converted to a HOT topic entity and some savvy fancy wording news release.

And then sell $50,000,000 in shares *to doctors*.

And why bother making the company plans a reality and having to work 24/7 losing millions knowing the plan that was pumped to investors will not work. Just take those millions, do nothing and enjoy the easy life. This happens all the time with Pump and Dump stocks.

How about that DELI scheme the SEC shut down before they could sell any shares, the scheme took a small NJ deli that made about $40,000 per year and manipulated the shares to $14 per share.

The market cap was valued at $100,000,000. If they sold 10,000,000 shares discounted to brokers for $5 and the brokers resold them for $14 to investors, the Brokers would have made $90,000,000 and the schemers $50,000,000 from a business that made only $40,000 in sales annually, *NICE!* And they almost got away with it.

Even if a P&D company says as a fact they made $50,000,000 and lied, the SEC will likely file charges with the company or CEO for fraud for stating a fact that was not true but the LIE sends the shares into huge buying volumes at higher prices.

The punishment is usually fines that are a fraction of what the company raised and the CEO being banned from being part of a public company but rarely jail time. But the ones behind the scenes just find a new CEO and reverse the company and do it all over with a new patsy president or CEO. That is why you always see they only INTEND or PLAN to make $50,000,000 and never say they DID or WILL.

Here in Nevada, I met a kid (Patsy CEO) of a Pump and Dump ticker sitting at a desk by the phone in a tiny empty office to answer calls or be ready to sign his name on SEC documents. Sure they are paying him $10,000 a month but eventually that will be used to pay his SEC fines and legal fees. And he won't even know there is some website promoting a new Canadian Gold Mine as $50,000,000 worth of shares are sold and that CEO just sits and plays on his cell phone all day.

With endless amounts of money, there will be endless amounts of Pump and Dump schemes and endless amounts of CEO's to keep the status quo.

While patsy CEO's are trying to come up with SEC imposed fines or paying defense lawyers to avoid prison,

The ones that took most of the money are here. SWEET!

There are about 400,000,000 people in the USA. At least 10% (40 million) will invest into penny stocks at some point. Some will spend $1500 more or less every month to try and find the one big winner while most will invest smaller amounts on cheap stocks more often attempting to make a killing on those very low priced stocks fast.

40,000,000 out of 400,000,000 people that does not include foreign stock buyers, comes to about $6 billion per month ($70+ billion annually) and that is on the low end estimate on what could be $500,000,000,000 ($500 billion annually) ***ALL on diluted schemes.***

The objective of Pump and Dump stocks is to get as much of those 40,000,000-sub penny retailers money by making each pumped stock more exciting than the others. The hotter the stocks topic and pump, the more of those shares will sell and the more money the scheme makes.

This may insult the 99%, but if the Pump and Dump stocks can make investor's part with ***$6 billion each month legally,*** then there is no reason to condemn but rather congratulate the scheme.

"Why congratulate them if they took investors money and ran?"

Pumped scheme stocks, "did NOT" take money from investors. Investors handed it to them willingly. HERE TAKE IT! TAKE IT ALL! And if you don't take it, I'll just give it to someone else.

Plus investors have to STOP blaming the company when the money they invested **did not even go to the company.** As a CEO, I have met some very interesting people over the years who keep this flow going that make Billions each week. Some are here in the USA, some in the tropical Islands and others overseas. Talk about a learning experience.

A man I became close friends with was part of various Pump and Dump schemes and a respected **FAMILY MEMBER!** I asked him at lunch: "Can I be completely honest?" he said SURE so I asked him, "Why do you pump and dump stocks to make an immoral (but legal) fast dime instead of a hard working honest dollar?" **He replied:**

"Because it takes them one day to make a Pump and Dump dime while it takes me 5 years to make an honest hard working dollar."

BINGO, Now I get it. If I work hard for 5 years at a loss and then finally see profits, it's hard work with significant costs and NO guarantees it will even work, and in those same 5 years they end up making a guaranteed $200 to each of my $1 and they hardly work at all.

Their fast dime in a day is a SURE THING. My hard work in 5 years for $1 is not. If I make $1,000,000 after working hard for 5 years, they make $200,000,000 doing nothing but selling worthless shares.

That's why Pump and Dumps never achieve their goal. It would cost too much, take too long and is too much work, TA DA!

These are not bad people I met and know, and to be honest, they are quite personable and I **respect** the ones I stay in contact with. They just use the system to make money that others view as unfair when it is totally legal.

One thing to mention is, a company that DOES take the long-term risk and beats the odds **(Like GNGR did)** can actually end up worth far greater than any individual pump and dump can achieve. The PUMP and DUMP is quick with low risk but the rewards are small by comparison to a valid ticker that does achieve their goals over time.

For a few to make lots of money, millions of investors have to lose a little money and the ones selling debt-diluted shares never lose.

Many CEO's I spoke to regret what they did, not because it hurt shareholders, but because they had to pay back what they made or even more in fines. In many cases, the CEO did not even write the PR NEWS releases, they just approved and signed them but they are the ones that get in trouble.

A desperate CEO going from legit ticker to a Pump and Dump had better know what they are signing at all times to make SURE they do not incriminate themselves or end up paying fines that are equal to or greater than what their percentage of the scheme paid them, or they will be right back to where they were before the scheme, **BROKE and in trouble.**

And you have to deal with 1000's of angry investors that can prove you DID screw them over when their shares are all cancelled.

BUT AGAIN! Losing ALL THE TIME, it seems investors just get used to it. You can't WIN if you don't play and you know you will lose if you do play, but playing (Lotto or Pump and Dump stocks) ends up in people's DNA like alcoholism and the only benefit is being able to *imagine* what you would do with all the money that never arrives.

If you don't bet you can't dream. The 99% bet, get angry, bet again and dream of more money that never arrives and the cycle continues. Hope is only what the 99% have. If they don't bet they lose all hope.

A group who set up a P&D OTC gold mine company with the state of Nevada created a new exciting website showing Gold Nuggets, Mines, Cranes, Dump Trucks and more.

The pumped OTC rented some land on the edge of town that was owned by a farmer who said they can rent that land for $500 a month but can't build on it.

The schemers then went to Home Depot and purchased a shovel for $19.99. Looking deeper into the pumped OTC, the company now had proof of the land lease and the receipt for the shovel, a 100% fact. But the AMAZING PR News that hit investors said this,

FOR IMMEDIATE RELEASE (OTC public company) Nevada ticker XXXX gold mine is about to start mining on our secured land rights to retrieve some of the possible $500,000,000,000 in gold deposits still in the earth underground. With the secure lease in place for the land and equipment being delivered next week, we are on schedule to *"possibly"* capture some of that $500 billion in gold.

The stock surges as people rush to buy the shares BEFORE they start mining and making millions in gold deposits. The stock shoots from $.01 to $.10 and people keep buying more and more shares. As the stock tapers off, people who bought just wait. NEW NEWS, the equipment has arrived and commencing mining, investors tell others they are mining the gold. Hurry before the share price EXPLODES!

The Gold Mine OTC Company goes to the plot of land and stuck the shovel in the ground and walked away and that constitutes they have begun mining. The land and shovel was legal evidence they did have the land rights and gold mining equipment and people invested.

Of course, investors only saw images of cranes and digging machines with 50 hard hat workers mining gold on some fake website.

Many scam gold mine companies will buy gold nuggets from mineral retail stores or online and post images of gold in dirty hands saying LOOK what we dug up today. *Say it ain't SO!*

$500 in gold nuggets bought from eBay and a website with no physical operations and they sell $80,000,000 in shares. Sweet!

Think of the GOLD stock you purchased. They say they will find lots of gold and when doing so the price of gold drops due to more supply than demand. That is exactly what happens when you buy the shares, the more they sell, the lower the price because there is more supply than demand. **They are, in reality, mining shares, not gold.**

Once the stock is all sold, the company will eventually say they found a few nuggets but that is all. After selling shares of stock for $80,000,000, they shut down the website, stop posting news, the cell phone is tossed in the trash and the P.O. Box left unpaid.

No mines, No office, No phone and of course, **NO GOLD!**

And brokers only care about one thing, lots of cheap shares and lots of buyers = lots of commissions and short sale profits.

If a broker does 100 transactions on a low float $.10 valid stock, they bill $700 in commissions. If they do 5,000 transactions on a low priced Pump and Dump stock with billions of shares available, they bill $35,000 in commissions. If you worked for a broker making 10% commission, which stock would you tell people to buy knowing your check on Friday was either $70 or $3,500?

This is why many **valid low float companies** have falling prices, No one is interested in them, not the investors or the brokers.

Pumpers on social media continue to make investors think they did the right thing buying the pumped stock.

Pumpers post to investors: *Good stock purchase BUD, Excellent stock grab BRO. How polite. Like I said if they say BRO or BUD, they are lying.*

I received this private message on a stock chat room.

Hey Bud!

Take a look at $▮▮▮▮▮ it is EXTREMELY thin, and they are announcing in the next two weeks the official closing of the business doing $20 Million in revenues, per the LOI Press release. After closing the PPS should be between $.50-$0.55 a share. Could be even higher since the float is so small! This is one you are going to want to load up on.

Highly recommend grabbing a nice position, you will be thanking me that is for sure! She is already on the move!

Have a great day!

As of Feb. 2024 the stock is at $.0005 and the LOI (Letter Of Intent) just means someone said they INTEND to post $20,000,000 in revenue but they never do. *If you ever see LOI or Intent, you can bet it's likely not accurate or even a fact.*

Another post asked me about a ticker. *"Excuse me, in my ignorance, but why is there so much volume on a stock that is failing?"*

The high volume of shares bought from brokers at less and less cost, are coming from the company debt shares, not the retail bid or retail investors holdings. It's an endless supply of shares increasing the float at a declining price.

The trade volume goes up while the price falls. Read page 7 again.

Your ignorance is excused. EOM.

More proof the 99% do NOT look at stock data.

Even if by some miracle the shares you paid $.001 for did go to $.02 per share, 8,000,000,000 shares held by 1,000's of investors would all rush and try and sell them at the same time and drop the share price so low no one can sell at a profit.

When that happens no one will want to pay $.03 on the asked volume to match a huge sell off. You will never see a stock with an asked volume of 8 billion at $.03 and 8 billion on the bid allowing everyone to sell at $.02.

8 billion shares at $.02 on the bid totals $160,000,000 which means the market makers would have to have the same 8 billion at $.03 on the asked which comes to $240,000,000 with buyers taking out those $.03 so everyone can sell at $.02 which will never happen.

If the bid went to $.02 (That likely won't happen) the brokers would just get more debt shares cheap and dilute more into the float taking the share price to $.000001. That is where all the shares being dumped into the dilution are coming from, the debt diluters, not the investors on the bid sells.

If the market makers initially get 8 billion shares from the company's debt dilution dump, what makes anyone even think for one second they would NOT just get another 8,000,000,000 shares to sell on the asked from the same source and not have to buy any on the bid?

The shares will continue to drop in price as dilution continues and the shares will end up at $.00001 or lower with some tickers posting 99,999,999,999 or even unlimited shares available. If a company that posts 99,999,999,999 shares authorized and they did go to the $8.00 they said could happen, that tiny little P.O. Box non existent company would be worth more then the company **APPLE**. Now ask yourself IS that really a possibility?

Share Structure

Market Cap	13,760,855,738
Authorized Shares	99,999,999,999

People who invest $100 on a $1,000,000 pay out dream are like, what else can they do with $100? I bet 100% of wives do not know the full amount their husbands are spending on scheme stocks. I say the wife, not to be sexist, but because for some reason there is a Gene in women's DNA to avoid stocks.

Sadly, many Pump and Dump stocks did not set out to be that way. Some were doomed legitimate public companies that failed for one reason or another and the CEO had to choose, walk away broke, or give into the P&D scheme and make a few bucks, or just sell the public vehicle and ticker to a lizard.

Artificial Intelligence, Crypto and Mushroom Drugs will be the NEXT HOT pumped tickers costing investors $30+ billion GUARANTEED. Many of those DEAD Marijuana or Delicatessen stocks will now become Mushroom, Crypto or Artificial Intelligence scam stocks.

Psychedelics should not be used for scamming retail investors.
*Looking at some stock market listed companies, especially on exchanges known for pump-and-dump schemes - that promoters with little or no biotech experience and very little or no self-generated scientific research behind their company's compounds are pushing very hard to attract **quick retail money**. Investors should carefully look at the business models they invest in, and look deeper into the company data and its management team.*

Pump and Dumps will often promote they acquired 40% of a newly formed private company that has $50,000,000 and that the affiliate will bring great value to the Pump and Dump share price.

This allows the public company to pump they have an affiliate with lots of cash even though no cash exists. Plus the P&D only owning 40% means they don't have to consolidate the false financial data.

This allows the P&D to promote the $50,000,000 lie based on what the affiliate tells them.

Well that's what they told US!

How can a new private company be incorporated and have a new website only weeks prior to the association with the public company and actually make $50,000,000 in revenue?

Maybe that company should go public!

Even top influencers can't help themselves.

Seven have been charged with securities fraud and were also charged with conspiracy to commit securities fraud by the DOJ. Authorities alleged the defendants used the social media platforms to manipulate exchange-traded stocks in a scheme going back to at least January 2020. Through widely followed Twitter accounts and stock trading chat rooms on Discord, these defendants allegedly "promoted themselves as successful traders," according to an SEC press release, and encouraged followers to buy stocks that they also purchased. But they did not disclose to their followers while promoting those stocks that they planned to sell shares once prices or trading volumes rose, the DOJ and SEC alleged. The influencers gained a profit by pumping the stock prices and then selling once they rose. *Earning them about $100 million in total.*

What most don't even realize...

When many of the 12,500 listed OTC companies that pump and vanish, you would think the number of listed OTC stocks would decline, right? The number of OTC companies listed stays about the same because the ones that took your money folded, reverse merged into a new company and assigned a new ticker with a hot new product to pump. And, the cycle continues and is never-ending.

If every failed pump and dump did *not* re-emerge as a new ticker, the listed tickers on the OTC would drop from 12,500 to 10,000 then 5,000 then 2,000 until the only ones left are the legitimate companies (Like GNGR) that the 99% investors don't want to invest in.

Stock scheme reverse mergers happen all the time like the NJ DELI that made $40,000 per year and artificially made the market cap $100,000,000.00! I am sure they did not use deli sandwiches to justify that market cap. They would have had to associate some HOT TOPIC company (Part 1) to add to the DELI public vehicle (Part 2).

Which pump news would work best to sell the debt shares?

"Get this gold mine stock quick before we file to go to NASDAQ"

"Would you like mustard or mayo on your ham and cheese hero?"

When a pump and dump is over, there is no reason to promote a company when the shares are all gone. There is also no reason to keep the company active. No news, No pumps, No website, No phones answered, No nothing. Not even a ham and cheeses sandwich.

Why work to have the stock rally when the scheme and brokers make no money when there are no more debt shares to sell.

All a pump and dump has to do after the scheme is over is do a huge stock reverse split from billions back to 100 million shares, add a new HOT topic company idea (Artificial Intelligence) and start the process all over again with the same or a new ticker.

The tickers change constantly on the OTC. What does not change is the 99% who keep buying into each new scheme.

The data can be looked at and show the schemes business plans and goals will never make any money because most of the companies are only on paper not reality. They only sell and dilute shares and never let anyone make money on the stocks other then those who run the scheme.

A pump and dump is very similar to a carnival game of chance but with NO chance of winning. Like a P&D stock ticker, play and win BIG and when you lose, just like the carnival game, you were CLOSE. **When you lose, TRY AGAIN!**

The trick is to make the carnival games and Pump and Dump stocks so impossible to win, they can charge very little for a BIG prize knowing you won't win and they keep all the money and not pay out what cost them money, carnival prizes or share value.

If a carnival game charged $25 for one try to win a worthless prize, no one would play. But millions of investors will spend $100 on a Pump and Dump stock to try to win big, but still end up losing.

If there was a carnival game with 100 soda bottles, and if you were given 1,000,000 tries for just $1 to toss a marble in a bottle, you win $1,000,000, many will give it a try because the prize is so huge and you get 1,000,000 chances for $1, (Like a pump and dump stock).

The pump and dumps are the same soda bottle game, INVEST a little to hit it BIG. And the stock is also set it up to be impossible to win at because it would be like paying $1 for 1 million tries with a marble that is just slightly bigger than the bottle opening.

The likelihood to get a small marble in a bottle is near impossible but to make sure, they show you the marble fits but they always secretly slip you the slightly larger marble when you play.

Pump and dump stocks or the marble in the bottle game, immoral or illegal cheating can be considered a crime but *not* if the small print (no one reads) says *"the marble only fits in the one bottle far away from the playing field"* that's blocked by the game attendant or the stock being sold says *"the company will not achieve their goal and investors will likely lose all their money."*

Playing the Pump and Dump stocks or playing the $1,000,000 carnival bottle game, the risk-takers always end up being the SUCKER.

Enforcing securities violations from any publicly traded company that also knows how to avoid detection has been quite difficult to enforce. Few get caught, most do not. FINRA and the SEC, a US Government organization that helps keep people as safe as possible when it comes to stock fraud also has a hard time enforcing fraud when it is done under the radar. No one can enforce all laws especially when there is not enough evidence to convict or if that evidence is even found.

It's illegal to play poker for money in your house but people do it and the authorities can't stop what they can't find. A person you meet at a bar can tell you as a FACT the stock will rise because they have inside information. They can commit securities fraud and not be charged because the fraud was not exposed to the law.

I met a man at a party who told me about a 20 cent stock that **was** going to $8.00 then move to NASDAQ, (that is securities fraud).

Little did he know who he was talking to. I looked at the ticker and data and said, "NOPE." I showed him that company did not meet the financial and structure requirement by NASDAQ proving they will be denied, and that means NO $8 per share. **THE DATA IS THERE for all to SEE!**

He told me his sister **had proof** it would happen. Probably some pumpers "SECRET TIP". He said she invested $50,000 at $.20 and he was going to invest $20,000. The company never went to NASDAQ and the shares ended up at $.0001 and their $70,000 is worth $35. I saw him years later at the same annual party and he was upset with me because he had no one to blame except the bearer of the bad news. That is one reason being right angers people.

Before going public, I was friends with a women whose mother said she would invest in my business but she had to wait until her $10,000 real estate investment made back $100,000 in about a month. **UH OH!**

I said to her, "What investment?" She said her and her friend met a wonderful woman from CA who told her about a HOT real estate TIP that will turn $10,000 into $100,000 in a month so they each invested $10,000 (Total $20,000) I thought, "OH SHIT no way."

I asked for the woman's name and where she was from and called the Hermosa Beach CA. Police, I told the detective her name and about the real estate issue.

He came back with a file and said, "OH YEAH, she is a dirty bird scammer." I handed the phone to the woman and the detective told her she was scammed then the woman blamed ME for her loss because I broke the bad news. She never said it was her fault.

She was mad at ME for ruining the dream of $100,000 she thought was on the way. The 99% of retail investors who buy pump and dump stocks do the same; they blame **others** for their loss that was no one's fault but their own. **In our case, GNGR was also a victim.**

What is interesting is her husband was a cop and he confronted me saying he wants HIS $10,000 back. I said, "I never got any money from your wife." He showed me a cashed check for $10,000 that was taken from his pension plan without his knowledge.

To cover her fuck up, she told him she invested in me because she knew he would find out she lost $10,000. She told him Grant is from NY where all the scammers are from and the woman is Grants partner.

I told him to call the Hermosa Beach PD and they told him the same thing. He apologized and I never heard from him again. So not only was I the one who gave her bad news but she actually told her husband she gave me the money. **Some people suck!**

These are the same stories over and over again. Scams or Pump and Dump stocks, snake oil and lies. When they all unfold, those who lost money blame others. In GNGR's case, a crooked lawyer created our mess. **I'll get to that soon.**

Now I keep my mouth shut mostly because I hear about these issues AFTER people already handed the scammer their cash or they bought some crappy stock, so I let them find out on their own so they can't blame me. **IDIOTS!**

But let's not dwell on things I think people know. I think I have also made my point having repeated many times specific data in this guide so let's move on to other business issues.

So with all the HOT SCHEMES and amazing new stocks hitting the market with AI, Mushroom, Lithium Batteries Elon Musk will supposedly be buying out before the stock shoots to the moon, Lets look at some quick numbers that are very persuasive to investors.

PUMP AND DUMP NUMBER LOGIC

When Amazon was only $2.00 per share 20 years ago, many who passed on that investment wish they invested and even if some did take a risk back then and spent $20 to buy 10 shares, today after the 20/1 stock split you would own 200 shares worth $23,000 and hardly enough to retire on, but still a good return.

Investment groups, who did take the risk and bought $250,000 worth at $2 per share, turned that into $300 million today, and most blue-collar working class people don't have $250,000 laying around to risk.

IPO's today are not as common and most working class investors don't have the big bucks to spend $100,000 or even $10,000 on an IPO's $10 priced shares. If you did buy 1,000 shares at $10 ($10,000) and they did rise to $40 per share, you would net (before taxes) $30,000 and hardly enough to retire on and a 400% gain is rare.

When a high priced stock rises up 400%, you would have to invest millions in order to make the same return you are told you can make on high-risk stocks with very little money and the only place to do that is on the OTC Markets (The pink sheet stocks).

Unlike buying one Amazon share for $2 20 years ago that was worth $3,400 (Pre split), OTC penny stock investors do not want to wait 20 years to see if a stock pays the same gains. And the Pump and Dump tickers also don't want to work 20 years to make the company a success. ***No one wants to wait OR work.***

To use existing math to compare Amazon to a low priced Pump and Dump ticker and how fast you can make money, has some very interesting numbers that give Pump and Dumps the advantage over the long term higher priced shares.

If you buy any given stock today at $2, per share and want it to increase 1700 times to $3,400 (like Amazons pre split price) and have that happen in a few months, not 20 years, is almost impossible. But many believe (and are told) it can happen!

The term HOT STOCK SYNDROME is exactly what it means. People are attracted to a HOT STOCK even though the company promoting that stock will generate no sales or even launch a product. The hotter the pump, the more people are affected by the Hot Stock Syndrome.

Most who jump into a HOT pumped scheme at $2 per share never take a large position, maybe $100 more or less, because they know it's a risk. And they don't have much money.

Investors get a few shares at the higher price just in case it goes up they can make a few bucks, and also anticipating the price will soon drop so they can cost average and keep buying more at a lower price.

Investors believe buying more for less, that it could go back to the original $2 price and they make a killing, but that rarely if ever happens. Penny stocks promote huge FAST returns cheap. If you buy an OTC stock for $.0001 per share, a 1700x gain means that stock only has to rise up to $.17 (cents) compared to a $2 share rising to a $3,400 share price like Amazon, but it's the same 1700x gain.

If you invested $200 for 100 shares of Amazon at $2 per share that rose to $3,400, you made $340,000 but you have to wait 20 years.

If you invest $200 and buy 2,000,000 shares at $.0001 and they rise to just $.17 (cents), you make the same $340,000 and it seems like that could happen in only a few months, not 20 years.

SAME $200 investment. SAME $340,000 gain. 20 years vs. 6 months.

Many OTC listed companies seem to always offer the low priced high return options FAST with little financial risk. And saying they could be the next Amazon or bought out by Elon Musk doesn't hurt.

Who would not risk $200 to make $340,000 on a sub penny stock in a few months? Many do as proven by the data in this guide. This is what attracts investors to the penny stocks. And those who sell those penny stocks know this and capitalize on it.

Questionable Pump and Dump *(P&D)* Penny stock companies know investors want a great return on low-priced shares and fast. They focus on having what investors are looking for and limit the risk with fancy news and website data. Plus, it's only $200 so you are not risking a lot of money to make a huge fast return.

Most retail investors will risk $200 on many OTC stocks to increase their chances of hitting a winner, but a $200 loss on many tickers can really add up, and Investors rarely ever look at the share trade data.

If a public company promoted *lies, fraud and admitted to being a Pump and Dump scam that won't work* and the shares went from $.25 to $.50 (Up 100%), they are seen as a success and a hot stock to buy that is a credit to the investment community based only on the share price and nothing else. *Give that CEO a cigar!*

If a profitable legitimate company had sales and profits and the stock dropped from $.25 to $.12 (Down 50%) the CEO is a loser, a scam crook and should be arrested. *Put that CEO in handcuffs!*

The share price is all that matters. Legit or scam, as long as the share price goes UP! The (Crook or honest) CEO is a hero.

1,000's of HOT STOCKS offer so many variations of investments to the millions of investors who want to find even ONE winner among the vast choices of tickers with share prices well under a penny.

Returns are possible and proven but you have to know what and when to buy and you usually have to wait years for them to pay off.

In 1975, if you invested $10,000 in Wal-Mart, today it would be worth over $75,000,000 and many other public companies did the same.

20 years ago, if you invested $10,000 in Amazon at $2 per share, today they would be worth around $13,000,000.

Remember Amazon used to only sell books so when I said if you start a private or public company, you will need to also change and will be key to your survival in the marketplace. That is a proven fact.

Apples first investor sold back his 10% ownership in Apple for $800 and today would be worth over $200,000,000,000 ($200 billion). *DAMN*

People won't stop playing the lotto or a huge jackpot casino slot machine, and they will not stop spending money on debt scheme stocks to find the American Dream. And neither will the pump schemers stop because,

They ARE living the American Dream.

I have shown that most stocks are worthless because they are based on what does not exist. So what REALLY has the most value?

THE MOST VALUABLE ITEM ON EARTH

Since most Pump and Dump tickers are a HOT TOPIC scheme like gold, silver, Marijuana, a lithium mine and soon to be AI or mushrooms, let's really look at the reality of what is: *More valuable than gold, Diamonds, lithium, marijuana and all the Crypto and bitcoin combined!*

Nothing can compete with the value of this item, it's that valuable.

It is so valuable you can use it to buy a $100,000,000 mansion, 4 $5,000,000 cars, a $10,000,000 diamond watch and the item is sitting right on your desk.

It's TRUE! A gold mine stock, for example, brags about gold being $2000 an ounce so they want to raise money to go mine the gold, right? Seems logical, invest so they can mine the gold, sell it and the stock value rises! *Do you all know what it takes to mine gold?*

Millions of dollars in equipment, land that is not under regulations to not dig (which is most land these days) so you can't even MINE the gold because digging is illegal.

Not to mention the chemicals to process the gold and professionals to do the work and first survey to see if there is even gold in them there hills. It could cost $10,000,000 just to put in place the professionals and compliance even before you start to dig, if that is even allowed.

PLUS! (And keep telling this to yourself), when you invest in most gold mine stocks, *YOUR money does not go to the company* so they won't even have the $10,000,000 to start the mining process.

Read page 7 again!

Here is the point to all this. Even if the pumped scheme company actually dug for gold and found $100,000,000 in gold, gold is *worthless* compared to:

A piece of paper.

What I mean is an ounce of gold is $2000 more or less and 10 stock certificates (paper) weigh in at the same ounce.

Those stock certificates cost the scheme company only $.25 each to print (total $2.50) and each of those 10 pieces of paper represents 100,000,000 shares. Yes they are legitimate shares and legally sold by the company cheap like any other company selling shares for debt and will soon be resold to retail investors for as much as $.25 or more per share initially.

10 certificates, 100,000,000 shares each, is 1 billion shares x $.25 is $250,000,000 for only $2.50 worth of cheap paper. That equates to 125,000 ounces of gold, that's **8,000 pounds!**

Paper, truly IS the most valuable item on earth.

The Stock (Paper) at $250,000,000 per ounce that costs only $2.50 to issue and nets the brokers, debt investors and CEO $249,999,997.50, is far more than $2000 for an ounce of gold. **YOU WITH ME?**

It's a no brainer. Sell paper; screw the gold and screw shareholders.

If paper is worth more than all the gold pump and dump schemes combined, WHY focus on selling anything other than just paper shares?

For each piece of paper (Stock certificate) here is the take.

- Brokers take in $250,000,000 (They keep $125,000,000)
- Debt investors make $124,000,000
- The CEO makes $1,000,000 (Or less)
- CAN YOU GUESS WHO LOSES? The 99% retail investors

I have yet to see anyone make any money off a ticker that only sells paper.

I also have yet to see any gold in them there hills.

COST AVERAGING

COST AVERAGE rarely ever works, investors just have to hope for the best and expect the worst. Cost averaging is a way for retailers to buy more shares cheaper to make their original higher shares seem like they paid less than the original higher price. If you cost average on a debt scheme that is adding billions of shares to the float, the more shares in the float means more people are buying to cost average. That means none of the 1,000's of investors will be able to sell at a profit.

Cost averaging only works when the company is real, and operational, has sales and profits and a low float and no debt like Gunther Grant is structured. With only 108,000,000 in our DTC float any attempt to cost average will force a run on the stock sending it higher.

There are less than 10 people that own 25% of the float in GNGR, that's 25,000,000 shares out of only 108,000,000 in the float. Since GNGR was shorted, many that may have cost averaged GNGR shares ended up buying some of the massive amounts of illegal naked shorted shares dumped into the market by the illegal actions of the attorney and the brokers. *That data is further ahead in this guide.*

What normally happens when the 99% cost average shares; Investors at the start of the pump buy (Not many) shares at a starting price of let say, $.25, and believe it's going to $3.00 per share. When the stock drops to $.01, they buy more to cost average to $.05 and make a profit if it goes back to $.25 per share.

It was supposed to go to $3.00? Now at $.25 it's a winner?

Then the stock drops to $.001 and they buy more to cost average down to $.01 hoping the stock goes to 5 cents and they make a profit.

What was a winner at $.25? Now at $.05 it's a winner?

Then when it drops to $.0001 they buy more to cost average down to $.001 and hope it goes back to $.001 so they can get out and break even. *But it rarely if ever happens that way.*

The reason why they can never break even is by the time they cost averaged down to $.001 or less, billions of shares are in the float preventing any rise in share price.

Since almost all of the 99% of sub penny investors cost average, the issuing debt diluted pump and dump ticker has to have billions of shares available for sale.

Many who cost average like to see the price drop even more to grab more shares cheap. DON'T WORRY; you will get your wish. Investors are also made to believe debt is good.

NO, it is not.

Paying off (Artificial) debt with shares that are dumped and diluted is FAR different than paying off debt from profits from sales in a fully operational and valid business that does not issue or dump and dilute shares for debt reduction.

Cost averaging stocks allows the scheme company to add more debt shares to the float for less, knowing full well everyone will keep buying more shares and attract the bottom feeders who get in cheap and they also end up losing. Everyone wins except the investors.

GNGR has ONLY 108,000,000 true float shares even though many more naked shorts are still held by investors that don't know it. The fact that the GNGR shares traded and the price keeps going lower and lower proves more and more naked shorts are being issued.

The issuing of naked shares also keeps the liquidity up to fool investors there is action on the stock and that triggers the 99% and new suckers to buy more shares.

If GNGR shares were not shorted and more people bought the shares, the price would go UP, not DOWN.

Since GNGR has not issued any debt shares with only 108,000,000 in the DTC float and the share price was manipulated down to $.000001, anyone with *$108 can buy the ENTIRE FLOAT!*

ALL investors want liquidity. In most cases a liquid stock means they can sell it easier but if it's always declining in price, why sell at a loss? That is when the 99% that praised liquidity at first soon accuse the scheme of diluting the stock but the 99% fail to understand they are the same.

LIQUIDITY IS DILUTION

Investors believe liquidity is good and dilution is bad but they are essentially *the same*.

Liquidity means lots of shares are trading and that can only happen two ways. Either the company shares are trading heavily back and forth between investors or the company is just dumping more cheap shares at lower and lower prices, diluting the float.

When it comes to these penny stocks, dilution is almost always the reason for the liquidity on any given stock.

The 99% believe when the $.001 liquid shares are all sold, the price will rise believing the same volume will trade at $1 when the only shares left to buy are held by the 99% and they reap the profits.

The problem is the scheme will never let the shares rise UP as long as the 99% keep buying at lower and lower prices. The 99% believe the more they buy for less, the more they will make at $1 per share.

When a scheme unloads 10 billion shares to the 99% at $.001 ($10,000,000) creating the liquidity, the scheme knows any rise in share price means the 99% will sell and keep the scheme from making more money so the scheme will keep adding 10,000,000,000 more debt shorted shares as long as the 99% keep buying them for less.

A declining share price on a liquid stock means more debt-shorted shares are being sold to the 99%. When the 99% see the liquidity stop with 10's of billions of shares in the float at $.0001 (Or less), it does not mean the price will rise, it means you're screwed.

The 99% use the term liquidity when lots of shares trade even for a lower cost, as long as they believe they will eventually go to $1 per share. But they soon change the term to dilution when the shares are all sold and the share price never goes up.

The endless shares added to the float for less and less, is always associated with PUMP and DUMP (P&D) stocks. These schemes know full well as long as more shares are available for less, the 99% will keep buying them.

This further explains how debt dilution works.

A public company has a bid (Price you can sell the shares) and an asked (Price you have to pay for the shares). If buying and selling shares is represented by glasses of water, here is what happens...

When shares are sold, water is moved from the broker's ASKED glass to the investor's glass. As more shares are sold, less water is in the broker's ASKED glass. Normally the brokers would buy back the water for more money and add it to the BID glass so they have inventory so they can refill the asked glass to sell those shares for more money.

In a normal honest market, the water is moved back and forth as buys and sells happen but no additional water is added to the glasses.

What a debt diluted P&D essentially does is: while the water is being sold from the brokers asked glass selling to investors glasses, the debt dilution keeps anyone from selling water back to refill the brokers bid glass because the debt Pump and Dump scheme puts a garden hose from the yard into the asked brokers glass and turns it on fully.

What was once a glass that holds only 8 ounces of water has now flooded the glass and has run over the table and is now flooding the market with 1000 gallons of water making it so the brokers never have to buy back water from previous investors purchases.

That is what a P&D debt diluted scheme does. They flood the asked with never ending debt shares so the brokers never have to buy back shares from investors.

The more water (Shares) they pump, the less value it has.

I guess the term, you have been HOSED has some validity

The 99% call it liquidity when they believe they have a chance at making money on the stock, the same 99% than call it dilution when they find they can't make any money on the stock.

Also the scheme was set up that way and was not due to any issues other then deceit. WHY would a pump and dump company want a share price to decline and not rise up? *Ill tell ya!*

A RISING SHARE PRICE IS BAD

A rising share price is BAD for a Pump and Dump ticker. Those P&D companies make SURE the price slowly declines so only they can sell shares. The pumped company also does not want to compete with 1,000's of investors that already purchased shares at a lower price who will also sell to new investors if the share price were to rise.

It's easy to sell 10,000,000,000 shares from $.10 cents on down to $.00001 with an average price of all the shares sold at about $.005 (half a penny). A half penny average x 10 billion shares sold comes to **"$50 million bucks."** All on a declining share price.

All that money comes from the 99% and never goes to the 99%.

It's obvious that these Pump and Dumps are competing for the 99% investors money and to get that money they also keep their ticker at the lowest price to attract the 99%.

The lower the shares are priced, the more investors buy.

When you see 100,000,000 shares trade each day and the price stays the same, it's because as long as people buy at that price, the debt diluters will add more shorted shares to accommodate those buyers.

If the 99% stop buying, the P&D will just add billions more shorted shares for even less and the 99% will jump back in and keep buying.

The share price rarely, if ever, goes up because the scheme makes more money when the price goes down.

Just to make sure you all know:

If you buy shares, you buy them at your broker's asking price. You hope more people buy and reduce the volume as the shares are purchased, causing more to want them than what is available.

In that case, the brokers raise the bid price (The bid is what you can sell your shares for) and, in a perfect world, the bid ends up higher than what you paid initially and you make a profit.

As shares are sold on a Pump and Dump, instead of the brokers raising the bid price so you can make a profit, they just keep buying more debt shares (Cheap) and sell them short to new investors.

Brokers know when a **P&D** is in play, and by securing debt shares that are not in the float YET, brokers will short the stock when the price is at its highest and buy the debt shares cheap to cover the shorts. That allows massive liquidity with a constant declining share price because the shares are coming from the company debt shares, not the retail bid or retail investors holdings. It's an endless supply of shares that do not come from those 99% who already purchased shares.

Naked shorting means the brokers are selling synthetic fake shares that don't exist but the 99% believe they are real, just for the fact they see they have that ticker in their trade account.

Debt diluted naked shorted shares are the same as schemers that sell counterfeit merchandise at a local flea market. People buy what they and others think is real when they are fake.

Investors who buy similar fake shares to help a company expand and trigger a rise in share price when in fact, the money those investors spent goes to the debt share counterfeiter, not the company. That is what happens when the 99% buy into a new scheme Pump and Dump that imply when you invest in the stock (ticker), it helps the company expand when it does no such thing.

The reason why brokers never buy back on the bid, is simple... they don't want to buy back the fake shares they sold you the same way a scammer at a flea market won't buy back the counterfeit items they sold you because they are in business to only SELL, not buy back.

The 99% that always lose in the market must be so frustrated they can't fine ONE winner so they can claim some emotional victory.

EVERY ONE of the 99% that keeps failing to find the one winner ends up also claiming fraud and the CEO is a crook and they will have them arrested. Some post publicly they are going to call congress to take action unless the CEO pays them back. YES they are that delusional.

Shorting shares is FREE money for brokers but the 99% think their money went to the actual company when it did not. I repeat myself in many chapters so the data sinks in. Here it is in a nutshell:

If the money investors paid for shares does not go to the company and the naked shares sold don't exist, brokers can sell as many as they want at any price. It's FREE MONEY and they keep it all.

SHORT AND NAKED SHORT DATA

One investor who bought **illegal naked shorted shares** in my company from his broker called me and said, "YOU TOOK MY MONEY!" He thought when he bought shares on the open market, the money went to my company or me but it did not (It went to brokers shorting GNGR shares). He said he has the check to prove he paid me and he will sue me. I said, "Show me a cancelled check that has MY bank deposit stamp on the back and I'll refund you double what you paid." I never heard back from him.

The broker **kept all his money**. Brokers know the 99% will always go after the CEO because the 99% believe their investment went to the CEO or company when that is farthest from the truth. That investor and 1,000's like him ended up buying naked shorted shares from brokers, not from our company or me. The shorted shares caused the price to drop and that is what makes investors angry.

What I also found is that some stock traders will short naked just to get their commission checks (Plus a little side bonus cash from the schemers to push the shares) knowing they can cause the Brokerage they work for to take the heat if a short squeeze happens. They can end up quitting or being fired but the short issue and responsibility to correct it falls on the brokerage firms, same as if a UPS or FEDEX driver causes a car accident, they sue the company, not the employee.

If brokers sold GNGR short 800,000,000 shares, they are deficient about 700,000,000 shares that must be delivered at some point or the brokers will have to buy back the shorts to close out what they oversold. Brokers believed GNGR would cover the debt shares like Pump and Dumps do. They were mistaken. **I never issued any shares.**

The brokers also do what banks do; they lend shares like a bank lends money. They use the accumulated shares held for everyone in ONE account so they can lend the shares to short sellers for a fee (Same as when a bank lends money for interest). Eventually shares and the bank's money both have to be paid back.

If a bank loan is unpaid, the bank repossesses the house. If shorted shares are not acquired to cover the shorts sold, short sellers are forced to buy back the shares they borrowed. **That is called a short squeeze.**

Debt dilution short selling is so common, brokers often rush to start selling short up to 20 times the float when the price is at its highest without making sure the company has debt or if debt shares will be available when they may not be. Once those shorted shares are sold, it also changes the $.25 investors paid to a new value of only $.0001 or less per share.

Brokers know selling shorted shares that **don't exist,** causes the same reaction as if they do exist with the plan to acquire debt shares cheap to cover the shorts. If they find out the debt shares are not available, they will drop the share price from $.25 to $.000001 in hopes all investors sell at a major loss for a **tax write off** and the brokers close the shorts and also prevent a short squeeze.

If brokers that over sold shares short 20 times the TRUE float, they can be forced to buy back those shorts for up to 100 or more times what they sold them for if they can't acquire debt shares or if investors don't sell them back for a tax write off.

The investor's goal is to **buy low and sell high** while the status quo short selling goal of brokers is to sell high to investors and buy them back for much less or acquire debt shares cheap to close the shorts.

Selling naked shorted shares is like counterfeiting money, but if the debt shares cannot be obtained, the brokers have to use their money to buy back the shares they sold or get shares from the company.

The difference between a bank and stocks is: Someone **cannot** print money after taking a loan to buy a house and just hand the bank counterfeit money, while a debt dilution scheme can acquire unlimited amounts of shares from the company (if the company is part of the scheme) and the company just has to increase the authorized from 10,000,000 to 50,000,000,000 or more to cover any sold shorted shares. Or brokers will just naked short sell shares on their own.

If you print $50,000,000 in counterfeit money, you will be arrested and end up retiring in a federal prison.

If you print unlimited shorted shares to take $50,000,000 from investors, you end up retiring in a Beverly Hills mansion. TA DA!

How fucked up is that?

IMPORTANT INDICATORS using two high profile stocks.

To spot a debt diluted short in progress can be as simple as doing the following: if you take the market cap and divide that by the share price on any given day, it shows the true outstanding shares. Keep in mind, the shorts are quickly corrected by updating the data before the SEC can take action but always before the data is seen by investors (not that investors even look at this or any data).

Amazon at $202.61 per share divided into the market cap of $2,130,446,380,331 matches the outstanding 10,515,011,008 shares.

The numbers MATCH!

AMZN
Amazon.com, Inc.

Common Stock

202.61 ↓ -8.87 -4.19%

Delayed (15 Min) Trade Data: 12:00am 11/15/2024

| Overview | Quote | Company Profile | Security Details | News | Financials | Disclosure | Research |

AMZN SECURITY DETAILS

Share Structure

Market Cap	2,130,446,380,331	11/15/2024
Authorized Shares	Not Available	
Outstanding Shares	10,515,011,008	10/18/2024

Now by comparison, the DJT Media stock, you can see before the update there were MORE shares outstanding based on the math. DJT has been diluted this way many times since going public. The float keeps rising and the price falls as shares are diluted into the float.

This is NOT in any way political bias against DJT or is in any way illegal. This is to show how ***a perfect storm of the 4 ingredients*** needed to short-sell is in play and explained in an upcoming chapter.

1. An ***exciting brand, name or hot topic*** to attract the 99%
2. Lots of corporate debt to allow debt conversion dilution
3. Billions of shares (or unlimited) that back up short sales
4. The company issuing shares as needed to cover shorts

Do the math! The outstanding shares show 194,715,772. If you divide the market cap of $5,392,653,306 by the share price, the outstanding ends up **MORE** than what is posted as outstanding. That means MORE shares are sold short from debt dilution before the data is updated.

DJT

Trump Media & Technology Group Corp.

26.96 ↓ -0.
-2.6

Delayed (15 Min) Trade Data: 09:34am 11/08/2

Class A Common Stock

| Overview | Quote | Company Profile | Security Details | News | Financials | Disclosure | Research |

DJT SECURITY DETAILS

Additional Securities

Share Structure

Market Cap 🔍	5,392,653,306	11/07/2(
Authorized Shares	Not Available	
Outstanding Shares	194,715,772	08/07/2(

Then they update the outstanding from 194,715,772 to 216,924,448. After the brokers shorted DJT 22,000,000 more shares, it allowed debt investors to make over $600,000,000! In one day, NICE!

DJT SECURITY DETAILS

Additional Securit

Share Structure

Market Cap 🔍	6,095,576,989	11/1!
Authorized Shares	Not Available	
Outstanding Shares	216,924,448	10/2!
Restricted	Not Available	

Personally I don't think DJT knows this is happening, but as CEO, he should be concerned about the continued rise in the outstanding and the falling share price as the outstanding still continues to rise.

In most cases the company says the increased float is due to insiders selling shares after their restricted waiting period. NOT true because the debt dilution conversion rule as explained in this guide shows how shares can be diluted into the float *at any time, even before any restrictions are lifted.*

What used to be **29,992,831** shares in the outstanding has ballooned to over **216,000,000** shares. As long as there are buyers of just a few shares, the outstanding will rise and the price will continue to fall.

29,992,831 shares outstanding at $66.81

DJT

Trump Media & Technology Group Corp.

Class A Common Stock

66.81 ↑ 8.82 15.20%

Delayed (15 Min) Trade Data: 10:28am 03/27/2024

| Overview | Quote | Company Profile | Security Details | News | Financials | Disclosure | Research |

DJT SECURITY DETAILS

Additional Securities ⌄

Share Structure

Market Cap 🔍	1,739,284,270	03/26/2024
Authorized Shares	Not Available	
Outstanding Shares	29,992,831	11/22/2023
Restricted	Not Available	

216,924,448 shares outstanding at $27.34

DJT

Trump Media & Technology Group Corp.

Class A Common Stock

27.345 ↓ -1.585 -5.48%

Delayed (15 Min) Trade Data: 10:15am 11/14/2024

| Overview | Quote | Company Profile | Security Details | News | Financials | Disclosure | Research |

DJT SECURITY DETAILS

Additional Securities ⌄

Share Structure

Market Cap 🔍	6,275,624,281	11/13/2024
Authorized Shares	Not Available	
Outstanding Shares	216,924,448	10/29/2024

The more shares issued to the float, the lower the share price goes. The more shares people buy, the more shares will be diluted to the float. The float is SUPPOSED to stay low so the demand causes the share price to rise UP so investors can make a profit. ***Not likely.***

If you calculate the outstanding (216,924,448) DJT shares and subtract the initial (29,992,831) it's 186,931,617 shares sold short on average for about $30.00 which means $5.6 billion were generated selling shorted debt diluted shares to the public.

If DJT Media is in debt $400,000,000, why is the debt not paid from the $5.6 billion taken from investors? *(Read page 7 AGAIN!)* With NO company debt, massive amounts of debt-diluted shares can't be sold.

This is not bias on DJT stock, it applies to 1000's of stocks. DJT is an example to prove my data is accurate. I sent my warnings to DJT, Devin Nunes and other Trump family members back when the 29,992,448 shares were at $66 about what **WILL happen**, but I am sure no one read it or even saw it but now it's to late, the debt dilution is here.

As a Republican, while respecting some liberal opinions, this data is just one of many examples that *is in play*. I questioned if I should use this data but the facts are the facts and not political bias. This is to show when there is money to be made on debt dilution, regardless of being at the **TOP** of the food chain or the bottom, **NO ONE, not even the President of the United States is off limits.**

CHINA and USA adversaries use these debt conversion rules to steal BILLION$ from USA investors to fund anti-USA activity.

And I know HOW TO STOP IT!

Also, I am thankful to be one of the main producers of TRUMP political collectible jewelry since 2016 *MADE IN THE USA!* More on my change from confections to castings is further ahead in this guide.

If the DEBT conversion rule was *not* used with DJT stock, DJT would still be at 29,992,448 shares in the float and those who paid $66 would be sitting with shares at or around *$2,500 per share* (just like Amazon from $2 to $3,400). The problem with that is the $5.6 billion would not have been raised selling those diluted shares to the market to get that massive amount of cash from investors who, in many cases, only purchased ONE share simply because it's EXCITING. And the investor's money never even went to help DJT Media or its debt.

I call this the *AMAZON Effect.* Many only own ONE share of Amazon just to have something EXCITING in their account. Same with the DJT stock as sales for ONE share were common and is clearly not for any financial gain, it's just EXCITING and that is what sells shares.

DJT ticker trades, only (1) share are very common. Same with Amazon and many other EXCITING stocks. OK Lets move on.

Open Price		Low Price		High Price		Close Price		Prev Close
48.50		47.51		50.75				46.69

Trades	Volume	VWAP	Dollar Volume	Avg Volume	52 Week Range
27,317	2,380,796	$ 48.69	$ 115,929,273	-	12.40 - 79.38

Last Trade Time		Type	Quantity	Stock Price	Currency
09:56:56			1	48.9388	USD

Trades	Volume	VWAP	Dollar Volume	Avg Volume	52 Week Range
27,345	2,382,335	$ 48.69	$ 116,004,699	-	12.40 - 79.38

Last Trade Time		Type	Quantity	Stock Price	Currency
09:57:04			1	49.00	USD

Trades	Volume	VWAP	Dollar Volume	Avg Volume	52 Week Range
30,666	2,716,852	$ 48.83	$ 132,663,650	-	12.40 - 79.38

Last Trade Time		Type	Quantity	Stock Price	Currency
10:05:45			1	49.65	USD

Trades	Volume	VWAP	Dollar Volume	Avg Volume	52 Week Range
30,693	2,718,529	$ 48.83	$ 132,748,867	-	12.40 - 79.38

Last Trade Time		Type	Quantity	Stock Price	Currency
10:05:56			1	49.6491	USD

MORE MARKET MANIPULATION

A stock chat room member posted a question to me: *XXXX is really moving up today, 200%. But cannabis stocks look to be in a freefall.*

My reply; Smoke and Mirrors, only 100 shares traded to give you that false data as if the stock is taking off. And was likely not a valid trade.

Cannabis companies that are operational will survive, while the scams are cleared out. *The 100 shares you saw trade is to send a signal to other brokers and market makers.* They do not want to send emails or any recordable data that can be illegal so they use signals.

When you saw 100 and then 300 shares trade, it was a signal to other brokers to react to those signals, 100 and 300.

The 100 share trade posted by a market maker means they need shares, and the other 300 trade means take the price down 30%.

When you see individual trades of 600 or 1000 then you can worry.

100 - I need Shares.
300 – Take the stock down at least 30% so I can load shares.
505 - I am short on shares
600 - Apply resistance at the ASK to keep the price from rising.
700 - Move the price up.
800 - Prepare for an increase in trading volume.
900 - Allow the stock to float and trade freely.
911 - Pending News/Press Release On The Way
1000 - Don't let it run
2100 - Let it run

End of reply

During the time I was writing this guide, XXXX marijuana stock reversed merged into a NEW Artificial Intelligence ticker, just as I said it would.

Another stock scammer combined a crypto scam saying he also uses artificial intelligence to *GUARANTEE* profits. He got 5 years in jail. If he had said he *INTENDS* to generate profits not say *GUARNTEE!* He would have not been charged.

READ THIS A FEW TIMES SO IT SINKS IN

Let's **PRETEND** (*Because this never happens in reality*) just **ONE** P&D scheme **allowed** investors to win. Where is all the WINNING money coming from? If the P&D scheme **did NOT sell any debt shares,** what's in it for the schemers? **NOTHING!**

The Scheme would still have to pay for pumped intent misleading news and pay dozens of pumpers (at great cost) to make a demand for the shares so the price rises initially. With **no operations or sales** to generate revenue, the P&D would have to spend lots of money they don't even have, all for nothing? **Not likely!**

If 10,000 investors each turn $100 into $10,000, the scheme ends up losing $100,000,000 by allowing investors to sell on the bid to NEW investors at the higher share price that the scheme would have made selling debt shares. The only option for the scheme is; **here it comes!**

Sell billions of debt diluted shares to new investors on the asked price that add more shares to the float that drops the share price and prevents any shares sold on the bid, so no previous or new investors can sell at a profit, while more and more of the 99% keep buying at lower prices.

The BID element in the market place is essentially SHUT DOWN allowing unlimited billions of debt shares to be sold to existing cost average shareholders and new sucker investors that buy in for less and less as the share price keeps falling. The P&D debt diluter wins and all investors lose. **The proof investors will lose all their money is:**

Pump and Dumps are not in business to let investors win. If investors win, Pump and Dumps lose, and Pump and Dumps never lose.

Schemers know, as a fact, that the 99% will buy billions of liquid shares even as they drop in price but ONLY if the Pump and Dump is HOT news and a $100,000,000 plan. And they need the brokers help.

Most of the 99% once again find they are locked out of profits or any chance of the stock breaking even. It was all set up that way.

THE LOCK OUT

That is when brokers no longer buy on the retail bid and sell short and then get the shares from debt sellers for a fraction of the bid to keep the price from rising and to continue to decline as the float grows.

More shares, less cost, more investors = more commissions.

A broker can take in $50,000,000 or more in commissions each quarter selling shares to investors that brokers know will never be purchased from the retailers on the bid. This lock out is because many brokers are in on the schemes. They may not be breaking the law but they obviously don't have investor's best interests in mind.

If someone buys shares, the brokers make MORE money getting the debt shares cheaper than the bid price. If the shares asked price is $.10 and the bid is $.09, brokers buy shares from the debt sellers for $.01. When someone buys $500 worth at $.10, the brokers make $450 not just the $7 commission. What would YOU do as a broker earning *10% commissions* each month?

Process 2,000 investors $500 transactions and make only $7 commission on each transaction that comes to $14,000 ($1,400 commission to you)

Or:

Sell 2,000 investors $500 in shares that cost $50 from debt investors and profit $450 in addition to the $7 fee comes to $914,000. ($91,400 commission to you)

Brokers keep the shares on a declining price to hide the fact they are also buying debt shares from the scheme for less.

Brokers need to hide the dilution debt dump and prevent anyone from selling on the bid even at a loss so as NOT to expose the trades that exceed the float until they get the next allocation of debt shares to cover the shortfall. Usually 3 months before the float data is updated.

Your "TRUSTED BROKERS" know full well the scheme will dump shares, kill the price and fold the company.

This is what the 99% retailers *lose, $300,000,000* on each trading day! And the debt scheme and brokers make BILLIONS giving the 99% what they want, lots of shares CHEAP!

Price	% Change	$ Volume	Share Volu
PRICE	% CHANGE	$ VOL	SHARE VOL
0.00045	-10.00	177,332	369,746,997
0.0001	0.00	36,039	355,575,353
0.0009	+12.50	176,806	194,179,721
0.0001	0.00	7,749	100,186,635
0.0003	0.00	29,411	98,035,708
0.000098	0.00	7,184	72,340,000
0.0001	+100.00	5,735	57,350,000
0.0004	+60.00	13,665	45,683,210
0.0001	0.00	3,987	39,867,985
0.00025	0.00	10,121	35,079,681
0.0041	-6.82	141,907	33,709,089
0.0614	+1.49	1,973,069	30,181,179
0.0004	0.00	10,481	26,577,550
0.0006	0.00	14,730	25,409,101
0.0002	0.00	3,493	23,106,000
0.0004	+39,900.00	8,963	22,440,250
0.0004	0.00	7,618	22,157,738
0.0001	-50.00	2,281	21,354,381
0.0001	0.00	1,357	21,319,799

The shares are not only diluted but also shorted when you see 20,000,000+ shares trade on any given trading day. When you see the *% change at 0.00* means the bid is locked out. The float keeps rising and the brokers stop buying shares from retailers on the bid side and millions of shares can trade with no price *% change.*

Some tickers will have hundreds of millions of shares trade each day with no change in the share price. Most of the 99% believe they have legal recourse but that is not true when you look at the disclaimers.

THE LEGAL DISCLAIMERS

I put this chapter in to make my point in this guide even though I know many won't read it since they don't read the disclaimers on any of the questionable scheme stocks they buy into.

A company with over $50,000,000 in debt, and no revenue that clearly stated they make NO money and investors are likely to lose all their money over time to pay for operational costs, had the shares rise to $50 simply because they promoted they were in the crypto space when the market was new to the Crypto excitement. I believe they sold over $2,500,000,000 ($2.5 billion) in stock and continue to sell shares today for much less.

Here is the disclaimer; I'm smart so if ANYONE can tell me what this all means PLEASE email me.

The Disclaimer as written on their 15c211 compliance data.

Carefully consider each Product's investment objectives, risk factors, fees and expenses before investing. This and other information can be found in each Product's private placement memorandum, which may be obtained for each Product that is an SEC reporting company, for each Product that reports under the OTC Markets Alternative Reporting Standards. Reports prepared in accordance with the OTC Markets Alternative Reporting Standards are not prepared in accordance with SEC requirements and may not contain all information that is useful for an informed investment decision. Read these documents carefully before investing.

Investments in the Products are speculative investments that involve high degrees of risk, including a partial or total loss of invested funds. These Products are not suitable for any investor that cannot afford loss of the entire investment. The shares of each Product are intended to reflect the price of the asset(s) held by such Product (based on digital asset(s) per share), less such Product's expenses and other liabilities. Because each Product does not currently operate a redemption program, there can be no assurance that the value of such Product's shares will reflect the value of the assets held by such Product, less such Product's expenses and other liabilities, and the shares of such Product, if traded on any secondary market, may trade at a substantial premium over, or a substantial discount to, the value of the assets held by such Product, less such Product's expenses and other liabilities, and such Product may be unable to meet its investment objective. This information should not be relied upon as research, investment advice, or a recommendation regarding any products, strategies, or any security in particular. This material is strictly for illustrative, educational, or informational purposes and is subject to change. The shares of each Product are not registered under the Securities Act of 1933 (the "Securities Act"), the Securities Exchange Act of 1934 (except for Products that are SEC reporting companies), the Investment Company Act of 1940, or any state securities laws. The Products are offered in private placements pursuant to the exemption from registration provided by Rule 506(c) under Regulation D of the Securities Act and are only available to accredited investors. As a result, the shares of each Product are restricted and subject to significant limitations on resale and transfers. Potential investors in any Product should carefully consider the long-term nature of an investment in that Product prior to making an investment decision. The shares of certain Products are also publicly quoted on OTC Markets and shares that have become unrestricted in accordance with the rules and regulations of the SEC may be bought and sold throughout the day through any brokerage account.

I read that 100 times and still have no clue what it means other than investors will lose all their money.

If you do read the fine print when investing, at least you will know you have NO legal grounds to sue them. Let's understand the disclaimer wording so you are aware of the warning signs. Almost every stock being pumped or marketed will have the small print that no one reads.

Here is some more fine print, READ IT then we'll move onto the warning signs. It's confusing and always in small print with no spaces to get you discouraged from reading, but it is essential.

The meaning of the safe harbor provisions of the U.S. Private Securities' Litigation Reform Act of 1995. Forward-looking statements also may be included in other publicly available documents issued by the Company and in oral statements made by our officers and representatives from time to time.

These forward-looking statements are intended to provide management's current expectations or plans for our future operating and financial performance, based on assumptions currently believed to be valid. They can be identified by the use of words such as "anticipate," "intend," "plan," "goal," "seek," "believe," "project," "estimate," "expect," "strategy," "future," "likely," "may," "should," "would," "could," "will" and other words of similar meaning in connection with a discussion of future operating or financial performance.

Examples of forward-looking statements include, among others, statements relating to future sales, earnings, cash flows, results of operations, uses of cash and other measures of financial performance. Because forward-looking statements relate to the future, they are subject to inherent risks, uncertainties and other factors that may cause the Company's actual results and financial condition to differ materially from those expressed or implied in the forward-looking statements. *Such risks, uncertainties and other factors include, among others. Such as, but not limited to economic conditions, changes in the laws or regulations, demand for products and services of the company, the effects of competition and other factors that could cause actual* results to differ materially from those projected or represented in the forward-looking statements. *Any forward-looking information provided in this release should be considered with these factors in mind. We assume no obligation to update any forward-looking statements contained in this report.*

Who wants to read all that, it's exhausting!

This is how the fine print relates to a pumped stock. WXYZ is for example purposes of a pumped OTC ticker.

"WXYZ" has a **plan** to enter the $100 billion dollar a year Marijuana industry and **intends** to open up 50 new dispensary locations with capital we **anticipate** will be invested from Warren Buffets Berkshire Hathaway after the review of our business plan they currently have at their offices. We are excited at the **potential** of a direct investment from the Oracle or Omaha Warren Buffet.

Mr. Buffet said this sector is a billion dollar industry giving confidence that he may **likely** invest, allowing WXYZ to achieve our **intended** goal with **disruptive potential** with the **plan** to grab some of that $100 billion revenue and **vertically integrate** our operations to all states that legalized marijuana.

To the moon!

Sounds Great but this is what you are really being told.

WXYZ is not going into the marijuana industry, we will not open any dispensaries and our business plan that was sent to Berkshire Hathaway was one of 1,000's sent that ended up in the trash. Warren Buffet does not even know about our plans and he will not be investing and we will not reach our intended goals.

But the promoted "INTENT" news sent the stock rallying allowing the pumped OTC to sell 2 billion shares between 3 and 5 cents and took in **$75,000,000. NICE!**

That IS Lotto money just not for investors.

That is why you need to read the fine print and wording that is about intent and what really is going to happen and combine that data with the company share structure and financials.

But to be honest, everyone reading this knows it and invests anyway so maybe I did not even need this chapter.

With so much money in the market ripe for the TAKING, Schemes will use laws to alter the perception of the scheme to detract from the normal status quo most know about that is so common. The UMBRELLA is fairly new and was attempted on our company GNGR but I declined the lizard's futile attempt.

I had a few SPACs contact me but I also declined the offers that almost always end up with dilution and a declining share price.

It is OBVIOUS to me, and hopefully those reading this guide, to understand dilution and declining share prices is how money is made and also proving the retail investors are likely to never make ANY money in the "stinky pinkies" as they call those shares.

Since pump and dumps have NO operations or product sales revenue, it's hard to attract the **non** 99% investors. The SPAC latches onto a valid exciting existing operation that looks AMAZING. Even though drowning in debt, the EXCITEMENT in the marketplace outshines the fact the company is simply a pump and dump hidden behind legitimacy and usually starts on the NYSE or NASDAQ before being delisted to the OTC.

STAY SHARP AND BEWARE OF SPACS AND LAWYERS!

Most of this guide is directed at being public but the same issues also relate to any private company that may end up being a target for a SPAC. DJT was a SPAC merger. *A SPAC is sort of like an UMBRELLA.*

A SPAC, *"Special Purpose Acquisition Company"* is usually a blank check company that is public with no operations with the goal to find a victim business and convince that company to be public.

The HOOK is to get the private company that has or can show potential but needs capital. The SPAC convinces that private company CEO they will get the needed capital to expand the operations. What I experienced is, they say one thing, and then do another. Remember they want all the money and you can't have any.

The new ticker on the SPAC deal will use an artificially raised highest share price so they can be listed on an exchange like NYSE or NASDAQ. But I also see that most SPAC mergers end up below the required price or requirements to remain on the exchange and are eventually delisted to the OTC Markets.

When the scheme starts (let's say, $30.00 per share) and the SPAC pays some of the 3rd party debt that the private company has, they receive shares they can sell with no holding period. The SPAC also tells the private company when 10 million shares are sold for $300 million, they will reinvest millions to help the company. *Yeah Sure!*

I have yet to ever see any merger private company get the capital they need or promised to expand and eliminate debt. With no debt, a pump and dump or SPAC can't work. Private companies facing financial issues that believe merging with a SPAC will save them are 100% incorrect and here is why.

The SPAC knows the company will likely never be profitable and they also know the private company has NO money to pay the SPAC for the merger. The SPAC becomes the debt holder and as they pay debt, they get shares, register those shares on the debt conversion rule and work with brokers to start shorting the stock at the initial highest price.

I DARE anyone to post a ticker that was part of a SPAC deal where the share price went UP and the company achieved their goal...

What follows is usually a reverse stock split to move the underperforming shares to a higher price to remain on an exchange. But, the shares will continue to drop and Investors who have 10,000 shares may end up with only one share after multiple reverse splits.

One example of a ticker that did many reverse splits and with each reverse, the stock fell back down while current and new investors kept buying more and more with each reverse split.

Working the numbers with their splits, 12/1, 1/12, 1/1,000, 1/10,000, 1/500. Here is what you needed to buy to end up with *1 SHARE!*

You would had to have bought *5 billion shares* that increased 12 for 1 giving you 60 billion shares that were reduced back 1 for 12 to 5 billion shares that were then reduced by 1,000 giving you 5,000,000 shares that again were reduced by 10,000 giving you 500 shares that again were reduced by 500 giving you *1 share.*

Today their price is under a penny and the SAME people are still buying it. And, soon it will be merged into a new ticker and scheme.

To end up with *ONE share* after all the reverse splits, even if someone DID buy 5 billion shares in 2008 (Unlikely) for even $.0001 ($500,000), your ONE share today is worth under a penny.

SECURITY NOTES

Capital Change=shs increased by 12 for 1 split, payable upon surrender. Pay date=11/09/2009

Capital Change=shs decreased by 1 for 12 split Pay date=12/27/2010.

Capital Change=shs decreased by 1 for 1000 split Ex-date=10/14/2014.

Capital Change=shs decreased by 1 for 10000 split Ex-date=09/27/2019. Pay date=09/27/20

Capital Change=shs decreased by 1 for 500 split. Ex-date=04/17/2023. Pay date=04/17/2023

SPAC investors are bigger players (even institutions) and jump in just like the 99% do on low priced schemes and suffer the same fate. But they lose MILLIONS, not just $100. In many cases, they are greedy money mangers that misuse client's money for personal gain.

The plan is to end up taking the SPAC share price so low on the OTC it attracts all the 99% retail investors. But, first they tell the brokers to oversell the shares up to 20 or more times the true float at the higher prices when on the NYSE or NASDAQ exchanges.

If shares start at $10 or more and the float is 1 million shares while the SPAC is in full swing, the brokers will sell short 10 million shares and take in $100 million the victim company knows nothing about because the CEO does not know his company shares were naked shorted.

To cover the broker's shorts at $10 per share, they drop the price artificially to let's say $1 and the debt holders legally are entitled to 10 million shares but they don't pay $10 million in debt, they only pay maybe $200,000 (take it or leave it) and a panicked CEO will usually take it just to get some capital to get through the month.

In many cases, the CEO does not know the stock was heavily shorted at the higher price so they get **NONE** of that money.

When the debt investors get hold of those 10 million shares, they have the brokers close out the shorts and the float now moves from 1,000,000 shares to 11,000,000 and the SCREAMS of dilution start.

Eventually many SPACs are delisted to the OTC and the broker's start selling short 100 million shares at $1 or less to the 99% who think they could go back to $10 and make a killing.

Since the brokers are again shorting the stock 100 million shares (but everyone only sees the float is 11 million) at $1, they take in another $100 million. Remember, the 99% TRULY believe when the 11 million are all sold, the stock will go TO DA MOON, as they say.

But what soon follows is the norm. After the brokers sell off 100 million shorted shares for $1, they again drop the price to $.05 and the debt holders legally force the CEO to issue more shares at the lower price on the agreement. That's called death spiral toxic funding.

Now the SPAC stock that once had only 1,000,000 shares at $10 ends up with 111,000,000 shares in the float at under $1. The float continues to rise and the share price keeps falling. **TA DA!**

When its all over, the brokers and debt diluters make $200 million or more all while the private company CEO that took the SPAC bait never gets the money they needed and also that CEO has to face investors, lawsuits and the SEC for any violations that may have been done by others but, **YOU'RE THE CEO so it's always your fault.**

Any company contacted by a SPAC is a sign the private company is in trouble and debt conversion diluters are **NOT** in business to help a losing company. Why spend more money on losses when they can sell $200 million on shorted shares fast and easy with no hassles or costs.

If you're a private company looking to go public, beware at all times. And beware investing in a SPAC.

Going public can also ruin your private company by spending precious time and capital trying to figure out how to get your share price up while others try and destroy your private company by toxic death spiral debt funding or to get you to give up and sell them the public vehicle ticker (Part 2). Or they just walk away with the cash.

Merging with a SPAC, your shares that may have started at $10 or more are quickly manipulated down to $1 or less. Even if your company is making money and growing, the stock will be worthless.

SPAC Merger contracts will often say you agree to be responsible for any investors prior to the vehicle being sold or merged. **So, watch what you sign.**

Going public by any means (SPAC, IPO, S1, DPO) will put your company in the crosshairs of 1000's of schemers who do and say anything to get the CEO to consider a change that does not benefit the CEO or the victim company or shareholders.

But NASDAQ or the NYSE is NOT where the BIG money is made by a long shot. The initial pump is to show validity and a solid company to invest in even when most if not all mergers ONLY target a company with debt and an exciting story to tell investors. The REAL money is made when things go south.

What would YOU do to make money if you sold shares as a SPAC?

Sell 1 million shares on NASDAQ to less people at $10.00 to make $10,000,000

Sell 20 billion+ shares to the 99% on the OTC Markets at $.01 to make $200,000,000

The LOWER the share price goes, the more people will buy them and the scheme will make more money than selling the SPAC shares at a higher price to less people on an exchange like NYSE or NASDAQ.

I did not know most of what is in this guide until **AFTER** being public. Once public, I ended up at the point of no return and had to figure a way to **not** end up like other ticker CEO's. Stay sharp! At least GNGR was already operational and profitable and we continue to keep the company alive while the stock ended up in the gutter.

Proving legitimacy has NO place in the penny stock market.

Taking the bait to merge a private company into a SPAC or taking your company public or agreeing to a reverse merger, never works out the way the CEO anticipated. It's as if the CEO went skydiving and jumped out of the plane, not realizing they forgot a parachute. You can think about it, realize you screwed up, flap your arms, pray, but you cannot go back.

In my situation, I never had to deal with that event because I was smart enough not to get on the plane in the first place. Be smart, stay sharp and don't panic.

SPAC's latch onto a victim company but the actual SPAC has limited information or who it running the SPAC. That is why most pump and dump or SPAC companies operate from a Suite or P.O. Box and use a cell phone, so when they vanish, you can never find them and they toss the phone in the river.

I took my company public because we had an existing operational company with paying accounts that expanded to more locations that needed funding and with no outlet for capital; we raised some money to go public with the belief that the much greater capital would be accessible after being publicly traded. **WRONG!**

We saw the data about going public and how it can help. The attorneys said GO PUBLIC! Everyone said GO PUBLIC and you'll get the capital. After being public, everyone had their hand out for money and the few we paid offered no help at all and were, in fact, the ones trying to get me to sell the ticker. **Everyone is in on it!**

The issue with going public and not being able to access more capital is, you still have to answer to those who invested before you went public and those you don't know who bought shares on the open market before the share price decline who are now all PISSED!

Raising money so you can go public or merging into a SPAC to raise even more money to make the business plan work is just digging the hole deeper. Once the SPAC or debt shares are depleted, most of those involved with the SPAC or merger vanish into thin air.

The CEO will then have to face all the compliance and investor relations alone with no idea what to do as panic sets in as the shares drop further and further. When the CEO is faced with NO answers as to how to correct the issue is when the Lizards jump in to break you down to get you to sell your public vehicle outright cheap. If you do sell, they all make MILLIONS on a new P&D and the CEO is left high and dry to deal with the SEC and a failed underfunded company.

The longer schemers keep your company down; and the more investors become agitated, the more confident the schemers believe the CEO will finally give in to selling the vehicle. But that is almost always from a ticker that has failed operations and the CEO is broke.

GNGR is a global selling brand and we're not broke, so I can keep moving ahead making money and expanding so I can wait the market out while I make changes, and never give into the schemes. That is why the Russian and Ex-Cop lizards kept cursing at me; they never heard the words **NO DEAL! And why SPAC's keep calling me.**

Some did try to destroy my private company to get me to fold and quit and with no option, sell them the public vehicle. But they failed their mission. Without DEBT, a pump and dump or SPAC cannot do the 3rd party debt conversion. When you see **hidden stock data and DEBT**, you can bet it won't end well.

The SPAC, the 3rd party debt holders and brokers make billion$, the investors do not. Ever wonder why brokers have **NO commissions** on many NYSE and NASDAQ shares, so how do they make money?

Brokerage's revenue comes from **(PFOF)** Payment For Order Flow, which are rebates from market makers. Since the market makers get **DEBT shares cheap**, they can offer **higher rebates** if brokers **push garbage stocks.** Here is one of many examples.

This SPAC recently opened on the NYSE at $35.00 that dropped to $.17 and my target price will end up $.01 or less. Today, they are in PANIC mode to remain on the NYSE and to do that they have to do a reverse stock split to get the shares back UP or be **delisted to the OTC.**

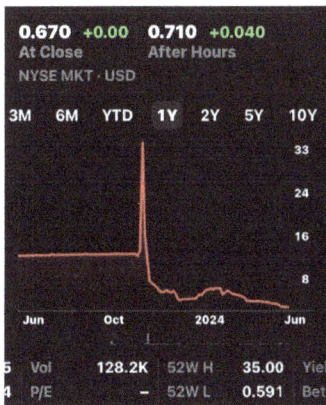

0.670 +0.00	0.710 +0.040
At Close	After Hours
NYSE MKT · USD	

3M 6M YTD **1Y** 2Y 5Y 10Y

most recent fiscal years. The Company must submit a plan (the "Plan") by July 18, 2024 to the NYSE American outlining actions it has taken or will take to regain compliance with the continued listing standards ▮▮▮ If the Plan is not permitted or the Plan is not accepted, delisting proceedings will commence.

Even DJT stock hit $79.00 and the PR NEWS informed investors that **ANY shares sold by ANYONE** would not be applied to the company. That includes the DEBT holder's shares sold to the retail investors **(Read page 7 again).** Sadly, and to be completely honest, I anticipate the same fate falling to DJT like most others that sell shares and the funds don't help the company as the float is diluted and share price declines.

But **DJT investors are similar to AMAZON investors** and JUST maybe the saving grace for DJT's share price. Many are buying only one or two shares just to be part of something exciting even though they are not in it to make money. This excitement is why a pump and dump or a SPAC attaches with something EXCITING. No one will buy shares in a shoe company for $79, EVEN IF they are making more profits than DJT. It's just not exciting.

SO WHO AM I? GUNTHER GRANT? (Ticker GNGR)

I am sure readers are wondering, since I am a CEO of a public company, am I a crook scammer or legit? Usually the share price dictates which one I am. Unjustified in our situation. *If GNGR or I were a crook or scam, this book would never have been written.*

GNGR with fewer than 109,000,000 in the float with an operational and profitable business cannot issue debt shares because GNGR has no debt. *With no debt, a company cannot be a diluted pump and dump.*

A publicly traded Pump and Dump debt diluted scheme, needs to have *4 specific ingredients* to make that happen.

1) A company's goals, based on excitement or an impossible plan

Billion dollar plans that never happen is what attracts the 99%

2) Billions of available shares priced as low as, $.000001

This is why the 99% buy into those stocks because *they are exciting and cheap* (Referring to the share price and the 99%ers budget).

3) The company has Lots of DEBT

Allows the company to issue shares below the bid to debt investors who then resell them to brokers who sold shares short to the 99%.

4) Someone in charge of being able to issue shares

To authorize the sale of debt diluted shares to debt investors knowing it will dilute the float and kill the share price.

GNGR has none of the 4 ingredients, so it's impossible for GNGR to be a debt diluted Pump and Dump scam.

People that accuse GNGR of being a debt-diluted Pump and Dump scheme, is based only on the share price, and the 99% never look at a company's *true* structure.

A person at a regulatory agency once said, *"If GNGR is trying to be a debt scheme pump and dump, GNGR is doing it wrong."*

If someone **DOES buy GNGR shares on the open market**, the money is paid to someone that already owns GNGR shares OR maybe MORE shorts issued by brokers to keep the price suppressed.

Neither GNGR nor me, the CEO, gets any of the money investor's pay to brokers, when GNGR shares are purchased.

When a company is not a debt diluted P&D scheme, it means the company has to generate revenue some other way.

How about WORK FOR IT like GNGR does?

AGAIN, since GNGR has only a TRUE DTC float of fewer than 109,000,000 shares, at the price **the manipulators** have us at, as of 2024/2025 is $.000001 per share. That means!

Someone can buy and own the entire DTC registered tradable float of the GNGR public Company shares for only $108.

GNGR has a great public vehicle (Or the lizards would not want it so badly) and **GNGR is also a valid operational company that is an established trademarked global selling brand** and the 99% rarely ever invest in a legitimate valid operational company.

To have a LOW float share price be taken down to $.000001 by the brokers puts the entire tradable floats price to acquire all the shares for only $108 was just a tactic used to scare buyers. But $108 is hardly a risk to be scared of since most of the 99% spend that much or more on shares in a questionable company that does not exist.

I also want to quickly point out this **FACT.**

Items can be made CHEAPER here in the USA than in CHINA!

Years ago, it was suggested I contact a man who makes embroidered hats to see if we can work together. He made it CLEAR he could make things cheaper in the USA, but companies just elect not to. He said when his business started to expand to $1 million in sales, he needed more machines and employees and a larger factory.

If China paid the same minimum wage as the USA pays, China would be bankrupt so they pay subpar wages and STILL it costs more to have items made in China than the USA.

When he hit $5 million in sales, he said his net profits were $1.5 million annually. It was when he hit that $5 million milestone he decided to close his operations and have it all made in China.

He said he now makes only $750,000 net profit due to the added costs of shipping and other costs. He actually makes 50% LESS profit than when he made the items here in the USA. ($1,500,000)

He said he had to constantly be at the business, getting machines repaired, dealing with payroll and insurance and spending all his time working. He said he knew it would **COST HIM MORE** to have items made in China, but because he was still making $750,000 instead of $1,500,000 he did not have to work or worry about machines breaking down or being at a factory all day.

He said $750,000 is more than enough for him to have a great life. Instead of worrying and working, he now plays golf and goes sailing while all his hats are made in China. I can understand his point. He wants to take it easy in life having paid his dues and built the business so much he could afford to take a loss of half his $1.5 million profits. 25 People lost their jobs and another USA company moved overseas.

All the news reports saying people should not support foreign made items also have to look and the USA-owned companies having items made out of the USA for the same reasons. *Being LAZY?*

As my company expanded and became known in the marketplace, I constantly get emails from Chinese companies saying they will cast our items for me so I can relax and enjoy the good life and not have to work. But that means I have to give them my technology.

My technology is not known in the industry (and why we have NO competition and are expanding) and is top secret how I do my molds and production." And I know some foreign metal casters want my intellectual property but they won't get it.

A school called me to ask if they can let a Chinese exchange student work for me for FREE so they can learn business as part of their class assignment. I searched the phone number and it was linked to a gold jewelry casting company in Chinatown in NY City. *NICE!*

GNGR ILLEGALLY NAKED SHORTED

SO what happened to my company (Ticker GNGR)?

As for GNGR, we were naked shorted *illegally by a criminal attorney* who forged my name to debt we did not have. When the brokers oversold GNGR's 108,000,000 float up to 800,000,000 or more (Believing the shares will be available) means those oversold shares have to be obtained or bought back eventually.

Brokers would have to get those oversold shares from me or the brokers have to buy them back from the people they sold them to triggering a short buy back, causing the shares to rise significantly higher. *So you can figure out what will soon happen next.*

Short Squeeze!

The problem now for brokers is: the debt diluter criminal attorney who assured the brokers more GNGR shares would be available knew I would *not* give him any but he told the brokers to keep selling by lying to them saying I will be issuing the shares. When the hammer fell, there was NO debt and NO additional shares issued by GNGR and the attorney, after he was arrested, charged and convicted, died suddenly before he had to serve his sentence.

The SEC file and arrest report of the attorney who forged my name and showed the courts fake non-existent debt to dump shorted shares into the market is posted under the GED to CEO chapters ahead. It will SHOCK you this happens every day illegally and in most cases legally.

In the **GameStop** short squeeze, brokers that sold shares short were done as a gamble that the company was going out of business not because more shares would be issued by a debt diluter. When the company did not fold and the share price went UP, the brokers now had to buy back the shares for more than what they sold them for short and got caught in a *$12 billion dollar short squeeze loss.*

What brokers did (To me and GNGR) was they shorted GNGR believing they would get the debt shares AND were assured GNGR would be bought out and the company and ticker cancelled and would hide all their short activity. They believed wrong.

This belief caused brokers to sell the GNGR shares short to flood the market with up to **10 or 20 times the true float** that makes it impossible for any chance for the stock price to rise on good news.

Those fake-shorted shares are also called Synthetic shares.

If I do not take action to correct the issues done by manipulators, the shorts can remain open for DECADES and cause the share price to drop and stay down until some action is taken to correct it. And most of the time the infected companies choose either to just fold, sell the vehicle or end up crossing the line to be a pump and dump.

Even trusted money managers have been known to invest client's money into pump and dumps. The PFOF debt sellers tell them, if they buy $1 shares using investor's money, they will get $.50 cents rebate for each share they purchase for their clients. They use investor's money that ends up at a loss just to make some quick money for themselves.

Since my company does not sell shares and we are fully operational, GNGR is making it hard for schemers to acquire my public vehicle. And with NO DEBT shares available, it has become too risky for brokers to continue to short more GNGR shares. And the probability of a short squeeze on the horizon is a reality they know exists.

I finally figured all this out and how to correct it and move our share price UP, and it does not include changing to a pump and dump diluted scheme or folding the company and not adding debt to the company, all of which makes the stock price go DOWN not UP.

Because of what I know that most CEO's do not, and investors have no clue about, I have a plan that will soon be exposed for the good of the company and shareholders. And just maybe, other tickers will follow, but I believe they will just give up like most do.

Someone has to be the best pilot, the best doctor or best chess player. And someone also has to be the best and smartest CEO. I won't say whom that is, but I am sure you can guess what I would say!

Those who want to watch and see how that happens put Gunther Grant's ticker "GNGR" into your list of stocks to watch.

DEATH SPIRAL TOXIC FUNDING

When I did get close to an agreement that seemed fair that also protected our company and investors and all involved to make money while expanding the business, I found that the contract agreement had some slight change at the end. *Sneaky changes!*

The wording is creative and I found changes were added after I read the approved agreement many times. When they leave the room to make 3 copies of the approved contract to sign (I kept one older copy in my briefcase), they swapped the contract before making the copies.

Since I have Dyslexia and it's hard to read contracts fast, when the final contract copy was given to me to sign, I got up and walked to the office window as they all wondered *what the hell was I doing.*

I put the individual pages of my draft (Older) copy over their new copy pages they just made so the sun shines through the two pages to make sure all the words line up. What I found showed some words and sentences were changed when overlapped towards the end of the contract. A simple trick that worked for me, ESPECIALLY when they said no changes were made to the final agreement.

This was what we ALL originally had agreed on and what changed.

I agreed to enter cautiously into an agreement for 50,000,000 shares for $.05 cents per share for $2,500,000 but not issue all the shares at once. In case they did not pay us, we would not issue any more shares preventing dilution. I agreed to issue them 5,000,000 shares before they pay us. Seems fair, FREE SHARES just not too many of them at once. They pay us when they get paid. *Fair and honest on MY part!*

For each 5,000,000 they sell for $.25 cents they issue back to our company $250,000. They make $1,000,000, we get $250,000 and everyone is happy and so are the shareholders as we expand the business. *That's good business! RIGHT?*

NOT SO FAST BUCAROOS!

That added data to the agreement on the new copies that most CEO's overlook, states (In long confusing words) that at **ANYTIME** the shares drop below $.05 (our agreed price they owe us for shares) that we have to issue them MORE shares to make up the shortfall.

Here is what they do. They take the 5,000,000 shares initially that they were going to sell for $.25 and owe us $250,000 but they instead work with the market makers to artificially drop the share price to $.0001 per share. The sneaky added contract data I would have signed says GNGR would have been **legally obligated** to issue them more shares to compensate for the price shortfall difference. What that means is, if the 5,000,000 shares we issued them dropped in price from $.25 to $.0001 they are worth only $500 not $1,250,000.

To bring the volume of shares to the agreed $250,000 they were to pay GNGR, we would be legally forced to issue them 2,500,000,000 (2.5 billion) more shares using the $.0001 price under the altered signed contract. At that point, they would end up owning the entire company and vote me (the CEO) out and because the $250,000 was backend money, I would be voted out before they have to pay the $250,000.

So what seemed like a great deal for all was just a way for a schemer to get hold of our valid public company, vote everyone out and turn the valid company into some hot topic Pump and Dump. That person who tried to death spiral scam GNGR also died suddenly just like the attorney who screwed us. Both ORDERED to leave me alone but tried to do a deal on their own outside of the chain of command.

Not a smart idea.

They would have ended up owning our entire company for $0 and all existing shareholders would have had their shares cancelled in a reverse merger death spiral scheme.

You would think they would have stuck to the original agreement and end up selling 50,000,000 shares for $10,000,000 and we get $2,500,000 and everyone (including the shareholders) wins! Not a chance.

Trusting a NIGERIAN prince's half sister in exile that wants to send me $500,000,000 is actually a better risk.

TODAY, ME AND MY COMPANY ARE STILL UNDER ATTACK

Gunther Grant and me personally was, and still are under attack by the status quo of the marketplace that **ONLY EXISTS** to destroy **ANYONE** who does not sell the public vehicle or play the game of debt, dilute, pump and dump.

By not playing the GAME, my Company was targeted, manipulated and was in *"illegal secrecy"* set up for destruction.

The schemers who infected GNGR created HOT TOPIC websites I knew nothing about. One investor thought GNGR was an Australian gold mine proving any pump and dump scheme can be whatever they want just by making a fancy website associated with any ticker.

They gambled that once they do the fraud and short GNGR, I would have no option but to accept the same fate and take part in the scheme like other CEO's ended up doing. *I did not.*

Investors accuse Gunther Grant of being a pump and dump because our share price dropped quite a bit due to the illegal fraud and shorts sold to investors. Since most stocks purchased by the 99% are pump and dump schemes, investors figure GNGR is no different.

Many CEO's I spoke to thought it was a way to exit with some capital but in the end, they ended up with very little or fines they could not pay. They all said they regretted what they did and said to me, don't take that path because it was the worst decision they ever made. I never even considered that path but I did want to know why other CEO's did choose to do that. Now I know why. **They GAVE UP!**

An honest peaceful caring man whose family is starving will steal and even kill for food just to survive. Many failed honest CEO's end up converting to a pump and dump just to survive. But what if a CEO does NOT choose either Failure or legalized fraud?

The people who say to me, *"OH you're one of those stock scam crooks"* is because most never met a legit honest CEO of a penny stock company and because most got taken on many pumped scheme stocks over the decades. **You can be a legit, honest CEO and be guilty by association.**

If any company decides they want to go public, once public no one will find your ticker. ALL tickers have to be pumped in some way or another and those that create that liquidity and dilution on debt conversions are the ones who find investors.

With no marketing, a legitimate company looking for capital will not have the shares rally because the 99% only react to pumped hot news. That lack of interest may cause the CEO to make decisions that head towards a pump and dump or be faced with closing the business.

And the CEO can't sell shares to the 99% because they would be restricted and the 99% do **NOT** buy restricted shares. The only shares the 99% can purchase, have to come from the 3rd party debt investors.

If you go public and expect capital, you won't get it, all while the debt investors walk away with $10's or maybe $100's of millions in cash.

Cost averaging GNGR with <109,000,000 in the true DTC float? There is really not much room to buy more shares to cost average UNLESS the shares purchased were part of the 800,000,000 *or more* naked shares that continue to trade as if they are real when they are not. Remember CNS shorted shares can be 20x the true DTC float!

GNGR could in fact be as high as 2 billion or more shares shorted.

Also at our low price, GNGR is not even worth selling if you own shares. The big question is, when someone does buy GNGR shares at the low price, is anyone really selling them or are brokers just selling more shorted shares to keep the price from rising and to make a quick few bucks believing the company will fold? *The status quo.*

If most pump and dumps have shares priced at $.0001 and there are billions in the float allowing everyone to cost average, how is it that GNGR with less then 109,000,000 in the (TRUE DTC) float allow investors to cost average more then what is in the float? *Naked shorts!*

10 billion pump and dump shares vs. less then 109,000,000 GNGR low float DTC shares yet both companies are perceived as the same just because the share price is the same. What is also interesting data is, the true DTC GNGR float of <109,000,000 shares looks to have **traded at least 8 or more times** the available shares.

With GNGR shares on a constant decline because of the illegal fraud, who would buy high and sell low, then buy more and sell lower then buy more and sell lower and do that 8 times? NO ONE! That can only mean one thing. GNGR was naked sold short and most or all of the transactions were buys not sells.

Time to close out the shorts on a short squeeze!

Many brokers sell short and buy from the debt schemers, NOT the bid. Since GNGR has no debt, and brokers are not buying from the bid, when GNGR shares are being purchased, they can only come from one place. ***BROKERS NAKED SHORTING GNGR SHARES!***

If brokers bought GNGR from the bid and resold what they bought from the bid, the share price would RISE, not fall. That further validates that GNGR was heavily shorted but was it 400,000,000, 800,000,000 or even 5 billion? *We'll soon see!*

If our low float <109,000,000 GNGR shares ***DID trade 8 times*** and were ***not shorted,*** investors who paid $.10 would be able to sell at $.25 then new buyers at $.25 could sell at $.50 and after a non shorted float traded 8 times, GNGR would be trading at $1 or more.

By adding shorts to the market, brokers supply the demand with shares that do not exist and they never have to buy on the bid. This causes the price to drop and also ***proves GNGR was heavily shorted.***

HIGH buy volume on a <u>non-shorted</u> stock and the price goes UP.

HIGH buy volume on a <u>shorted</u> stock and the price goes DOWN.

In most cases, brokers will not naked short shares without having the debt shares available. In GNGR's case, a well-known attorney assured them the shares would be available, when he knew they were not.

Think about this! If the lizards wanted 100,000,000 shares to do an UMBRELLA, why don't they just buy the 109,000,000 shares in the float for only $108 and then do the umbrella? Because they know any public buy back for GNGR shares would run up in price causing the lizards to spend more to get shares and also expose their scheme.

PLUS, they don't want to buy shares, they want them FREE from ME!

HOW TO STOP PUMP AND DUMP FRAUD

How does this DEBT conversion rule end up being the main reason for pump and dump fraud and how do we STOP it? This would work but no one will rule on this regulation because of the Billion$ at stake.

Under Rule 144, issued shares from the company are restricted for one year. So how is it that billions of **RESTRICTED** shares can be added to the float each week on so many pump and dump stocks within days of the debt investors receiving *restricted stock certificates*?

There is a rule that allows restricted shares to be converted to free trading if company debt is paid off by those debt investors. This rule, if eliminated, would **STOP all Debt conversion fraud the same day**. Here is how it works. And I'll use an existing listed ticker to make the case.

A NEW listed ticker had 200 million shares in the float. That company had no debt and no operations or means of revenue. Then they acquired a private company with debt from a 3rd party member with no traceable ties to the public company. Now the public company has debt that is owed to the 3rd party private company.

Now you have a public company with $2 million in debt.

Once that debt is on the books of the public company, the CEO (who is in on the scheme) allows debt investors to pay off company debt and change the company to a HOT topic ticker pump and dump.

Private debt investors will be issued lots of restricted shares in exchange for paying off very little company debt. The debt payers can now file to have those shares converted to free trading electronic shares by proving they paid some of the company debt.

The 3rd party company owed the debt is always someone involved in the scheme, usually the CEO's friend or relative so the CEO actually gets the money paid by the debt investors but it's not as much as you think and the money does NOT go to the company.

This event means the company can issue any amount of shares for a little or a lot of debt paid depending on how HOT the pumped price is.

It's usually starts with 100 million shares for a debt payment of $200,000 that decreases with each new 100 million issued shares because as the debt shares are sold and added to the float, the share price drops and also the cost of each new 100 million shares issued are also sold for less and less and the price never rises up only down.

This event of unlimited debt shares being acquired from the public company for much less than the posted bid price means the debt shares will always be more available and for less than the actual bid so brokers can keep the asked low so they can dump more cheap shares to buyers and not have to pay more for shares on the bid.

If the debt rule was eliminated, there could be NO debt dilution and the brokers would have no option but to raise (And buy from) the bid on VALID OPERATIONAL companies.

If the company were only a share-selling scheme that can't sell debt shares, they would fold and brokers would lose millions in commissions and lose billion$ not being able to short and buy unlimited cheap debt shares to cover the oversold shorts.

There has to be someone in the regulatory arena that sees the debt conversion rule as the main reason for debt diluted pump and dumps thriving. It's right there for all to see and is a regulation that allows it to continue. I call it *Legal Fraud.*

Debt dilution is so rampant that regulators can clearly see investors paying off debt to have shares unrestricted to dilute to the pump and dump float, and the forms that are filled out to do that are like applying and being *approved by the US Government to commit legal fraud.*

The debt dilution pump and dump scheme is legal and just part of the process that is the main cause for billions lost in the marketplace by legalized fraud.

The debt scheme to pump and dump rule is there for all to see yet no one will even stop it. Instead some 15c211 regulation is voted on that just says Buyer Beware that offers no investor protections. *NONE!*

There is NO question that something has to be done in the securities space to stop fraud and that is:

Eliminate the debt conversion rule. NOW ASAP!

15c211 and the amended rule was created by the SEC but the OTC has jurisdiction as to how those rules are implemented to OTC listed stocks. The OTC is not a regulatory agency so why are they in charge?

The OTC stated that the amendment to rule 15c211 is in place to offer "INVESTOR PROTECTIONS"

The problem with that statement is that the protections are not by changes to rules or to stop fraud by regulations. The rule is made to allow investors to have access to data so they can decide if they should invest in a specific public company.

And I already proved OTC investors do not look at data, just HOT PR NEWS! 15c211 is sort of like the warnings on cigarette packs. The warning is there but people still smoke.

15c211 is **not** a rule to enforce or stop fraud but instead is a rule to educate and school investors who are playing hooky and they will never be educated on how this works.

When a listed company becomes 15c211 compliant, they have to be transparent according to the rules. Those rules are: ***File your financials and data and warnings and pay the OTC fees.***

Since OTC investors do not look at warnings or financials, or even what is required by a company to be 15c211 compliant, they will continue to invest regardless of that compliance data being transparent under rule 15c211. ***Investors THINK 15c211 will protect them but it won't.***

15c211 is a regulation to warn investors the company will never achieve their goal and they will also likely lose all their money and investors say:

"BE RIGHT BACK! LET ME GET MY CHECK BOOK!"

If investors did look at that 15c211 disclaimer warning data and they can buy 1 million shares for $100 dreaming if they go to $1 they make $1 million, they will still buy the stock regardless.

Gambling is a sickness and the gamblers still gamble. Same with the pumped stock gamblers. They know it's bad and they continue just like people who smoke who see the warning.

15c211 is forcing companies to warn people they are going to be scammed but the investors already know that and keep investing.

15c211 also allowed the OTC to get rid of listed but not active zombie tickers and to punish legitimate companies for not paying the OTC fees. BUT in some ways it also HELPS legitimate companies like GNGR!

YES, HELP! You'll see in the EM Grays chapter coming up.

Eliminating the debt conversion rule STOPS companies from scamming investors with never-ending debt diluted cheap shares and not just issues a warning. But, as stated many times, you can't STOP anyone from tossing money into the fire. No warning will stop the OTC investors. *The only protection investors' need, is from themselves.*

Investors cannot blame the SEC, the OTC, or even the pump and dump schemes when buying shares in a company that clearly says:

"The company may not achieve their intended goal and investors will likely lose all their money". Seems fair, LET'S INVEST!

15c211 amendment rule also **protects the public companies that do not comply with 15c211** that electively moved off the OTC to the Gray Markets. 15c211 also protects the accredited, sophisticated investors who largely stay clear of OTC listed companies.

15c211 protects some and fools the 99% they are protected

SO why even create this new rule if the OTC allows the pump and dumps to thrive and knowingly allows those schemes to continue to rip people off?

P&D retail investors know they are being ripped off and there is no way to stop investors from putting their CASH in the fire and burning it, which is exactly what those P&D investors are doing every day to the tune of about $300 million dollars per trading day ($300,000,000) PER DAY on sub penny priced pump and dump stocks.

The OTC is NOT a regulatory agency but a free enterprise public company. The OTC is not an exchange; it's a place tickers pay to **ADVERTISE!**

FINRA is the actual owner of the stock tickers listed on the OTC, and the OTC was granted the rights to decide what companies need to do to be 15c211 compliant so they can list on the OTC ad platform.

The requirements were, in reality, PAY the fees to list on the OTC and warn investors of the risks or move to the grays where you can't be a pump and dump scheme, plain and simple!

I have seen 100's post on many pump and dump ticker stock chat rooms: *"HEY, what gives? I lost all my investment in a 15c211 compliant company and I thought we had protections?"*

Remember this, everyone.

15c211 is to warn you and has NO effect on the share price or the shares being debt diluted on any given pump and dump scheme. 15c211 does NOT guarantee a company will be a success or create a higher share price. And 15c211 offers no investor protections.

The OTC makes money-selling services to OTC listed tickers and **STOP sign** listed tickers who were not paying the fees, allowed more and more tickers to elect not to pay the fees and still allowed them to pump and dump on the OTC advertising platform. That also caused the OTC to lose millions in revenue. *1,000's of non-paying stop signs!*

And since investors don't look at data, it didn't matter the tickers became STOP sign companies and more and more pump and dumps said WHY pay fees if no one even cares about STOP sign warnings.

The (Now non existent) **STOP sign** tickers that did not file the 15c211 warning AND PAY the OTC fees were moved off the OTC to the Gray, EM markets.

There are, let's say, 12,500 public company tickers listed on the OTC and most pay about $10,000 annually, more or less, to be OTC yield or OTC current and more than $10,000 to be on the higher tiers. That comes to $125 million more or less in annual revenue for the OTC.

If **MY** new rule was created called 15c211-ETD to **Eliminate The Debt** conversion rule, the following would happen.

Out of the approximate 12,500 listed OTC tickers, my guess is 5,000+ listed OTC tickers would vanish because they only sell shares for money. With NO debt conversion rule, shares cannot be sold and diluted and with no products to sell, they would fold or they would have to find some of that GOLD in them there hills.

That would be a HUGE financial loss for the OTC's public bottom line. Losing about $10,000 x 5,000 listed tickers is a loss of over $50 million (I don't have the accurate financial loss, but it's a lot).

The OTC does not create regulations, the SEC does. If the SEC (Congress) created that NO DEBT regulation, the OTC would have to conform.

And ALL pump and dump debt schemes would vanish the same way the 99% of investor money does now.

Still a major financial loss for the OTC and probably their public share price as well. But the OTC is in the middle between tickers and regulations that the OTC does not create rules for. The SEC or Congress has to create new rules.

Here is a simple way the OTC can be seen as.

Think of the OTC like a magazine that sells ad space for companies. If you are a "STOP" sign company (that now has been eliminated), you were not paying to advertise. So why would any business let people advertise for FREE? *This is business!*

It's weird in a way, you have to pay the OTC and be 15c211 compliant to list on the OTC. If you became 15c211 compliant and did not pay the OTC fees, you would not be allowed on the OTC.

NOT complying with 15c211 and moving to the EM or gray markets actually protected investors and the companies themselves. If you were a pump and dump, you can't sell shares on the grays to those 99% retailers who buy P&D stocks, and if you're a company that elected to move to the grays, you legally cannot be shorted.

That is exactly why I electively moved Gunther Grant to the Grays, to take that step back and move ahead stronger and smarter.

OTC tickers that were Yield and Current (Many that were existing pump and dumps) who were paying the OTC fees and filing their financials and warnings did not have to do anything to be 15c211 compliant.

So it was business as usual for many of those P&D tickers and proof they did not have to do anything to conform to 15c211 allowing them to continue to debt dilute shares to the 99% retail investors.

It's pay the OTC fees and file your horrible data to continue to pump and dump debt shares, or close the cash cow scheme.

The OTC doing away with the "STOP" sign tier meant no more **non paying** freeloading pump and dumps on the OTC making billion$ selling worthless debt shares unless they pay the fee and move to yield or current.

I have to give kudos to the OTC who made it so there are no more STOP sign tickers that overwhelmed the OTC listed companies.

MOST ACTIVE

$ Volume Sha

SYMBOL	PRICE	% CHANGE	$ VOL	SHARE
Pink HCMC	0.0035	-12.50	30,797,586	8,790,062,:
TGGI	0.0032	-21.95	11,341,639	2,832,604,:
MDCN	0.0013	-27.78	2,770,563	2,142,579,
SVTE	0.001	+11.11	1,957,642	2,111,205,:
Pink MMEX	0.0056	+14.29	12,026,812	2,025,196,(
IDGC	0.002	+66.67	4,821,983	1,947,185,(
HAON	0.0008	-20.00	1,024,356	1,335,401,:
MNGG	0.0017	-26.09	2,369,767	1,109,262,:
BDGR	0.0013	-23.53	1,475,434	1,054,256,:
GNCP	0.0011	-38.89	1,266,124	1,025,703,:
BNGI	0.001	-28.57	1,053,647	983,068,:
GABB	0.0008	-11.11	811,578	965,524,:

A public company can file to be SEC reporting (P&D's usually won't be approved) and not have to pay the OTC fees and the OTC would have to list them on the OTC as an SEC reporting company that may attract some serious investors, but not the 99%.

If the "STOP" sign companies posted the financial data under the 15c211 rule, why were the OTC fees part of the process? The mix of regulations and fees is just the cost of doing business, I guess.

No one can fault the OTC or the SEC over the confusing definition of 15c211 or the way it really is defined. It's a warning, not protection.

The OTC should have said 15c211 is to educate and warn investors, not protect them because 15c211 does not in any way protect investors. *A huge difference.*

Another way I can easily describe the OTC (Pink Sheets) Market is:

The OTC is like a HUGE casino and tickers that attract the 99% are slot machines that all say PLAY AND WIN BIG, but most machines are rigged to never pay out, not even once.

Investors go into the OTC casino with $500 and bet $100 on the slot machine named *"To Da Moon"* and LOOK OVER THERE! There is the slot machine *"Don't miss the train leaving the station"* and investors dump another $100 into that machine.

A popular machine is the *"Don't miss the boat"* and another $100 is lost on that machine as well. When the day is over, the investors leave broke but they come back the next day and do it all over again.

Since most of the people I meet say, *"OH you're one of those scam pump and dump crooks that everyone loses money on all the time"*

My questions to those people are: If that is the case, *"Why in hell do you keep buying into those scams?"* So whose fault is it? Not mine!

It's a combination of mostly scheme pump and dumps or UMBRELLA tickers and investors who just don't know any better. That again, puts GNGR in uncharted territory since GNGR is neither.

We are a valid operational public company. We don't pump intent lies and lotto dreams and we sell globally the products we make. GNGR is that needle in the haystack because we proved it as a FACT.

To further show why regulations have to change to TRULY protect investors, you have to look at the TOP of the food chain.

$20,000 GOVERNMENT TOILET SEATS

To Change Regulation You Have To Change Congress. **GOOD LUCK!**

Many of the problems with the way stocks are traded are not the SEC's fault. There are 435 people to blame but you are powerless to sue them or get them to change.

They are called THE US CONGRESS.

They make the laws used by the SEC. And most of the laws that are in place allow Congress members to inside trade by allowing members to buy stock in a company *before they issue a government contract*. If you all recall the Trump nominee for Health and Human Services was *Tom Price* who served in congress. The democratic congress members grilled him in public hearings and constantly accused him of buying stocks based on non-public information to get him to look like he did something illegal to prevent his nomination (Insider trading).

He testified numerous times: "I did what I was congressionally allowed to do with regards to investments as all congress and senate members are also allowed to do by law"

Definition: legal congressional Insider Trading.

Congress members were trying and keep him from being nominated to the HHS position when the fact is, all the congressional members did and still do exactly what they were accusing Mr. Price of doing. If congress members used that stock issue to publicly shame Mr. Price as doing something illegal to anger the public that would mean they are also condemning themselves for doing the same?

You see how this works for congress but not you the public investor? Congress made laws to suit their own needs but for the regular people, it is a criminal offense. Also, as of 2022, Congress made any businesses they own exempt from the new tax laws. **NICE!**

That is why the SEC has their hands tied. The SEC operates under congressional rules and regulations and they will likely not be changing the debt rule anytime soon. Not when $100's of billions are at stake.

Remember the news about the $20,000 toilet seats and $10,000 hammers the US government bought decades ago? I'm sure most older investors remember. But do you all know why? It all comes down to congressional laws and why certain people are allowed to do things legally when others would face jail time. **Here is how it works.**

Congress and senate members buy shares in a company BEFORE they issue a government contract. Sounds like insider trading, but it's worse and costs the taxpayers billions all so some can make millions.

Congress members get together in private and say, "let's make some money." **Mua Ha Ha!**

The government needs things (light bulbs for buildings, tiles for floor repairs, paint for government-owned facilities, etc) and even TOILET seats for the Pentagon. Congress then votes to award contracts to suppliers of items using taxpayer's money to fund the process.

Congress also looks for companies that are public with a low share price and not much in sales but can make something Congress can order for the US Government's needs. Congressional aids locate a company that makes plastic molding castings that has a share price of only one cent.

A report is sent to the congress members who will appropriate funds for items needed.

Finding that this company is publicly trading at only a penny, and that the company can make items that seem justified, they get started with the process.

These Congress members come up with the need for "TOILET SEATS" for the Pentagon (the Pentagon has 284 bathrooms). Hey, they need updated toilets seats, RIGHT! Or do they?

ME? I have never ONCE IN MY LIFE said, **"DAMN, my toilet seat has worn down to the porcelain bowl so I need a new one."**

My grandparents 1950's house still had the same (unworn) vintage yellow toilet seats.

So they contact the plastic company saying, "This is the US Government. Can you fill a government order for toilet seats?" Of course, the company says YES! But they need money to cover the costs. The contract is not official and not valid so the plastic company cannot tell anyone about the contract until after the official order is placed.

Once the few congressional members know this public molding company can supply the toilet seats, they each secretly have others who work for them (kids, family etc) who have set up small financial companies on the side, start buying up the molding company shares at $.01 cent. With 100,000,000 available shares that no one is interested in, the only ones buying the shares were the congressional members using 3rd party people acting on their behalf.

That is why many congressional members have kids or relatives who own some sort of financial holding company. GOP and Democrats have set up these financial companies in other's names to eliminate conflict of interest.

Each of the 10 members of Congress gobble up the 100,000,000 shares each putting 10,000,000 shares into their respective 3rd party accounts, at only 1 cent costing each member only $100,000. When the shares are all secure in their accounts, they commence with the government contract and tell the mold company they are giving them $5,000,000 up-front for toilet seats *(your tax dollars).*

It's taxpayers money so WHO CARES! Congress can't take the money directly or they would be arrested for embezzlement so they simply issue it to a public company they now own shares in. The CEO of the molding company gets $5,000,000 in advance and posts news about this AMAZING GOVT. CONTARCT that is legal and valid and as the news hits the investment community, higher-level investors all rush to acquire shares.

Remember; those 10 Congress members bought the shares before they issued the government contract when they were only one cent and now people are scrambling for shares driving them up to $2.00 per share. Congress members quickly have their 3rd party investment companies sell the shares to the market makers for $1.00 who buy them all at half off.

It's definitely not insider trading that's for sure...it's much worse.

Each of the 10 Congress members spent $100,000 for 10,000,000 shares, and then sold them a month later for $10,000,000. Not bad for one month's work. So what happens now? The plastic company has to deliver the toilet seats but with no real direction, they call asking how many do they need to make? Congress replies "just make one toilet seat for 250 Pentagon bathrooms and deliver them to the warehouse." Congress used $5,000,000 of taxpayer's money to have a company make only 250 toilet seats at a cost of $20,000 each.

TA DA! $20,000 toilet seats! Same with the $10,000 hammers.

Also what I believe is, the company did not even make the toilet seats, they just bought them wholesale or from Home Depot for $10 each which is EXACTLY what Congress should have done. If congress did that, they would not have been able to make million$ on the taxpayer funded stock deal.

Congress members can make millions using taxpayer money to secure contracts for things that were really not needed or necessary but are a justified expense nonetheless. To this day, I am sure those toilet seats are sitting on some pallet in some warehouse just waiting for the current seats to wear out! In 2023, this article was published after I sent data to the media about this issue. POLICY DECISIONS? I think so.

By Joseph Morton
06:00 AM on Dec 26, 2023

WASHINGTON — Members of Congress and their families execute stock trades worth hundreds of millions annually, raising questions about whether lawmakers could be profiting from insider information or making policy decisions with one eye on their portfolios.

Why would anyone spend $20,000,000 to become a congress member that only makes $174,000 annually, unless they plan to make that $20,000,000 back *five-fold* during their term? *TA DA!*

129

AMAZON AND GUNTHER GRANT

Moving ahead to how all this works.

Some but not many Penny stock investors will also buy a well-known stock like Amazon and buy only 1 or 2 shares. This is not an investment strategy at all. I call it the Amazon affect.

Most know they can't brag about the pump and dumps because they are always at a loss so having a blue chip or name brand stock allows investors to have some feeling they have ONE winner in their account they can brag about. When you also look at a stock like Amazon you see further how sometimes a corporate action does not work as well as they thought.

At the time this guide was written, Amazon's post split 20/1 shares were $120. Let's look at it before the split and why all 20 shares after the split ended up worth less than the pre-split single share price of $3,400. I emailed Amazon and told them why the 20/1 split would not help and should have been 1700/1 but I'm sure no one read it.

Many people who had an extra $2000 (More or less) bought one share of Amazon stock (Pre-split) that went to $3,400 and didn't sell for only a $1,400 gain. They kept the one share so they can brag they own Amazon stock and it made them feel good. And if you did sell it for $1,400 profit, you also have to pay taxes that made it hardly a financial success. Owning one share was just to brag they own Amazon stock with many not saying they only own one share.

If you looked at the (Pre-split) $3,400 price trade data on any given day, you would see 1 or 2 shares traded more often than larger amounts. NO ONE buys one share as an investment strategy.

It's just to brag you own it.

I met one of these types at the local bar who was with his wife and he bragged about his Amazon stock. I said, "Wow, how much do you own?" He replied he does not like to talk about his finances. Than why bring up that you own Amazon stock in the first place, schmuck?

Then his wife later said he likes to brag about his Amazon stock, but he is too embarrassed to say he only owns one share. *Nice wife!*

After the 20/1 split, NO ONE can do that now and I am sure with no split it would have risen even higher as some only wanted ONE share and not selling it kept the demand up.

I guarantee it would have hit $5,000+ pre-split price. Now the shares are worth about $120 (At the time I wrote this guide) and no one is bragging any more so that was a very calculated mistake on Amazon's part and knocked Bezos down from the top richest spot.

I also have formulated a plan for Amazon that would drive their post split $120+ share price well above $750 and also save them $100's of millions in company costs annually while also knocking out competitors like Wal-Mart, and it **DOES NOT** rely on drones.

But again DEAF EARS. And hey WHO AM I to make that claim?

Because I'm never wrong as you will see.

Before Amazon did the 20/1 forward split, many that bragged about owning Amazon stock are now silent.

More demand before the split, and less demand after the split.

More demand/lower float makes share prices go UP

Less demand/larger float makes share prices go DOWN

That goes back to my point about the 99% who buy shares. When Amazon did the 20/1 split, they increased what is available in the float causing the shares to regulate for less, and also because $120 after the 20/1 split was not affordable to the masses that would have LOVED to get shares cheaper.

If Amazon did another forward split, about 60/1, to bring their price back down to $2.00 per share, **Then the masses would all jump in** and say I'M not missing it this time again at $2.00 per share as they figure it can go back to $3,400 per share.

50 million people trying to buy 200 shares for $400 would exceed inventory and the shares would rise up fast, from the same people that declined to use the same $400 to buy only 3 shares at $120.

The main reason anyone would buy Amazon stock ($400 more or less at $2 per share) is NOT because of Amazon sales or revenue, but because they are affordable. I bet, for sure, the stock would move up to $25 per share or more after that 60/1 split. **GUARANTEED!**

$3,400 that was split 20/1 to $170 that dropped to $120.

Do another 60/1 split to take the $120 down to $2

If you had ONE share at $3,400, after the TWO splits I mentioned, you would end up owning 1,200 shares at $2 per share, and most of the 99% would buy in at $2 causing the demand and share price to rise. At $25 per share, the 99% that bought $400 worth (200 shares) valued at $5,000, would **STILL NOT SELL** but instead **start bragging again** as demand rises further.

And Jeff Bezos would be the first trillionaire...

Jeff Bezos didn't do anything wrong, the 99% investors want lots of shares cheap ($2) or they want one share at a higher price to brag. Either of those strategies would exceed inventory and the price would SKY ROCKET! Reducing the price below $3,400 but much higher than $2.00 to $170 means Amazon lost the 99% entirely and those 99% are what moves the markets. Amazon will rise the same way Facebook did but it will be a long slow up and down process.

The 99% are like those who purchase 1 Hershey kiss at a candy store for $.20 and save it or they buy a bag of 25 for only $2.49 ($.05 each). That is what the 99% do, they buy fewer shares for more money and hold or buy lots of shares for less, creating more demand and that is what makes a share price rise FAST! There is NO middle ground with the 99%.

Amazon stock is fashionable, Joe Mamas, gold mine stock is not.

Amazon does not sell debt-diluted shares while pump and dumps only sell debt-diluted shares, never giving them a chance to rise.

Owning Amazon stock has nothing to do with sales, revenue, and fundamentals or as an investment since mostly 1 or 2 shares traded more than larger amounts.

It was only about fashion and to brag.

GUNTHER GRANT vs. AMAZON vs. PUMP AND DUMPS

It took *$8 billion in trades* to move Amazon's pre-split stock price up less than *1%.* It took only *$2,500 in trades* to move GNGR up *273%* while debt diluted pump and dumps shares go *DOWN* in price because of endless amount of shares that are dumped to the float making any rise in price impossible. The more pumped shares people buy, the more the pump and dump scheme adds to the float at lower prices.

Amazon has 9 billion shares in the float at $120 per share. Many P&D's also have 9 billion shares in the float at $.00001 per share. GNGR is far below 9 billion with only 108,000,000 in the float and structured better than any P&D (That GNGR will never be). This again puts GNGR in unchartered territory not for the worse, but for the better.

Amazon, *ROSE <1%* when **$8 billion** in shares traded. (Not Great)

GNGR, *ROSE >273%* when only **$2,500** in shares traded. (Great)

P&D's, *DECLINE* as unlimited shares are added to the float (Worst)

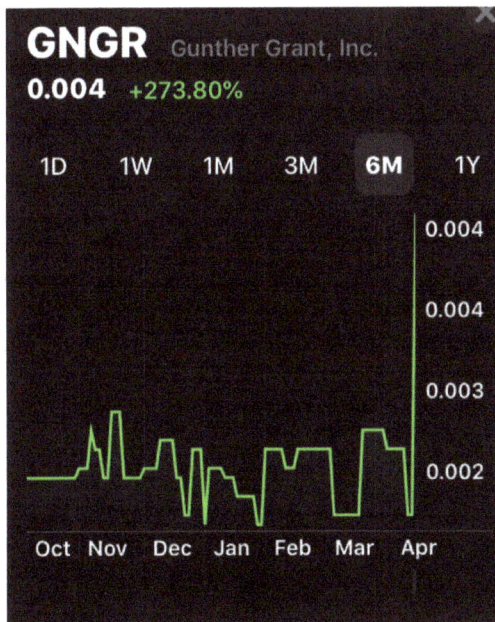

GNGR Gunther Grant, Inc.
0.004 +273.80%

| 1D | 1W | 1M | 3M | 6M | 1Y |

0.004
0.004
0.003
0.002

Oct Nov Dec Jan Feb Mar Apr

GNGR TAKING A STEP BACK AFTER BEING SCAMMED

Instead of having to choose between *failure and legalized Fraud*, I have decided to turn around and go back a few steps.

This new path of my own design, no other OTC ticker has thought of because other public companies just accept the status quo, since most who fail never take a step back and just surrender to *failure or fraud.*

When the SEC fined the market makers $12,000,000 in 2012 (The same year Davies scammed GNGR) for not being able to deliver GNGR shares to the brokers, the brokers still owe the shares to the investors that placed (And paid for) orders for GNGR shares.

Here is how I found out how things work and by deceit.

When the attorney Davies forged my name to create (fake) debt to have 100,000,000 shares unrestricted, Davies told the market makers not to worry, more shares are on the way from GNGR, not just 100,000,000 but billions or more. Davies then tells his associate brokers, who are in on the scheme, to short sell as many shares as they can at the higher price while Davies pumped the shares up.

Davies did not tell anyone GNGR was NOT issuing any more shares causing the market makers and brokers to keep selling naked shorted shares to 1,000's of investors when the price was high and sell more shares to cost average buyers as they killed the share price. Because what Davies did was multiple high-level felonies, he may have figured he would take the money and vanish out of the USA and avoid persecution.

Rarely does a person in the chain of the scheme lie to others in the scheme but when they do, is when the whole scheme falls apart and ends up reversing the pump and dump into a short squeeze buyback.

When that happens, some people ended up missing!

I met a group in the Mineola years ago that wanted to convert GNGR to a new ticker (A disabled veterans investment scam) and I would be the CEO. I thought I recognized a person at the meeting who was banned from being a CEO and fined $5 million from some previous pump and dump scam.

When the lawyer at the meeting introduced him by name, I knew it was him and knew right away he was setting up some scam to screw disabled veterans out of their benefits. I got up and walked out. *Screw veterans? No shame at all.*

It was a ploy to get me to reverse merge to bury the open naked shorts and at the same time, allow them to set up a new scheme. I think that attorney was the same one that worked on other schemes.

The resume of another attorney who has been bashing GNGR for over a decade states he *USED* to have the following securities licenses:

The Series 4: *is an exam and securities license entitling the holder to* **supervise options sales personnel** *and compliance issues.*

The Series 7: *is an exam and license that entitles the holder to* **sell all types of securities** *products except commodities and futures.*

The Series 24: the candidate *can supervise* all areas of the member's investment banking and securities business, such as underwriting, *trading and market making, advertising.*

The Series 27: *is a securities license that entitles the* holder **to prepare and manage the books and recordkeeping** *of a member firm.*

The Series 53: *exam is a licensing test that permits an individual to* **supervise the municipal securities activities of a securities firm** *or bank dealer.*

Series 63 exam: *is designed* **to qualify candidates** *as securities* **agents.**

Isn't it ODD that the same ex-trader attorney has spent the last 12+ years on IHUB bashing GNGR and questioning where our products are located and even posting to others if the CEO (ME) is even alive?

I know he's trying to get to me but like I said I'm numb to those idiots. But the bigger issue is why is he so worried about a company he says he owns no shares in or has any association with? In his bio, he states he *works with the SEC to shut down fraud* and the SEC told me they *don't know who he is*.

The SEC said GNGR is not a scam **(See page 305)** so why would an ex-trader attorney (and lizards) keep posting that we are? An attorney accusing a valid company of being a scam when the LAW says GNGR is not? I think he knows his assets and his time, as a free man is limited.

This attorney on IHUB is not an investor yet he knows so much about GNGR you have to wonder did he just search all 12,500 tickers and said "I'll bash GNGR for no reason" or did he already know about GNGR, our stock, our products and other fine details not by chance but by ASSOCIATION in some way with the *DAVIES Scam? It's starting to look that way. Plus he was a boiler room securities trader.*

He posted:

Re: MallenNV post# 14432   **Post#** 14433   of 14446 `Go`

How does anyone know Grant's alive?

The confessions of a paid pump and dump associate shows:

*Lesson 1: BASHERS NEVER Bash A BAD STOCK. Check the boards for stocks with no potential. They never have any Bashers. Bashers only go after stocks that are moving up or have excellent potential to do so. Bashers work to bring the price down to either increase their position at the expense of others or help a **Short make their bones.***

With NO shares to cover the shorts, it's short squeeze time!

The one problem for brokers is they would have to get all the short holders to sell back 800,000,000 or more GNGR shares so they can close out the oversold. That would drive the price way UP to $1 or more. So bashing GNGR to get the shares lower has no purpose other than to buy time to get me the CEO to just give up the vehicle.

You can't close out 800,000,000 or more open shorts with only 108,000,000 shares in the float unless you can get the company to issue shares or sell the vehicle. Getting neither can force a short squeeze. Pump and Dumps are also set up to protect brokers from facing a short squeeze. But in our case, the attorney failed to offer that protection and also failed to tell brokers no shares will be available.

Davies told (lied to) Brokers GNGR has debt and that is the signal to naked sell shares. If the brokers actually looked at the OTC GNGR data, they would have seen **GNGR has NO debt** and say, "HOLD ON, how can Davies guarantee them unrestricted debt shares if there is no debt?"

If there were NO open shorts in GNGR, a $2,500 buy-in that once took GNGR UP 273% would have also created liquidity on a rising share price and higher-level investors would have jumped in.

How can non-shorted shares be bought without having the price rise? **They can't.** The proof GNGR was and continues to be shorted is any trades, big or small, the price never goes up. There are too many illegal naked shorted shares in the float and more likely added.

With no shorts, trying to buy all 108,000,000 shares would drive GNGR up to $1 or more per share. That is why the pressure to do a short squeeze forces the brokers to buy back not just 108,000,000 but more like 800,000,000 or even billions they shorted.

Brokers would have to buy all the shorted shares back and cancel them because they can't resell those shares. That would cause the price to rise higher and higher.

Short selling involves having a broker who is willing to loan shares with the understanding that they are going to be sold on the open market and **replaced at a later date**. Then the borrowers re-lend them 20 times or more causing the naked shorted float to create fake dilution that kills the share price.

- There is no set time that an investor can hold a short position.
- The key requirement, however, is that the broker is willing to loan the stock for shorting.
- Investors can hold short positions as long as they are able to honor the margin requirements.

If you take away the initial 108,000,000 float shares that were the catalyst for the multiplied shorted shares, all shorts have to be closed out because without the initial DTC shares to back them up, the borrowed shares have to be returned to the original lender like a bank loan.

So which GNGR shares are the real DTC 108,000,000 float shares?

They ALL ARE. If there are 800,000,000 or more shorted shares, they are all considered real and no different than all the other shares. The only way to expose the fakes is to buy back 108,000,000 shares and request the certificate to have the DTC officially say yours are the TRUE shares. **First come first serve.**

Like the play **The PRODUCERS**, the schemers sold too much percentage of the play to investors and tried to make the play a FLOP. When the play was a success, the share sellers all went to jail. Same with GNGR, they tried to ruin GNGR to cover the oversold but, guess what? GNGR did not a flop, GNGR succeeded. SO NOW WHAT?

Someone has to pay for the crimes and fraud committed on **our great company**. The market makers got fined $12,000,000 and two schemers are no longer alive. Now it's the broker's turn to pay.

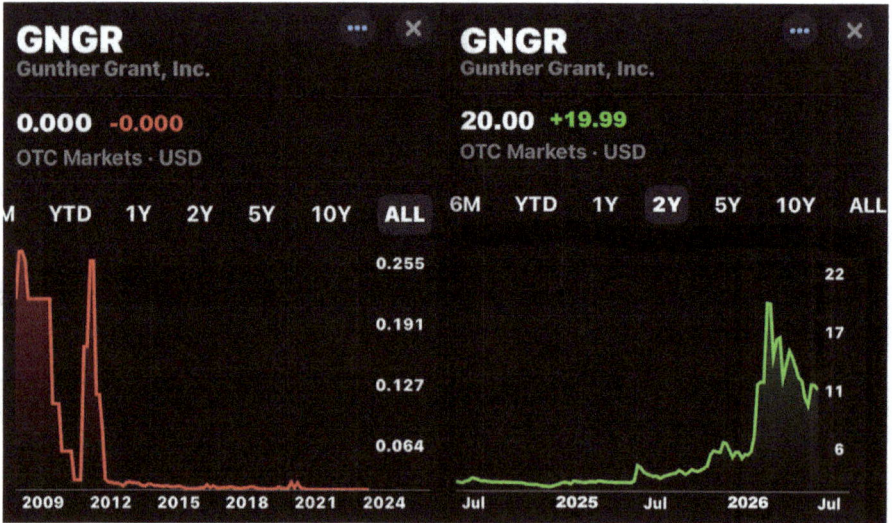

In **2012**, Davies **illegally shorted** GNGR between $.10 and $.25 then caused our share price to drop to $.000001. If a successful short squeeze is implemented, there is NO telling how HIGH our share price could rise. If we just surrendered and walked away, they win. We did not walk away and GNGR is working on changes that involve a **short squeeze.** Our plan is to fight and WIN and cause a major defeat to the status quo. Moving to the EM Gray Markets is, **PART OF THE PLAN!**

EXPERT MARKETS (EM) THE GRAY MARKET STOCKS.

Sophisticated and accredited investors will also look at Gray Market stocks that actually do protect them thanks to the rule 15c211.

Expert Markets (EM) as the OTC calls them or Gray market stocks have protections in place to attract the accredited sophisticated investors due to elimination of pump and dump and shorting schemes not being allowed on the Grays that is rampant on the OTC. *Shorting a gray market stock is illegal and retail investors are not allowed to trade in EM Gray tickers. PERFECT FOR GNGR!*

No schemes and no cheapskate retailers allowed on the EM Grays!

That may be why the OTC labeled those tickers as the EXPERT MARKET tickers on the OTC data. Because unlike the pump and dump gambler investors you have to be an EXPERT to buy the *less risky EM Gray* stocks and have to be *accredited or sophisticated.*

Seems like the OTC *(Not me)* are calling all pump and dump 99% retailers *not accredited and unsophisticated*. But then again, look at the data and financial losses of the 99% and make your own assumption.

Some very large companies started on the Grays like Facebook, Twitter and Porsche, to name a few, and has essentially *banned retailers* from buying gray listed stocks. This also prevents a pump and dump from operating on the EM Gray markets because P&D stocks need the 99% gambler retailer's money that makes a P&D work. The EM Grays are actually a place to find value and ground level stocks that can really pay off, without the worry of the company being a P&D (Pump and Dump).

ANY company that is a scheme pump and dump would NEVER electively move to the EM Grays like I did with my company because you can't pump and dump debt shares and brokers cannot short EM Gray stocks. You need BOTH to be a pump and dump scam that is not allowed on the EM GRAYS.

Further proving GNGR is not a scheme pump and dump.

EM Grays are where companies start out or elect to move to and take that step back before moving ahead or where zombie stop signs go to die.

That means if a company is on the grays, they are one of the three operations:

1) A previous P&D stock that ran its course and became a ZOMBIE STOP SIGN that already took retail investors money and just left the ticker abandoned causing the company to drop to the grays. If no one buys shares in 18 months, the ticker will be deactivated.

2) A valid operational company (like GNGR) that has electively moved off the OTC to show they are not a P&D scheme that may want to move above the OTC to the NYSE or NASDAQCM

3) A new company just starting out that intends to move up to an exchange. A new company, as you read about, has the odds stacked against them UNLESS they become a pump and dump.

GNGR may be the ONLY ticker to take that step back to regroup while most just give up, quit or sell out to a lizard.

The OTC also had to have known that so many ZOMBIE tickers (STOP SIGNS) needed to be dropped knowing there is no one left associated with those tickers any more and were just abandoned. So doing away with the STOP sign was a great move by the OTC to clean house.

Because Gray listed stocks can't just dump and debt dilute shares to retailers, accredited or institutional investors will look at gray company data and protections in place that the 99% retailers do not.

Also, to clarify, most retailers believe a ticker moving off the OTC to the Grays means they are delisted. That is *incorrect.* OTC (Advertised tickers) are all delisted stocks because the OTC is not an exchange or government entity. They are the place where delisted stock go!

When a NASDAQ or NYSE stock does not meet the requirements to remain on those platforms, they are *DELISTED to the OTC.*

Pump and dump debt diluted tickers that file to stay on the OTC being 15c211 compliant and also paying the OTC the fee to advertise on that platform, can still debt dilute, pump and dump.

Intent hot topic non-existent hype, increased authorized, no actual business operations, lots of debt and endless amounts of shares added to the diluted float.

- *15c211* will not protect investors

- Doing away with the *DEBT conversion rule* will!

It's that simple but no one will change that regulation.

I have to add in this tidbit of data.

While writing this book, I spoke with an ex-trader who told me they buy pump and dump stocks with some of the investor's profits. They act in the client's best interest (yeah sure) and investors are not aware the brokers will kill the share price on purpose.

Brokers use this tactic to use profits clients made on other stocks and sell them scheme shares. When the shares drop to $.0001 or less, they tell their clients they can get a tax write off against profits.

He said they do this so brokers can make millions selling naked shorted shares at a high price and buy them back very cheap allowing investors to write off the loss while at the same time, they close out the open shorts. Doing this, they eliminate a short squeeze.

Brokers figure WHY SHOULD investors have all the money so they devise a way to get some of it without raising red flags in the process.

Brokers will also naked short a valid honest company (like GNGR) knowing they will do the same damage they do to pump and dumps.

Many brokers have ZERO emotions and don't care if they ruin people's lives or businesses as long as they make money!

GNGR ON THE MOVE!

GNGR is not out, down or finished by any means, just a few things I have to take care of and it will all come together to make our great company even greater in the investment community. AND, as a global leader in jewelry and casting services, that is already proven.

In FACT, there is **not ONE company (private or public), like GNGR** with our company structure, operational excellence and global sales. **NONE!**

After some major changes to my company, I set out to make GNGR a one-person operation (Just ME). By taking my new approach to how to run a business and also changing directions, I made GNGR castings a global trademarked brand in less than 3 years.

If it fails, it **will** be my fault. But it's not failing as mentioned in this guide. **It's EXPANDING** faster than any other business I've ever had.

This is business and change can be good. Many companies that are failing refuse to change directions when that change can be what saves the company and also ends up a huge success.

I had to make serious changes FAST. Realizing time was not standing still, it had to be done as fast as I was able to make it happen.

Make smart changes and take intelligent risks based on what you have learned. Focus ahead with what works and leave behind what does not work. **Don't trust ANYONE but yourself.**

One day of change can quickly correct 10 years of struggle

So who the hell am I and why did I decide to go public? I wanted more in life and trusted people I should not have. I have been through and created more than what most people ever will while also being surrounded by those who wanted me to fail. I trusted the data saying going public can be the best business move and it was **a complete lie.**

What you read in this book is a fraction of the things I had to face that cannot be mentioned in this guide without me being sued by dozens of people that know full well what they did. I had to use my smarts to bypass what an education does not teach you in life and my journey is far from over, and in many case has just begun (Again).

The status quo never takes into consideration that **ONE person** may know more than everyone. Someone has to be the BEST even when it comes to changing the status quo and I know how to do it, and has already begun.

If I did not make business changes for the better and instead chose negative moral changes and gave into the pump and dump lizards plans, my company today would be gone and all investors would be out in the cold. **That's if you quit trying... I did not quit.**

It can take one bad decision to lose everything.

It can take one risky smart decision to become a huge success.

How I went from a GED to CEO and how I was able to make changes and fight to emerge the victor and not just take the hits and just lay down for the count. **I kept getting back up, bruised and beaten, but never stayed down.**

Being public, my goal was to stay focused on the business side and not spend too much time trying to get people interested in our shares because that is a waste of time. Focus on the business first and worry about the share price later and prepare for changes! If you don't:

BOTH the company and stock will fail.

Here's what I went through and how I eventually became a publicly traded company and why changes along the way are part of the process regardless of going public or running a private company.

And why you should not trust ANYONE when greed is in the mix.

The next chapters lead up to **ONE change with $3 in the bank and a half bottle of scotch on a freezing cold winter night,** that turned GNGR from a failed publicly traded candy store to a successful global selling trademarked jewelry brand.

If any of the events in the second half of this guide had taken a different turn, I do not know what would have happened. Would I be a Billionaire or dead? I would not wish to go back and risk finding that out. I know what I did in the guide was the right path.

Be patient, it will all make sense and explains a lot.

FROM GED TO CEO

Due to my Dyslexia, that was not diagnosed early on, caused me to repeat 3 grades, and I only went to art classes and eventually was kicked out of high school since I never went to any other classes.

My Dyslexia was detected many years later when my Aunt said how is it Grant is so smart yet can't read or write well. Some reports I obtained from my grade school shrink wrote that Grant might be deaf and mentally retarded. I ended up getting my GED.

My aunt had me tested over 3 days at a NY City aptitude medical center at age 17 where they diagnosed me with Dyslexia with an IQ of >159. Some of the visual dexterity tests I took, the doctors said I broke records solving them because I can see things from all angles at once and solve complex depth and dexterity visuals but am not able to separate words and letters that seemed to always jumble as I read.

That's why the lizards get so pissed. They think they are smarter than me, and you can imagine how HARD it was writing this book and, over time, I think I also became much smarter than at 17.

After my GED, I went to a college admission show and at the booth of a well-known NY School of Architecture; they had a huge blueprint of a house designed by some famous architect that had an A+ grade.

Within 5 seconds I told the professor that house would not have been able to support the second floor bathroom and would have collapsed into the first floor. He said, "Are you NUTS? That was a masterpiece of mid-century modern architecture engineering."

I showed him the error that was only detectible from the 3-D perspective in my mind that was not on the two dimension plans. One beam was 5 foot off center from the combined side views and the 3-D image in my mind proved the second floor bathtub would have nothing but weak sheetrock under the bathtub.

He said, "HOLY SHIT! You're RIGHT!" He called over 6 colleagues to show them and they all said this should have been an F grade, not an A+. He then removed the A+ award certificate from the art. They said, "HOW IN HELL did you pick up on that?" I said, "I don't know" and every time I do speak my mind, I am told I'm crazy, wrong or stupid so my life was pretty much keeping my mouth shut.

This was not isolated. From a young age I would always correct people for visual things I saw that were wrong all the time and many saw that as me just being a pain in the ass know it all, which I am.

This is also why I just may be the best mold maker there is. HA!

That hatred toward my ability is why the companies you will read about tried to keep me down, suppress me, not let me be creative, put me on some leash, all with the goal to STOP me from helping better them and those companies I worked for that have all since vanished. ALL of them hated the fact that without me, their company was doomed yet they still did not want to pay me a good wage.

One employer said *"WHY do you need more money since what you do comes so easy? It's like FREE MONEY"* **Really?**

Today my molds are superior and many do not even know how I can do what I do so fast and so good. I took chances with many plans in life, changed course and in 2020 to the present; my business has gone global with NO signs of slowing down.

If I can piss off Fortune 500 company CEO's, FORBES billionaires and others, then I must be doing something right! I'll get to that

I was, and still am, very smart (maybe even smarter) and can do just about anything but was unable to get higher caliber work with no degree so I went from the bottom up, GED to CEO of a publicly trading company.

Let's move back in time...the past is key to our present situation.

My first interview after getting my GED (16 years old, I think) and having had some basic high school printing experience, I applied at a Millburn NJ printing company and the owner asked if I could run a printing press. When I said YES, he said, "Can you do art and negatives?" I said YES. He said, "Can you do bindery and collating machines?" And again, I said YES. He said, "You seem like you're just the amazing everything know-it-all guy" in a nasty tone and I was not hired.

This was how it was all the time, so in many cases I just shut up. I also hated my name Grant so much that at an early age I used to tell people my name was John.

When playing Go Fish or other board games with other kids or at birthday parties, they would say "JOHN, it's your turn" or "John, do you want cake?" I never responded forgetting I was John, not Grant.

One parent told my mom she should have my hearing checked she thinks I may be deaf.

So as a kid, they called me retarded and deaf and today lizards call me mentally disturbed, inept, and a conniving fraudster. So far none of those designations have been proven medically or legally.

This was the way it was when I was young... shut up, struggle and sent to the reading lab at school to learn lip reading and sign language. And today I'm still given those amazing titles by people that I don't give a damn about and most I don't even know or care who they are.

Call me what you will, anything is better than being a broke lizard.

Moving ahead, with no help or guidance at an early age or when moving into business, I had to just take it as it came and did what I could to figure things out.

After my GED, I looked in the papers for jobs and my aunt thought I would be good at jewelry *(HA)* and there was a vocational school in NY to teach jewelry. Since I want to summer art camp at age 13 and cast some silver pieces and Dyslexia prevented me from regular school that required lots of reading, I went to the interview.

At the interview I found out the jewelry school was for bad violent drug addict kids who needed rehabilitating and the school supervisor said: "If you do not do what you are told, you will be hit and disciplined by the instructors", I said fuck this and we left.

So back to the job section in the newspaper.

The only jobs that seemed to pay well with only a GED was a printing pressman at various print shops like Minuteman Press, Alpha Graphics, Sir Speedy and other printing franchises that were bought by investors who did not know how to run a press.

I applied to a job that paid $8 an hour when other jobs were less back when minimum wage was $3.35 if I recall, so $8 was KILLER PAY with a GED back then.

146

When I was hired, the pressman there was fired while I was there and he said to me, "I GUESS they think you are a better pressman." He had INK all over his arms, clothes, face and the shop was a MESS.

I knew very little about operating a larger press but saw it was dangerous, motors moving parts spinning cylinders, chain drive sheet feeders, I figured I would lose at least ONE finger before the year was up and took that risk.

I never ran a large press before but at $8 an hour, I lied to the owners and said I need ONE DAY to reorganize the pressroom which allowed me to get the press manuals and look them over to figure how to run a press in one day that took 6 months to learn at a vocational school I never went to.

Because I was not good at reading, the saving grace was the manuals for the press were mostly images and what to do. I was able to look at the images and like a computer scanner, I was able to remember everything and in about an hour, I was running the press.

The problem with the job was I could never get the printing to look good, it was always spotty, streaky, too much ink, smudging etc. The boss kept seeing me struggle, wasting paper, and not being a GOOD pressman. But he kept me on.

One day I was eating lunch and manning the office and saw in the paper a job for a pressman for $9 per hour so I called the number and when I did line two rang so I hung up to answer thinking is was a customer but no one answered. So I called the number again and line 2 rang again. I thought, OH SHIT, that line two number is for MY job!

I knew I would be fired as they hired yet another pressman. I moved on and answered another ad for $9.50 and went to take the test from the head pressman. It was the same model press I knew how to run but what about the ink, and smudges and streaking? If they see that I won't be hired. The head pressman "Jessie" tested me at the shop "Budget Instant Printing" in Westfield NJ and I set up the press, loaded the paper, added the ink and LET HER RIP! The printing was PERFECT, no issues at all. Russ (The owner) asked Jessie, "How is Grant?" He nodded YES and I was hired.

I found out that the ink issue at my previous job was not my fault! It was in a back room that had no heat, and INK can't print that is cold. And also the ink was thick, not smooth so the ink they used was also OLD and was not usable.

Here I am at Budget Print Center when they made their annual company Christmas cards to send to clients. I am next to the tree in the blue plaid shirt. Great people to work with.

bingle jells

I made good money at the time and got bonuses for doing multi-color work. I lived far away in rural Mendham NJ with my brother on a horse farm in a house we rented cheap. I mowed the large lawns to offset the rent on weekends and also got paid $8 for each horse stall I cleaned on Saturdays.

The problem was to get to work with no car I had to get up a 4am, walk to the main street and take the bus from Mendham NJ to Morristown and catch the Erie Lackawanna train to Newark and switch trains at Newark to Westfield and then walk a few miles to the print shop to get there by 8:30am.

Going home was worse. I did the same trip backwards but by than the bus from Morristown to Mendham stopped running so I had to take an expensive taxi home.

I made $380 per week before taxes but it cost me more than half that to get to and from work. I had to move or get a better paying job or work closer to home.

I knew printing very well, all aspects from pre-press, bindery, negative dark room work, graphics art and design. I went to other print jobs as I moved on from Budget Press and ended up in NY City working for BILLBOARD Magazine. My aunt just got hired there and needed help.

She had a good position but needed help with printing and design. I actually did a lot of the work that she was supposed to be doing so I saved her and she saved me. I never asked her for money but at least BILLBOARD gave us all free lunches.

I took the job and commuted from Mendham, NJ to NY City on the LAKELAND bus line. It was perfect! ONE bus to Penn Station NY, then a few blocks to the office on Broadway. PLUS, getting up early, I had 2 hours to sleep in the nice bus with deluxe seating like a recliner.

I was also BROKE and was not anticipating any money for two weeks. I think we had half a loaf of bread, some cheese, milk and eggs. I had purchased a monthly pass for the bus and that took away most of the money I had.

I think it was 10 days later we drove to the post office with my brother's old car running on fumes. I went to the PO Box and there was an envelope from BILLBOARD. I opened it and it was my first check for $1,350 after taxes. That was GREAT money back then. More than what college kids made once out of school.

I had NO bank account and there were no check cashing places so we went to the local bank and a girl I knew whose horse I took care of at the farm worked there and knew me and I asked her if she could PLEASE hook me up and cash the check. She said "NO problem Grant" and we walked out with $1,350 CASH!

That fits in with "Its WHO YOU KNOW" in business advice.

We filled up the car with gas, we got a house full of groceries and I opened a bank account with the rest. From $0 and hungry to $1,350 and lots of food, you have to know that was two contrasts that I never want to be faced with again.

Since I knew printing and Billboard started to send out marketing material to match the art I drew that was used in magazine ads, they also needed printing done for the mailers. I said I could get it done. I had a budget and found some printers in the NY City area to print the material but GODLY expensive. I told the printer in NY City, Come on, the card stock is only $10 and the ink and negatives were maybe $5 why are you charging me $250? "He said, "HEY KID, if you can do it better, go do it yourself!"

LIGHTBULBS!

I called a print shop owner I knew from years ago and asked her if I can print a job using my paper and just pay for the time on the press. she said, "SURE you can use the press for $10 an hour."

She knew me so she knew I was not going to break or damage the machine. I took the jobs from Billboard and bought the paper, spent an hour to print and brought it back to work on Monday and they said, "WHO gets the $250?"

I could not say ME so I said, "I forgot to get the receipt so I'll go get it next week." The girl at the bank said you need a business account but I had no company or name. She said she would add a DBA name to my personal account so I created the name *American Quality Printing*.

We had no computers back then, so I hand designed a purchase order and submitted it to Billboard and they sent a check the next day to my PO Box for $250. My cost was about $30. I started to do so much printing on weekends it exceeded my pay. I told my aunt I have to leave the job but in doing so I did not realize that a few days later, she was fired. The new director stopped using me for printing and used his contacts.

I lost my good pay and the extra money printing the mailers for them. Lesson learned. DO NOT burn your bridges unless you have a guaranteed alternative. In this case, I went from GREAT MONEY to ZERO revenue. I did have savings but... *TIME TO START OVER!*

TIME FOR CHOCOLATES

I did some odd jobs but was not sure what to do. My brother moved on and at that point, my father was in the confection business in upstate NY and asked me to help him. So I took a chance to see how that would work out.

I moved to UTICA and he had one chocolate machine in his kitchen and was making various items for wholesale and local retail. Nothing huge but was still interesting. He had a small operation that soon moved into a retail location and we hired 3 people and eventually the operation moved into a larger facility.

But he was focused on the same custom markets and products while I wanted to expand and go national and into larger retail sales. I used my art, graphics and sculpting to come up with new ideas that he was not really looking to do.

I went to various trade shows and in Texas, I met Don Morris of DISNEY who wanted Disney characters on chocolates and I also met the owner of HORIZON Candy Company who also wanted items we could make for his retail markets.

HORIZON used to put jellybeans in champagne bottles and colored jellybeans in plastic crayon tubes and Lifesavers plastic tubes and so much more. He made millions! I found this on Google.

Home › Vintage Toys › Vintage Unopened 1990's Horizon Creations Orange Crayon Jelly Beans Sealed Candy Container

Time Warp, LLC

Vintage Unopened 1990' Horizon Creations Oran Crayon Jelly Beans Seale Candy Container

$20.00

Add to Cart

151

After meeting Don Morris and HORIZON, I went back to NY to the factory and used my sculpting and art to create a new line of DISNEY chocolate pops and HORIZON wanted chocolate bars with sayings like I LOVE YOU, etc. that he sold in HALLMARK greeting card stores.

I made the new sculpted molds and samples to show Horizon and Disney for approval. Without getting into the details, the Horizon and Disney sample I made never left the factory.

Other issues that contributed to my business decisions, I cannot write about for liability reasons that were not approved by other parties allowing that data to be printed.

I wanted to do things differently and expand the business into retail and the company wanted to remain a custom ad specialty shop. For financial reasons and lack of long-term confidence, I decided to leave the chocolate business.

After I left the chocolate business, I was hired at Palozzi Mazda to sell cars. I know it was 1989 because the MIATA just came out and we had the first models at our location. I became the #1 salesman, selling over 30 cars per month, and making great money and no stress. I also decided to move back to NJ around 1990.

I found an apartment and made great money at the MAZDA dealership and I had some capital on hand. I figured why not start brokering printing again and paying to use a press to do my own work and keep doing that until I make my next move. I started to make more money and even bought a laminating machine to put plastic on menus for even more sales.

Eventually I moved to a house share with a large cellar to work from and most printers in the area gave me their laminating work. They dropped off menus and I laminated them and I also helped with their printing as well as my own sales.

Between printing and laminating, I opened up a print shop using the name I used before, ***American Quality Printing.***

I opened the print shop in North Plainfield, NJ and the orders started pouring in. This was around 1991 when no one really had digital printers or computers.

Many years later, the guy at the Millburn printer called my grandmother asking if I want to come in for work and she said, "UP YOURS! Grant owns his own successful print shop." **GO GRANDMA!**

I used a local lady for setting type on a line-o-type machine for flyers and business cards, using the old film and developer system, but it was horrible quality.

One day a graphics guy, Steve, came in and needed printing and said he would trade my printing services for a word processing and art layout program computer. I said OK! He gave me an OLD 286 computer and monitor that had ALDUS page maker and an HP printer.

The ALDUS page maker program let me create flyers, business cards, letterheads and more with different fonts and spell check on the fly, fast and cheap. I was like "HOLY CRAP, this is awesome!" I upgraded to a 386 computer, TOP OF THE LINE back then.

My business took off and I eventually was at my capacity in my neighborhood and I tried to get printing jobs from outside my area but those businesses said they use their local printer.

I realized then that I am never going to grow and with home computers and printers hitting the market, I may lose business to people doing it at home. Plus STAPLES and Office Depot started to offer services I could not compete with.

Being a visionary and always looking ahead, I knew this may not last and today print shops with presses are all but obsolete. So I decided to create an advertising company and combined it with my printing.

If some reading this has ever seen the placemats in diners with ads on them, I was one of the original pioneers of that product.

I started with Carousel Diner across the street from me. The original design was black and white with square ads on the placemat. I went out and sold 40 ad spaces on the mats for $299 each and printed enough placemats to last 6 months at the diner.

I think I used to print 60,000 placemats and gave them to the diner for free but they were REALLY UGLY! Not fun or even pretty to look at. I did this in a few diners, then found out I needed help with sales.

I found sales help, and to be fair, I would take the paper cost out and split the rest 50/50 since I had the print shop so I was only out the paper and ink costs while the regular sales paid the rent and overhead.

NO labor or overhead applied to the placemats. She agreed and was a super sales person. She would sell 40 ads and we had another DINER then another and another and we were making MONEY outside my area from ads, not printing services.

The numbers were amazing. 40 ads x $299 is $12,000. The paper cost and ink and negatives were only $2,000 so we netted $10,000 and we each made $5,000 and did one placemat per month. And every 6 months, we just renewed an existing placemat we had in diners.

She sold 3 weeks and I did the art she got approval and collected the money. Then on the 4th week, I printed and delivered while she went out to get more sales for another area.

We had diners all over NJ and it was EXPLODING! But I was not happy with the placemats. They were still UGLY and boring. One day, out of the BLUE, she said she couldn't work with me anymore. WHY, I don't know, but OK it is what it is. NO it was NOT. She decided she did not want to be 50/50, she wanted it ALL! 100% of the money.

Other issues that contributed to my business decisions, I cannot write about for liability reasons that were not approved by other parties allowing that data to be printed.

What she did was she decided to sell her own placemats and have someone else print them and she keeps the entire $10,000 and not split it 50/50 with me. **She was now my competition.**

I tried to find sales help again but it was not so easy to get good sales people. I lost 90% of my diners and the money stated to dry up, as I once again was a one-man show and could not do it all. I decided to make a BIG CHANGE for the placemats where I did not have to print them and also make them better than the old ugly mats and also eliminate her as a competitor. I sent the mats to a color web printer.

I came up with a new FULL COLOR MAP "Called PLACE-MAPS" with search and find games and also put the ads on the BACK and every diner wanted the new style. I even managed to get the CHESTER Diner in NJ that never wanted the other ugly mats. He LOVED the new color mats! I hand-drew the color art on one side and printed the ads and coupons on the back so people could take one with them when they leave or pick one up on the way out.

And they were nice looking and complemented the diner and was also a map of the town. Businesses got daily advertising morning, noon, and night every day for 6 months, all for only $299. That came to $1.50 per day to be seen by 1,000's of consumers each day for half a year.

What the salesperson, who became my competitor, did was she took all the money from her mats and spent it and went to her printer and said, OK print the mats for $2,000. But that was MY COST, not what other printers charge. To print 60,000 two color 11x17 placemats cost about $7,500. She said to them, "Grant said it's only $2,000" and they said, "RIGHT he did it at paper cost, we have overhead and have to pay a pressman and make a profit."

She actually would have made more money staying with me since I owned the print shop. Greed and stupidity!

And my new color mats KICKED ASS so much that she could not draw or compete, so she ended up moving onto another business. As further proof of what she did, my first color placemat around 1991-1992, I added to the map. TRY COPYING THIS IDEA because I knew she could not draw like me. She eventually folded.

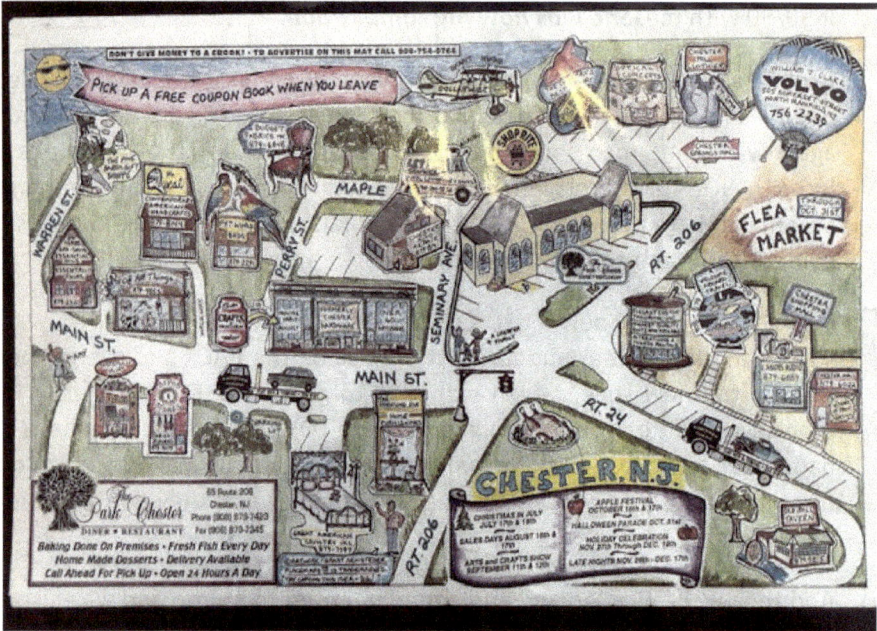

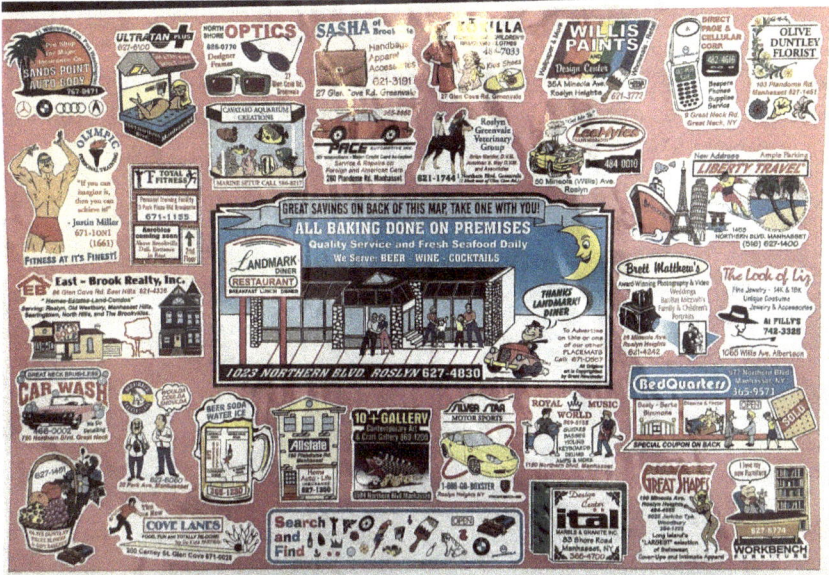

Since I sent the color maps to a larger web printer, I did not need the print shop anymore and I knew print shops were going to be obsolete anyway so I started to sell the equipment and close up shop.

Some other events done by others were done to financially destroy my business to the point I decided to move away from others who had one goal... TO STOP ME from succeeding.

Other issues that contributed to my business decisions, I cannot write about for liability reasons that were not approved by other parties allowing that data to be printed.

I decided to move to Idaho from the NJ area to get away from others who wanted me to fail and who worked hard to make it happen.

I did the graphics in my apartment and sent the last placemat to the printer and made $9,000 and was preparing to move out west.

OFF TO IDAHO 1993

A friend said come to IDAHO and get away from all those people and family. I ended up heading to IDAHO with about $10,000. I even did a place-map in IDAHO but I was just not into it and needed a break.

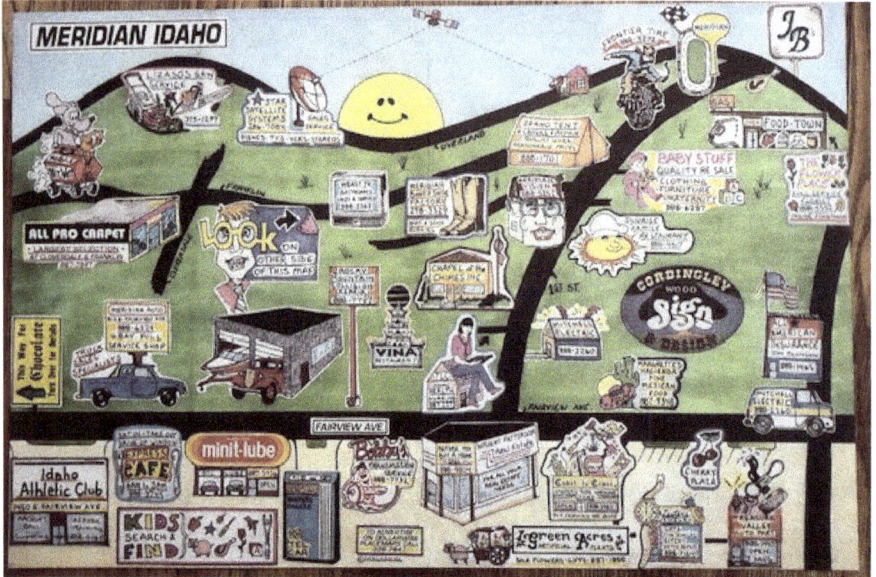

I did talk to some people at a bar about my past and ended up showing them what I did in NY with confections and one asked if they could do a little story about me. I said SURE why not.

They wrote an article in the local paper saying Transplanted Confectioner from NY lands in IDAHO, but at that time, I was not in the chocolate business any more.

OR WAS I

A man saw the article and contacted me and said he wants to

CAN YOU GUESS?

Invest in a chocolate business.

I said OK. We met and made a deal and he put up the money and we opened KASTLE CHOCOLATES in Boise Idaho and opened up a factory and retail store. I made the rooftop chocolate bar sign.

I put up ZERO MONEY and we were 50/50 partners BUT my partner had other motives.

We needed equipment and I knew how to set up a factory. I was out west so not sure where to get local equipment. It was then when I think my brother called and said our Dad's factory is closed.

I called NY and his equipment was up for sale.

I told my partner in Idaho and we flew to NY and we bought the equipment. We rented a huge U-HAUL truck and loaded it up and headed back to Idaho.

Other issues that contributed to my business decisions, I cannot write about for liability reasons that were not approved by other parties allowing that data to be printed.

I know it was around 1994 because we listened to the OJ Simpson Bronco car chase on the radio while driving back to IDAHO.

Back in IDHAO, we set up the factory and equipment. I called a large food distributor who delivered mostly to gas stations and small food stores. I can't recall their name. Associated Grocery, I think.

Rather than get a sales rep; I came up with a plan. I told them to give me a list of ALL the locations and I will call them to make an offer to take our KASTLE CHOCLATES bucket of mini chocolate bars. Each bucket had 250 mini bars in various colored foil and we made them for holidays as well.

I also made what was one of our best sellers, the Chocolate Pickle in milk chocolate with LOTS of rice crisps in green foil. The SLOGAN was they are DILL-LICIOUS! *And they were!*

I was able to focus on whatever markets I wanted, Retail, wholesale and ad specialty.

We also did jobs for Nintendo, Kodak and also had a huge retail store.

The distributor trusted me with the SECRET customer list and all I had to do was call every location and say, "HEY I'm with Associated and we have a SPECIAL item to add to your next delivery." They were all like, "OK, in fact send 5, one for each register."

So it was ALL GOING GREAT! Factory, Good workers, making sales and expanding and we controlled the sales.

We agreed not to take a paycheck for one year and my partner had capital, I did not. I took some retail sales money but needed more just to live. HE KNEW THIS! And he knew I needed a car. I found a car for sale up the road, a 1965 Mercury Marauder with 390 CI duel exhaust in MINT shape for $4,000. He said let's have a 3rd person buy in and he will buy some of MY shares for $5,000 so I said OK but I want vote proxy for one year on his shares so I still control 50% of the vote and he agreed. I got the money and bought the car and had some extra cash plus some savings.

My 1965 Mercury and me in Boise Idaho.

Soon after I got the car, my partner got WEIRD, distant and aggravated. Not sure why.

WELL I'LL TELL YA WHY!

My partner wanted to be in total control of the company. It seemed he wanted me OUT, but who would make the molds, do sales and production that I was doing? He knew NOTHING about mold making or production.

I had my thoughts and than proof who he was talking to behind my back, but again...

Other issues that contributed to my business decisions, I cannot write about for liability reasons that were not approved by other parties allowing that data to be printed.

I said to my partner, I have 50% of the vote for a year so he said he would buy me out now or he and his 3rd party partner friend would vote me out next year with nothing. I guess I had no choice so I agreed to sell my ownership to my partner. When the deal was complete, I packed up a U-HAUL trailer and headed cross-country BACK to NY.

The Idaho company eventually folded and I know why and my ex partner decades later ended up being part of some questionable OTC ticker that never achieved their goal and he made millions on the debt shares being sold to the market.

CHOCOLATE AGAIN IN 1997

I went back to NY and started to work for another chocolate company on Long Island, NY.

I was hired to work 9-5 and punch the time clock and did production in the factory and eventually made chocolate molds for them using some techniques I developed and various hand sculpted designs and molds for the ad specialty markets.

I managed the factory production and made new types of molds that were previously sourced out at great cost. Eventually we were making all molds in-house saving them $350,000 in just mold costs that expanded to more orders.

I was paid hourly which was fine because they were getting so much more work faster with me and also I had to work 50 hours a week to keep up with the increase in orders and molds to make. I believe I was making $1500 a week with overtime so that was ok and they gave me an annual bonus and promised me more when they expanded.

They had a meeting and told me they want me to be part of the EXECUTIVE TEAM. WOOHOO! Me an executive! I agreed and got my fancy title. I even came in on weekends as a team player to make even more molds for the next week's production so I think I was up to 60+ hours a week (more or less).

I loved to work as most know about me.

When I got my first EXECUTIVE paycheck (Salary) it was for $1100 for the week. I was working more hours than when I was hourly with overtime, I figure at 60 hours a week they would have paid me at least $2,200 a week. Plus, what I saved them in mold fees.

I told the owner I want to go back on hourly and punch the clock and he said "No, you cant. You're a BOSS now." I said, "But I am working twice as much for half the pay before I was a boss."

Since I had NO agreed hours when I was hired, and on the hiring forms that said work hours are 9-5 Mon-Fri, I did not come in on the weekend and on Monday I did not come in at 6am, I actually came in at 8:30 to eat my bagel and coffee at my desk.

15 workers were standing around doing nothing without any molds made to make the chocolate orders.

The owner came in mad as hell with his son and said, "YOU were supposed to be here at 6am!" I said read this and showed him the work contract 9-5 and said "Come back at 9, I'm having my breakfast," and they walked away.

They came back a minute later and the owner said, "If you're not on the team, then what are you?" I said, "I want to be hourly and punch the clock" and he said, "You're an executive. Act like one." And I said. "I do but 60/80 hours a week at $1,100 comes to $13 an hour, that's not calculating over time."

That is when the owner's son said to me "making molds is so easy for you so it's like FREE money for doing nothing".

Really, nothing!

When I was on the clock hourly they gave me a year-end bonus of $2,500. If I applied that to my 80 hours a week as a so-called executive, it comes to 60 cents more per hour. ***HIGH FINANCE!***

The owner and his son stood there and he said, "If you're not going to be a team player, then you couldn't be on the team."

I said what team? He said ok then you're off the team and I said what are you saying and his son (foaming at the mouth) yelled, "LEAVE - NOW!" I said OK, got up took my plant my coffee and bagel and walked out. The owner said to his son, you maybe should not have done that.

Then the owner said to me, you will never ever get work and pay like you had here, that they rule this industry and anyplace I work will not last. Little did he know his company was one of the ones that didn't last.

At $13 an hr, I can make more money as a busboy, AND get free meals!

That company was a MESS, dirty, so many hazards and issues. The guy who was sort of the maintenance guy who I heard passed away was a train wreck. Really nice guy but loved the booze.

I looked in the huge chocolate kettle one day and saw tiny burn marks all over the surface of the hard chocolate then noticed solder on the rim on the machine. The maintenance guy had soldered up high near the ceiling and solder dripped down hitting the machine rim and splattering into the chocolate.

I made a report but no action was taken, **NICE!**

I was pulled off production and a complete moron was hired to manage the factory. This CLOD went to turn on the water to 3 in line kettles and did not make sure the drain was open and the pressure in the kettles crushed them like an empty soda can, I heard three loud BOOM noises and knew exactly what that was.

All I heard was GOD DAMN IT! In 10 seconds he destroyed $50,000 in equipment.

One morning when I went in to work early, I heard a grinding noise, the moron manager forgot to turn off the conveyor motor after the air compressor that kept the belt on track and it moved off track into the motor over night. They had to cut 1 foot off the 3-foot wide belt, which meant 1/3 less production. I'm sure he told the owners I did it. My key was taken away that day.

The plant manager and maintenance guy were like Dumb and Dumber. Every so often they knocked over a kettle full of melted chocolate and we put a skid on it so no one walks in it until it hardened.

I had one of the ladies in the factory take a Polaroid photo as if I was Huck Finn and his sidekick Jim on the raft paddling down the chocolate river looking out for Indians.

Interestingly James was the name of my co-worker. Wherever you are James, I hope your ok!

So it's easy to see what a joke this company was. A moron plant manager, a crazy maintenance guy and also shit pay.

OBVIOUSLY leaving was not a big deal especially seeing the writing on the wall that this company will not last (Without me) so why waste time here?

SO that was the end of that. I moved onto yet another chocolate company.

ANOTHER CHOCOLATE FACTORY 1998

The next day I was hired at another confection company. You think saving the prior company I worked for $350,000 by making molds in-house, they would pay me $100,000, not under $13 per hour (Executive pay).

As soon as the previous chocolate company found out I was at a competitor, they threatened to sue that company claiming I stole technology. It was MY technology and they failed to have someone learn it while I was there so they now had a company, employees, chocolate machines and NO MOLDS, which means NO PRODUCTION.

I would have not trained ANYONE what I know.

The new company I worked for was told by the other Chocolate Company's lawyer, I was under a no-compete contract, but there was no contract. If they intended to get me fired, they must have figured I would go back and work for them, for what? $13 per hour?

This new place was also a MESS; they made basic items, novelty items and no real mold-making talent. They made what they called "chocolate ART frames."

They take a wood frame with a chocolate slab and the workers would just dab edible paint colors on the chocolate to look like famous paintings and they also made other things like bears, ducks, lollipops and bunnies, etc. Nothing spectacular, but they did have a good-sized operation with about 10 employees.

They said they would pay me $400 a week for 2 weeks to see how it goes and I agreed. So I set up a mold making room and got to work on new items to expand their product line and sales and also oversaw production. But unlike the other places I worked, the owner was not as mean, she was worse! Down right nasty and rude with no consideration for others and she and her daughter treated the workers, and me, like garbage. I nicknamed her the warden.

All the workers were mostly underage and illegal. One kid (I think he was 15) who was really smart, I made him my production assistant. He learned production and how to use some equipment and also trained others to do new jobs using new molds I created.

He was quiet but really smart and a HUGE help to the company and had a great positive sense of humor. He also had a really bad cleft upper lip but no matter, he was a great kid. I went to the owner and told her he's doing a great job and he should be given a small raise and she said...

"WHY give him a raise if he knows he can't work anyplace else with his ugly face".

THAT is the first time in my life I ever came THIS CLOSE to knocking out a women (If you could even call her that). I was livid and I said take $1 an hour from my pay and give it to him. She said NO because everyone else will want a raise. The next day the kid quit. He got a job with a landscaper for **$10 more** per hour. **Good for him**.

Owners forget very quickly who actually makes companies work and if the owners can't or don't know how to run things, they need to realize who is really running the show.

The owner's husband did most of the day-to-day business activity while her daughter also belittled the employees and the son-in-law did the accounting (Tried to, at least) and those 4 were always arguing, every day.

During the 2 weeks, I overheard the fighting and bickering about money and other issues. It turns out the company got in trouble because previously (What I was told by the owner's husband), the son-in-law over-charged the illegal workers paycheck deductions and each quarter, he would file the corrections and take the refund, not give it to the workers and he would keep it. Something like that.

A worker I heard, checked with an accountant and filed a complaint with the employment agency that investigated, and made the company issue back to employees the overcharged deductions and fined the company a large amount. Perfect accounting procedures.

When I got my first shitty $400 paycheck, I looked at it and told the owner's husband that it looks like too much is being deducted.

He grabbed my check and left to go to the accountant and when he came back, he threw a rock at the son-in-law breaking his computer screen (But was aiming for his head, I'm sure) and said, "YOUR AT IT AGAIN! You're going to have us all end up in jail!" The son in law just laughed.

Anyway a TOXIC situation everyday fighting and arguing non-stop. At least there was no chocolate all over the floor.

One day a man came in who was a consultant hired to spend a few days at the company to Assess why things are not going well. I already knew why but they hired him to look at all aspects of the operation including me.

The consultant made his rounds each day looking at production, the books, and everything and while he was doing that, calls came in from ASI Ad specialty people looking for quotes on corporate orders that this chocolate company was not really doing much of.

The owner's husband came into the mold room and said, "Grant, an agent is on the phone from SHOLASTIC and wants some CLIFFORD the BIG RED DOG chocolates. I knew them; they used the other company I worked for and were also looking at other suppliers.

I got on the phone and they said, "THANK GOD we found you. We need your help for a new idea for the CLIFFORD promotion."

I told them how about a large hollow chocolate dog house you can put the stuffed Clifford in with the Clifford blanket in cello bag and they said DO IT! It was a $100,000 account. I said, "What about the other Chocolate Company? He will be pissed."

They said they came up with a Clifford box that the dog went in but it looked more like a coffin. *NICE!*

Scholastic told me they told the other company they decided to use MUGS that year just so they would not have to say they went to another chocolate company.

At the ASI trade show in Texas, the other company's owner and son (the one who fired me for not being a team player) were walking around and saw me at the booth with the NEW HUGE CLIFFORD chocolate doghouse and when the son saw it, he KNEW we got the account and was pissed.

I said to them, "*I THOUGHT YOU RULED THIS INDUSTRY!*"

I figured I not only saved them $350,000 on molds but also they expanded to an additional 10,000 sq ft. so I probably was the reason they made more sales and why they hired 10 more people before I was fired. Eventually they went out of business, as predicted.

When I met with the consultant while working at the new chocolate company, I also was making the CLIFFORD dog house mold. I got some supplies from the dollhouse section of the craft store to make the doghouse roof and made the house part from wood from Home Depot.

I vacuum-formed the top and bottom separately and when clipped together, it was a 3-D doghouse. We filled the mold half way and rotated the mold so it hardened hollow like a hollow Easter bunny.

I then cut the dog door out and we put in the cello wrapped stuffed Clifford dog. I made the sample mold in a few hours after the consultant met me. I brought the chocolate doghouse sample to the office and the consultant said, "DID you just make that mold this morning and the chocolate is ready to go?" I said, "yes, why?" He started jotting down notes.

We did the Clifford job and it came out amazing. Wish I hade a photo of that to show you all. ***ANYWAYS!***

The consultant kept following me asking questions, watching me, interviewing me more than anyone else. He eventually left a week later and told the owners he would send his report next week.

A week later I was working early before the owners came in and a FEDEX envelope came in from the consultant. I knew it was the report and I WANTED to read it.

I called the owners at home and said, "I'm at work. Can I turn on the office air conditioning?" He said yes.

I called him at home to make sure he was not on his way and I know they lived about 10 minutes away so I didn't have much time.

I took the FEDEX and carefully cut open the glued seam and took out the report and made a copy of it but it was lots of pages so I had to hurry! I got it copied in about 8 minutes, then put it back in the FEDEX envelope and had a glue gun all ready to reseal the seam and put it on his desk.

Just when I sat at my desk, they came in to work. Got it copied just in time. He saw the report and he and his wife and the two kids want out and the owner said, "YOU run things till we get back. We have to have a meeting."

When they left I sat back in my desk to read the report. It was really bad. The company was in serious financial trouble.

But I only wanted to know if it had anything about me. There was a chapter that said GRANT so I skipped over to that. The consultant said, "to get to the point"

If you lose GRANT, your company will GO out of Business.

It talked about my molds, how well I treated the workers and that the daughter was MEAN and NASTY to workers and should not be allowed to interact with them and to have Grant manage the shop, make the molds and also handle customer service. HE said if you do NOT PAY GRANT at least 4 times what he's making ($1600) a week plus bonus, he will end up leaving, and your company will go out of business. MORE reasons for another owner to hate me.

It went on about my molds, speed, ability but I had to hide the report in my car before they came back. I knew they also read it so it was fun to watch how they reacted to me.

The owner said we want you to stay here and run the company factory and we will increase your pay and offer you bonuses even per order. I was like this, may be good. That week they took in an order for a big retail store for the ARTWORK chocolates. It was actually for Wal-Mart and had to be done in 2 months.

They panicked thinking there was not enough time. I told them I'd get it done. They said if I can get this order done in 8 weeks, they would give me an $8,000 bonus. It was a $250,000 order.

The next week my paycheck came and my increase pay went from $400 to $440. WHAT THE HELL! But an $8,000 bonus, I was OK with that. *For now.*

We got the order and I set up assembly lines and the chocolates were made, colored and packed so fast I got the order done in 4 weeks, not 8, saving the company time and lots of labor costs.

After all the trucks picked up the order and left, everyone was able to take a sigh of relief.

Finishing up the production report I put on the owner's husband's desk I saw checks to be signed and saw one for ME that said $6,000 (Not $8,000). I took the check to the son-in-law and said, "This is supposed to be $8,000" and he said, "NO, that's your bonus." I said, "Why $6,000 not $8,000?"

READY FOR THIS! Are you sitting down?

The son-in-law said *I made more money;* I said how do you figure? He said $8,000 over 8 weeks is $1,000 a week but you did the job in 4 weeks and $6,000 over 4 weeks is $1,500 a week so instead of $1,000 a week, you made $1,500 a week.

I said, "So I should have taken longer and had you spend another $10,000 on payroll to get $8,000?" He said that's your bonus and walked away.

SERIOULSY! I am not making this shit up!

At lunch I went to MidLantic National Bank to cash the check and the teller had me go into the managers office. OH NO they can't cash it? The manager sat me down and said, "Don't worry, we'll cash the check but we want to talk to you about your job."

He asked me if I am still going to work there because they got some big bank credit line and used ME as part of the reason they will expand and grow. I said, "OH YES, I'm going to help them make millions!" He said, "Great!" and told the teller to cash the check and she brought back the cash and gave it to me.

When I got the $6,000 cash, I said, BY THE WAY I JUST QUIT! He ran after me and said, "NO you have to stay there!"

I said, "Tell them to pay me what they owe me." I never went back to the company after lunch. I went to Ruth's Chris Steak House and had the best damn steak lunch ever!

I can't imagine what they talked about when I never came back after lunch, and I don't care.

SO, once again, back to square one with $6,000 in my pocket and some savings. Time to regroup my thoughts and plan my next move

AGAIN!

CHOCOLATES SEA CLIFF, NY 1999

After quitting that other job, I moved to Glen Cove, NY and decided to open a 1950's style café in Sea Cliff that was called CHOCOLATES. In the winter, a lady used to ski to my store.

I sold ice cream sodas, shakes, burgers, and fries. I even bought the old red and blue spinning seats from an old Woolworth's café. You can sort of see them through the window. We had a pinball machine and jukebox as well.

I gave a FREE meal to anyone who could beat my record of spins with only ONE Push off the counter. My record was 87 spins. No one was able to beat that. We had pinball contests and even had a guitarist come in on Friday to play for customers. It was a fun, relaxing time in my life but I had bigger plans than to just own a soda ice cream shop.

I also sold CHOCOLATES that I bought from suppliers. One day, a sales rep from a fudge supplier came in to sell me a program so I can make my own fudge. I ended up buying a kettle and their supplies, mixes ingredients etc.

I had NO clue what I was doing.

Me at my CHOCOLATES ice cream fudge shop with our first kettle before there was a Gunther Grant Company, Sea Cliff, NY 1999

We were **NOW** in the fudge business and I also knew how to make chocolates so I used the fudge kettle to also make our own truffles and other candy. The store was a success, fun and NO STRESS.

But there was a PROBLEM with the fudge!

The fudge was so damn sweet, it hurt your teeth and it was hard and didn't last long. I hated it, it really SUCKED, fake vanilla, oil based just really horrible. Over the weeks to tone down the sweetness, I added bitter cocoa powder and it helped a little.

The fudge was hard as a rock in a few days. I threw away more than I sold. I took a step back and over the months I started to move away from the ingredients I bought from the supplier and started to create my recipes. I think I had 100 or more and each one was NOT acceptable to me either.

This was not candy making anymore, this was SCIENCE!

I won't get into how many times I threw away 35 pound batches one after the other but it was A LOT! And also the flavor was not what I liked and being in the Candy industry for many years...

If I don't like it, I know you won't either.

Other candy stores I knew who used the fudge program and never altered the recipe stopped selling the fudge and I ended up buying their fudge kettles. That is how GNGR ended up with 3 kettles.

To make a long fudge story short...

I eventually perfected the FUDGE that got even BETTER over time, so enough about that.

For now!

I ended up making fudge to resell to other stores. I even sold some of our 8-ounce fudge to a major candy distributor.

But they took my package design and put their own label on it and decided to get the same fudge kettles but were never able to replicate MY gourmet fudge recipe and they stopped selling what they tried to copy from me.

I did sell to other small stores in the area, delis, markets and other candy stores so it was a start. I called STARBUCKS to offer our small trays of FUDGE for the local coffee store locations.

STARBUCKS wanted 2" x 2" fudge squares wrapped in cello but first I had to PASS the STARBUCKS health teams inspection. They set up a date and time and a team came to my CAFÉ and they checked all the certifications and they even sent a camera into the air ducks for heat and air conditioning to see they were clean (I read they would do that so I had the ducts professionally cleaned the day before they came).

The STARBUCKS team came and approved my facility and they sent me a request to make $5,000,000 in fudge for the chain locations. WHAT? I wanted to only make them for maybe 10 locations, not 1500.

When discussing this with customers at Soda counter gossip, one man said he would help and invest. ***HERE WE GO AGAIN!***

He said he wants to do the STARTBUCKS order and make the store a franchise and open other CHOCOLATE locations. He said first things first, let's get NEW equipment and expand.

He invested $25,000 for 25% and I gave him shares in the business.

Months after I left the other chocolate company, the owner's husband came into the café, sat down and just sat there like he wanted to say something. He looked stressed and totally dejected.

He brought me the coffee mug I left at my old desk as if he wanted to ask me something or ask me to come back but he just looked around at the café and equipment and my employee and must have known I'm staying where I was and he just walked out.

A week later I got a call from a business liquidator saying that a chocolate business folded and the equipment is up for sale so I went to the location because we needed a chocolate machine and pump and maybe they had one. Turns out it was the company I worked for that had folded just as the consultant said they would, all because they screwed me out of my $2,000 bonus.

The factory and office was a mess, papers and things strewn all over but I went there to buy the chocolate machine and pump.

While moving the machines, I saw my resume on the floor of papers. Not sure why but that memory still makes me feel somber. I picked it up and sadly looked at my life and all my past year's employment. The liquidator asked me what is that? I said nothing and just let it go and what seemed like slow motion, it landed back on the floor.

Back at the CHOCOLATE café, we set up the equipment and got things in place and ready to get the fudge perfected and work on the Starbucks samples. Everything fit into place EXCEPT I never issued shares in my own company to myself.

I did issue the investor his 25%, but the reality was his 25% was 100% since I did not take any shares for myself.

One day the investor came in with the POLICE! And they said you are ordered to vacate the store. I said, "WHAT? WHY?" The investor found out HIS 25% was in fact 100% and he went to his lawyers and got a court order to VOTE ME OUT!

NO WAY! But it happened. I went to get my jacket and briefcase and the police said I couldn't legally leave with ANYTHING. So I left in total shock. While that investor just stood they're smiling saying now he's going to make the $5,000,000 with STARBUCKS!

I walked over to 7-11 to get a hot dog and go home. I really thought I was dreaming this but it was all too real. ALL the equipment I paid for was GONE and worth far more than $25,000. The 3 kettles, the phone booth, the pinball machine, the spinning stools, the grill... ALL OF IT was gone.

Also, his $25,000 check bounced after I gave him his shares. But even if it did clear it would have been in the company bank account that he had control over.

NOW you all know why I ALWAYS maintained control of GNGR. If I had let others control GNGR, the company would no longer exist and all shares would be cancelled after a pump and dump scheme.

When I was in 7-11 getting a hot dog and soda, the police followed me. They always came to my café to hang out with their family and kids and got free food, coffee and ice cream but they were under legal orders to have me leave the store.

I was well seasoned at getting screwed (remember those punches I mentioned in the beginning?) I was like OK, time to start over.

AGAIN!

When the police came into 7-11 they paid for my hot dog and soda and took me aside and said, "LOOK GRANT, we are under a court order BUT if you are around tonight at 2AM, come back to the store with your spare key before the investor changes the locks in the morning and we will meet you there and I can go in and take whatever I wanted."

AWESOME!

I went there at 2 am, with my friend's van and they helped me load the fudge kettles, the chocolate machine and some other things I needed and they told me DO NOT take these to your house! Hide them where no one can find them. I did just that. I put them in my friend's garage and the next day the investor was PISSED!

He got a warrant to have my house searched and NOTHING! NO kettle, no chocolate machine, NOTHING.

About 3 weeks later, I was asked to come to an attorney's office and there was the investor and his lawyer. They wanted me to go back to the store and make it work like I had it working before being DRAGGED out.

I said, "I want my 75%." They said, "You are mistaken. We want you to WORK for the investor to make the STARBUCKS order as an employee." I walked out.

A month later, the store was for rent.

If the plan was done as agreed and GNGR did achieve the goal with STARBUCKS and we went public with millions in sales, his 25% ($25,000) today would have been worth closer to $25,000,000 or more.

Greed kills deals, remember that.

FARMINGDALE NY 1999

I met Marcie around 1999 when the Seacliff CHOCOLATES cafe closed and we are still together today. We eventually moved in together into the house apartment she rented in Farmingdale, NY and I moved the equipment into the basement to store there.

I was one of the first independent chocolate companies on the Internet. If you searched the Internet for CHOCOLATE, the top spot was MARS, then NESTLES then HERSHEYS then ME "Got Chocolates"

Since I did not make chocolates, I would go to a distributor and buy bulk and also to outlet stores to buy fancy discounted chocolates to list for sale on our website. I was shipping all over the USA... Cellas cherries, BACI, Guyllian Shells, and much more.

I think back then people just liked getting chocolates in the mail and did not care the delivery cost more than the items they bought. I also set up a fudge kettle to keep working on new flavors and ideas. Soon, more and more companies got in on the net and paid to be on top spots that I could not afford so we decided to open a store in Farmingdale, NY.

And also around that time maybe 1999-2000 if memory serves me, I read that a large company filed bankruptcy, many years before I took my company public and before Gunther Grant was incorporated. I ended up calling the Cayman Islands trustee and some other attorneys and asked them if I can make a deal to acquire the public vehicle so I can merge my confection company into a public ticker. I knew about being public but not sure how to execute it.

My idea was simple; turn those existing shareholders into customers. I thought what if each shareholder purchases a $12.00 fudge 4 times per year? We would make $28,800,000 and open a large factory and expand FAST!

I spoke to a few attorneys and some trustee in the Cayman Islands who said WHATS IN IT IF FOR THEM; I said shares of stock, I guess. I posted on the bankrupt companies Facebook page that I want to take over the public vehicle while the trustee sells off the brand, equipment, name and other assets. Many Facebook page fans loved the idea. ANYTHING is better than nothing.

Over the weeks I had about 2,500 shareholders siding with me and then one day a wealthy well-known investor said he's buying the company and everyone was really excited, except me.

When I had called the trustees in the Cayman Islands (BEFORE the news of the buyout), they told me about the buyout plans before the news was public. I think they told me too much too soon.

The trustee said they would see if they could make it available to me (Just the public vehicle) but word got out about my plans and who knows why, but they told me it's not for sale yet.

The Cayman people said the buyer **does not want the Ticker or public vehicle since his company is already publicly trading** and since the company's failure was not his fault, he had no responsibility to any of the previous company's shareholders. So why keep it if the investor does not want it?

I knew he did NOT want the public vehicle but he still posted he did not **INTEND** to cancel the shares with the buyout that excited all the bankrupt company's investors. **Something stinks in suburbia!**

So then why pump the stock and telling shareholders he does not INTEND to cancel the shares when he and I knew he was?

I think he paid about $800 million for the bankrupt company. I went to the company Facebook page and all shareholders CHEERED at the fact he **_INTENDED_** to take them all with them to the new journey but I knew otherwise. **Remember, intend means WON'T!**

I posted to all the shareholders on the Facebook page that you're not going to be taken to the new entity and the shares will likely be cancelled. The buyer only wants the name and product line that already had established markets.

The 2,500 I had voting on my side quickly said NOO WAY Chocolate Boy, we have a major WELL KNOWN investor on our side. I said OK but be warned, he said he's **_INTENDING_** to take shareholders with him, he **did not say he WAS!**

I posted on the two company's Facebook pages many times to warn people before I was kicked off. I posted to everyone to ask the investor to PLEASE tell shareholders YOU ARE TAKING THEM WITH THEM, (not Intending), and no reply.

I did get a hostile email from the investor's son saying I better back OFF or else. Threats? I Think so.

I said just tell your dad to tell the truth that he is not taking the shareholders with him. My guess is he was pissed because he knew full well they planned to dump the shares on the news they intend to take current shareholders knowing they were not. And, they were pissed because I knew about their motives.

Based on the mention he **INTENDS** to not cancel the shares, the shares (If I recall) shot up to $3.

People told family and friends to buy shares. One said he told his mom to mortgage her house to buy lots of shares. She's going to be rich. Some told me they used credit and others used retirement savings and kids college funds to buy shares.

Once again, I said DON'T DO IT! Unless he says he **will** take you all as a fact, not intent! No one listened and most told me to just fuck off.

When the hammer fell, he did NOT take shareholders with him and the shares were doomed and the stock went to a penny from $3.00 and soon the ticker was no more.

SO WHY would he buy the company and not sell me the public vehicle and only **INTEND** to take shareholders with him and then kill the shares and ticker and have his son threaten me?

This is my GUESS as to what happened and sometimes I even think and say, "WHAT COULD I ALSO HAVE DONE?"

My guess is... This is what the investor could have done, knowing how the markets truly work and what COULD have been done based on this guides data.

FIRST: Accumulate 25 million shares cheap (maybe $.10 per share costing $2,500,000) before releasing the news of the buyout.

Even if he purchased 25 million shares and knew he is going to kill the ticker, he could have had brokers short the HELL out of the stock well above the TRUE FLOAT just like GAMESTOP, but this time, NO SHORT squeeze but a killed ticker to bury the shorts. Or buy them all back for $.001 or less.

People who rushed to buy the stock believed they would not be cancelled and my guess is the brokers shorted the shares 10-20 fold at $3 to 275,000,000 shares and could have easily had 150,000 investors buy $5,500 each on average. Most may have bought much more.

That comes to $825 million (The price to buy the company)

Then, when he buys the company, he decides not to take the public vehicle or investors and kill the ticker burying any open short positions. He would have duped the public and could have used their money to buy the company costing him $0. The ticker shut down, the shorts closed out and all those that rushed to buy at $3 were left with total losses.

Most of the ones I spoke to kept saying where is the chocolate guy? Maybe he can save us but, by then, the Cayman trustees were told not to speak to me and the layer who told me inside info about the buyout before the news was made public would not return my calls.

Question: Why would the investor not let ME save the shareholders since he did not want the ticker or public vehicle? If the trustee sold me the ticker or I acquired it, he would not have had the option to be able to *sell shares short.*

Why keep what he did not want and dump it after the share selling event? My guess and gut feeling is he figured why not just have retail investors buy the company for him then after the purchase say, LATER SUCKERS! And most actually believed that the shares would easily go back to $44+ per share like in 1993, only 6 years earlier.

With the well-known investors name behind the deal, people believed they would go even higher. Some posted on the Facebook page, their mom's house was going to be foreclosed on and many posted they lost their retirement accounts and used credit to buy the shares and some said they lost their kids college savings.

100's posted they're facing financial RUIN but just like a pump and dump scheme, NO ONE cares about the investors.

The ticker was doomed before anyone but ME knew it and I tried to warn others and posted that publicly back in 1999-2000. In some published data the investor's representative said to shareholders:

"There is a small group of miscellaneous **assets" not being purchased**, but the deal covers **"basically** all of the company."

Basically definition: *in a general or basic way — used to say that something is true or correct as a general statement even if it is not entirely true or correct.*

And was the small miscellaneous asset not being purchased the ticker? *It sure looks that way as I warned everyone.*

A class action lawsuit was settled in 2006 for $42,000,000 due to lies to analysts to boost the shares price just like I said would happen.

Today you can find the 2002 **worthless certificates** for sale on line with the caption, "Original investors lost their shorts"

So sad, but I did try to help. OH WELL let's move on...

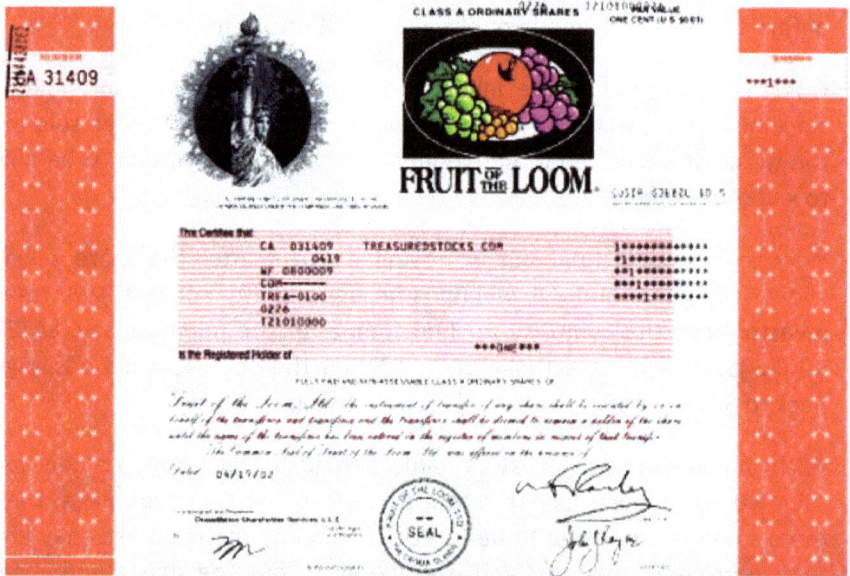

Fruit of the Loom 2002 Certificate (Original Investors lost their shorts)

List Price: $89.95 $69.95
(You save $20.00)

FARMINGDALE STORE 2001

We moved to our new location in Farmingdale right before the TWIN TOWERS attack in 2001. I opened Got Chocolates and Fudge and retail was OK but I wanted to do wholesale. We did a lot of fairs in NY City and all over Long Island, and eventually Oyster Fest that turned out to be a cash cow. I even went to Fairway Market stores in NY City and secured wholesale accounts.

When the Twin Towers were attacked and the rescue and fire workers were at ground zero everyone was donating so much food they actually had too much.

I called the groups that took food to the rescue workers and said I have chocolates and fudge, they said YES they need candy and sweets they have too much FOOD. They sent an NYPD van to my store. We took EVERYTING in the store and loaded it into the NYPD van. Our store looked like Cindy Lou Who's house when the Grinch took all the gifts. EMPTY.

I focused on wholesale and went through many packaging design changes and sizes of fudge. I started with different toppings on the fudge like M&M's Reece's Pieces, sprinkles, adding peanut butter, Mint and other flavors.

Most worked out, some did not like the malted crunch used in malted shakes. Malted crunch looks like gray kitty litter and on top of the fudge in the 8-ounce tray looked like a mini kitty litter box. I had 100 of them made and, as a joke, I put a fork in the package so it looked like a cat litter scoop and made the label "KITTY LITTER CRUNCH" AND THEY SOLD OUT! But I never made them again.

THE ONLY thing that was a complete flop was a mold I made of a 44 cal. Bullet and made them in chocolate with foil and called them "BITE THE BULLET" to compete with Hershey's kiss. But in the display bucket, they looked like suppositories so that was the END of that idea.

Valentines Day we sold Chocolate roses and next door was a TANNING SALON and all the guys flirted with the girl who worked there. A guy came in and bought 2-dozen chocolate roses for $60 and gave them to her.

185

When he left the salon, she brought them back and said she hates chocolate so I took them back and gave her $30. Was this the start of a way to make sales that I never did before? It sure looked that way.

Every guy that went to the salon and the gym next door for the next few days kept buying her chocolate roses and each time she brought them back and we split the money. I think we each made over $500 selling the same dozen roses over and over. I'm **SURE** she may have said to all the guys she LOVES chocolate. **WAS THAT WRONG?**

Joe Albertson of the supermarket chain put a broom by each register and told cashiers to ring it up as if the buyer put it there even if the person did not want it and only refund the money if they questioned it.

My friend in Idaho, Jack (JR) Simplot's wife Mimi told me that story.

When I tried to sell our 5 pack chocolate bars to Albertsons, I put 5 ½ ounces of chocolate on the label beating the price of Hershey's and MARS prices. Only I got caught because it was (5) ½ oz. bars making the weight really 2 ½ ounces not 5 ½. EH, I gave it the old Joe Albertson's try.

In Islip we had wholesale accounts and good retail sales but the store was a problem. The landlord next door had to let us use his bathroom in his Tanning salon because the store we rented did not have a bathroom (We did have a kitchen) and when we got inspected by the health department, we were denied the license because of no bathroom, so we had to move.

ISLIP STORE FRONT 2002

I opened Got Chocolates "OH FUDGE" shop on Main St. in Islip, NY. After we set up and started to do ad specialty items again, I focused on new exciting items for the retail and wholesale markets that were unlike anything ever created to get an edge on our competitors.

I also decided to raise capital to go public. After the investors who cost me the store in Sea Cliff and the business in Idaho, I knew I had to maintain FULL CONTROL.

First we raise some private equity to expand to get a bigger hold on the markets we were in. I hired an attorney and after speaking to the SEC and other compliance people, I found out that to take Got Chocolates public, I would have had to endure a complex time consuming 2 year audit that could have cost $50,000 before applying to get a stock ticker. I also found out that if the company was NEW with no sales or data, I could use that new company and bypass the audit.

It was in Islip that I developed our "Strawberry and Cream" products that were approved to be in 1,000's of big box stores in two areas of each store, the candy and produce aisles.

But with no capital, we could not fill the orders. It would have been close to $10,000,000 annually for starters. The pressing issue was to expand and become a publicly traded company and in order to bypass the audit, I came up with a new company and name that would not require an audit or someone saying Got Chocolate is too close to their name.

I put all larger production ideas on hold until after we became publicly traded to raise the needed capital. I did sell our strawberries and cream in the store and every time we made them they sold out.

The packaging was as good as the product. Red foiled

freeze dried strawberries and vanilla chocolate!

Around 2004, I formed Gunter Grant, Inc.

Gunther was my dog when growing up, and Grant is me!

"Gunther Grant"

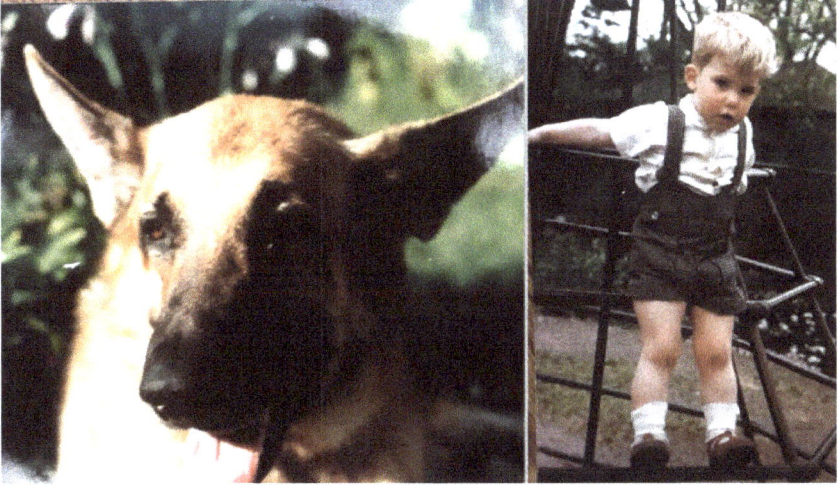

On the phone outside of our Islip, NY Main Street confection store

I think I was ordering a pizza, I don't recall.

MOVE TO EAST ISLIP, NY 2005

With the initial investors and our own personal capital, we moved from the small store front with little space and no parking in the town of Islip to the larger facility at 133 East Main Street, East Islip, NY (free standing building with lots of parking).

We upgraded the building with 220 electric for the fudge kettles and other things we needed, commercial water heaters, office space, and many other tasks to get the building ready for opening. Once we were approved by the Department of Agriculture (we passed with the best rating) we then purchased more equipment and set up a retail store and factory.

During the transition from Small retail to the large facility, we had some down time with the move and getting 133 ready for production. The rent was $3600 per month. We ended up at that location for 4 years on the lease and renewed the lease so I recall, we were there for at least 7 years. I believe it was from 2005 to 2011.

6 years x $3600 per month came to $259,000 for just the rent. The problem with confections is you can't sell much during the summer and shipping is not easy with the heat and shipping candy bars in the mail was impossible.

We were making many orders for the ad specialty markets like I did at the other chocolate companies only now I WAS the boss. We were actually holding our own and we had the best team of workers and the facility was in many ways state of the art.

I also tinkered with printing on M&Ms, corporate logos and other art that MARS candy company also offered at the time. It was a pad printing method and the molds M&M used were very costly to produce. But no one else besides Mars was doing it, so I gave it a go.

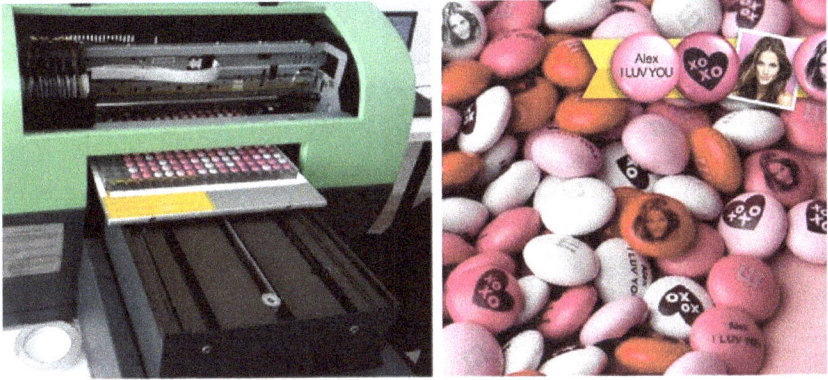

At the 133 East Main St location, I made logos printed on M&M's and offered the product to the AD SPECIALY market. MARS wanted to monopolize this so they had their attorney call me to say stop using and advertising M&M's in my sales and marketing. I said what about all the bakers that make M&M cookies and advertise they are using M&M's and the fact I advertised our M&M topped fudge they did not care about.

It was the logos on the candy they wanted to monopolize. I was able to make the dies very cheap and fast while they had to tool metal etched dies at great cost. I still believe they never made profits on the logo candy back when it all started.

The lawyer told me MARS will shut me down and sue me if I did not stop advertising logo's printed on M&M's so I agreed but what I did was I took images of M&M's and rotated them 90 degrees and called them 3&3's, he called back and said HEY WISE GUY, those are still M&M's and to stop advertising 3&3's, Again I said, OK.

I then rotated them another 90 degrees and advertised them as W&W's and again the lawyer was so pissed I think he busted a vein in his neck. HE said you're going to face MARS, you wise ass chocolate wannabe. I said OK OK, YOU WIN. He said GOOD and hung up.

Then I turned them again 90 degrees and called them E&E's and when he called he had to have had a stoke.

I could feel the HEAT though the phone! He said ONE MORE TIME (but I was out of letters and number anyway) I said, OK OK, but I have just one more thing to do that is *FAR MORE important* than your call.

I yelled to a coworker, "Could you make my McDonalds meal large size!" HE Started SCREAMING on the phone and I just hung up. I did remove the M&M's or whatever you want to call them and went back to production.

The attorney tried to bill me $125,000 for legal fees but were not justified, MARS legal department called me to apologize for the attorney's behavior and the woman I spoke to said the CEO saw the M&M events and attorney reports and he actually laughed out loud and got a kick out of it knowing I was just messing with the lawyer.

I can't imagine him in the office when he got off the phone with me. They said they would not pursue legal fees and that was the end of that. They had no case.

What I had pioneered before M&M was a threat to them trying to monopolize the process that they failed to control. So I guess I was the first threat only to end up being threatened by them and today, anyone can print on M&M's.

IT was FUN I have to admit and I laugh every time I think about that day.

3&3's, W&W's, E&E's. And of course M&M's *HA!*

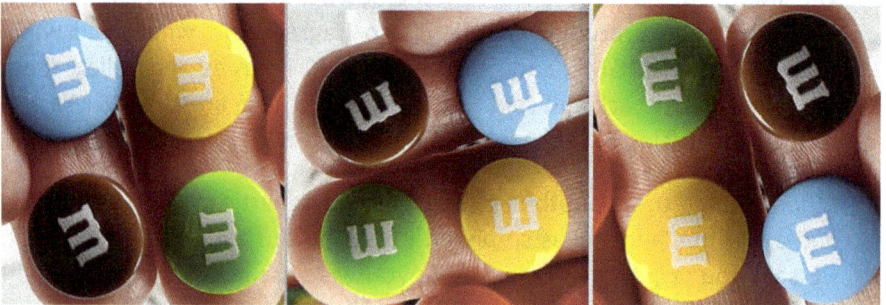

ANYWAY!

At the 133 location, I also perfected the best fudge available and proven time and time again to be a major winner with sales at WholeFoods, BJ's Wholesale Club, fairs, events and retail.

The way I mixed and timed the fudge at various temperatures kept it shelf stable for 6 months without drying out or hardening and it also would not melt in the hottest summer. In fact our fudge beat Hershey and Nestle's chocolate sales in BJ's during the summer months at the 5 locations.

No one wanted chocolate bars that would melt in the hot car.

People also bought the fudge as gifts and for summer BBQs and parties. Plus, many can share the one-pound fudge. Some said they loved to put it in coffee to make it MOCHA and others said they microwave it so they can pour over ice cream. We even added a FUN WITH FUDGE menu inside each box.

Our Gold Box (Vegan) fudge in Whole Foods was not just candy, it was edible art!

A distributor made a sales sheet for grocery store promotions.

EXCLUSIVE
"NEW"
ROUTE MARKETPLACE
SPECIALTY
CONFECTIONS

Gourmet Belgian Fudge
One pound - Serves 16
Perfect for gift giving
Great for holiday sales
Repeate purchases

BJ's Wholesale Clubs was our BREAK OUT moment moving into BIG BOX store sales territory. Our facility was to be used for retail, production and for wholesale and to expand into larger big box stores (that we DID achieve) before we went public.

We got a check each Saturday from the previous week's sales from 5 locations. They averaged about $2000+ per week. At the time, I recall BJ's had 200 locations. We were asked to supply all 200 stores with the same average sale of $400 per store per week. That comes to about $80,000 per week ($5,000,000 annually) for starters with more sales during many major holidays totaling about $25,000,000 annually.

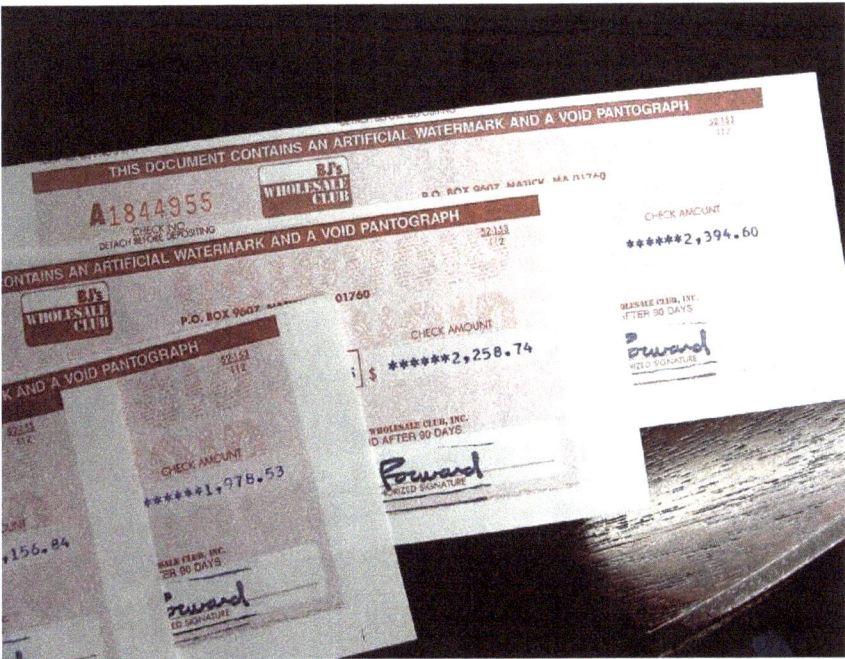

My sales rep, who was the one responsible for getting us into BJ's was also the person who took me to Bentonville, AK to meet with Wal-Mart and SAMS Club buyers.

Our products were approved and a $14,000,000 order was on the way. BUT, we needed capital for such a large order. Many companies dream of going to big box stores, we actually achieved that goal.

Our Fudge production and store displays we made for BJ's.

FUDGE PRODUCTION KITCHEN

BOXING ASSORTED FLAVORS

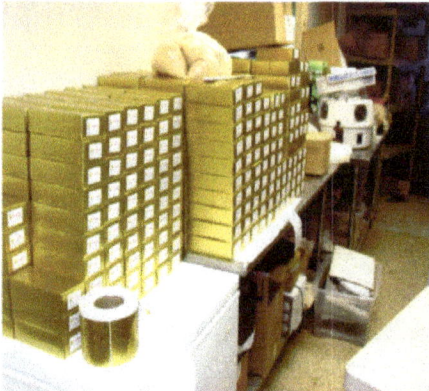
LABELING AND BAR CODING BOXES

CASE PACKING, READY FOR DELIVERY

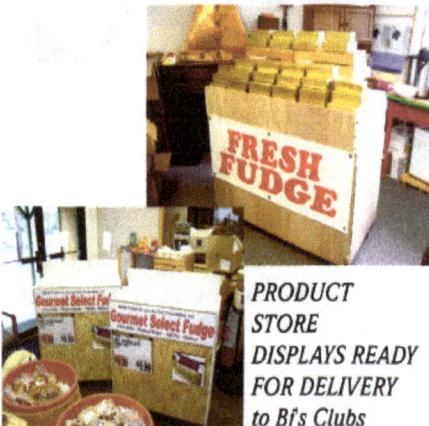
PRODUCT STORE DISPLAYS READY FOR DELIVERY to Bj's Clubs

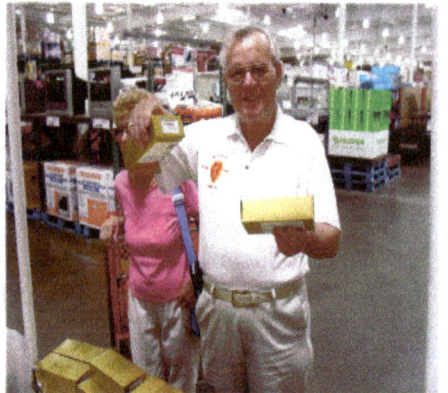
HAPPY WHOLESALE CLUB CUSTOMERS

With BJ's, we set up a table to give samples and it took lots of time and labor to do that in many stores. To get on the shelves was very costly and required more compliance and to have fixed floor displays cost millions. SO I came up with a PLAN! Shhhhh.

I created our OWN displays to leave behind at the stores when we left for the day and SLOWLY we stopped setting up tables and started our own store delivery of fudge just to restock our own displays.

We snuck in the displays and used them as the sampling table and when no one was looking, we stacked up the fudge and wheeled the display in the aisle right by the registers before we left for the day.

One day I was restocking the display and an executive was touring the store and he saw my display and I figured the manager would say you did not get authorization for these but the executive said to me "NICE DISPLAY! Keep up the good work." **HA!**

Other companies spent MILLIONS to get to that point with a free standing display in the FRONT areas of the store. I just figured let's do it on our own, and it worked!

GNGR went from a small candy shop in Islip, to products on displays in the big box stores and became a publicly traded company. We did what much larger companies wanted to do that were unable to do.

That was not an easy task, but we did it.

With the OK from SAM'S Wal-Mart, the order they asked us to fill totaled just over $14,000,000 and the sale guaranteed (meaning they will pay whether it sells or not) but they saw the BJ's sales and knew it was a sure thing.

We only had to sell 116 units per month on a half skid display. I even created the FUDGE VAULT. Since the fudge looked like gold bricks, the display looked like a bank safe. Our East Islip location had room for numerous large trucks to take the fudge away.

Working on the new custom 30 fudge case pack containers.

To do $14,000,000, only 4 individual fudges per day per 1,000 locations needed to be sold and our BJ's sales exceeded that. Wal-Mart/SAMS also wanted larger orders during holidays that would have exceeded the $14,000,000 with Mothers Day, Christmas and Thanksgiving.

My chocolate variations and pumpkin pie fudge to this day has never been replicated. I still have my **VERY SECRET** recipes and production methods hidden away in my files.

Just 4 fudge boxes per day in 1,000 locations for starters to gross $14,000,000 with another holiday influx of another $14,000,000 annually is $28,000,000 for 1,000 locations. Moving to 5,000 locations comes to $140,000,000.00 annually with the proof already with BJ's Wholesale Club and the Whole Foods test sales.

So how in HELL can I make that much fudge?
Not to worry I knew how to do it.

I continued to raise pre-public capital with the plan to use most of the funds to go public while also filling BJ's orders with the 800-pound fudge kettle the size of a HOT TUB I purchased and additional equipment. We also supplied a large gift basket company with various items they resold to their florist customer's individual locations.

We continued to do corporate ad specialty and product replication like this Chocolate cable connector with edible silver dust that was an exact replica of the Swiss metal connector (Bottom right in image). *Remember, whoever makes the molds, get the orders.*

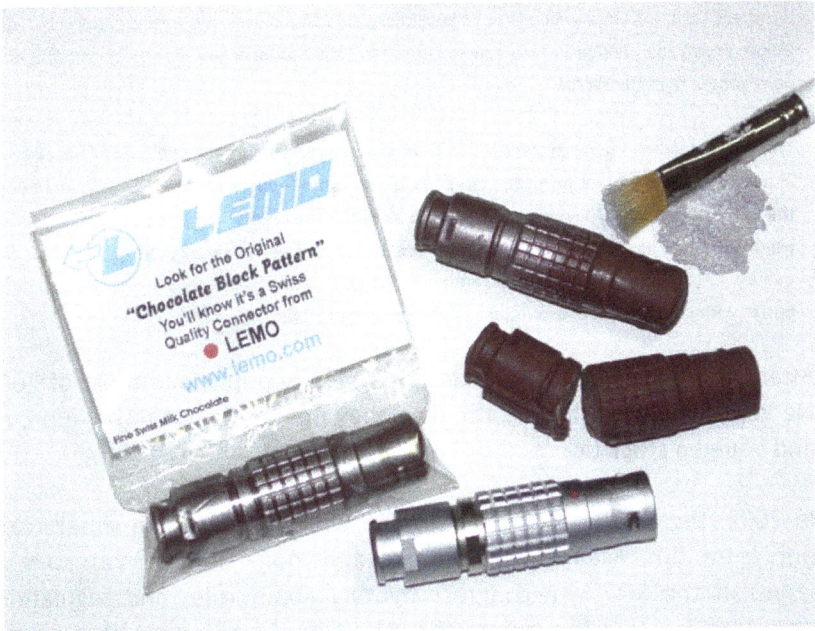

Whole Foods also wanted my gold box fudge in all stores but it had to be vegan so I altered the recipe and replaced butter and cream with almond milk and cocoanut oil. It was INCREDIBLE!

A magazine picked up on the vegan fudge and printed an article but we needed money FAST and from all the data I read, said go public and you'll get the capital you need.

YEAH SURE! Whoever wrote that was mistaken or insane.

Gunther Grant announces Vegan Fudge

09.26.2012   *By Timmy Trabon*   f ⊙ ⊙ in ✉ 🖨

Gunther Grant, Inc. announced that its subsidiary, Got Chocolates, Inc., has created a non dairy Gluten Free Vegan Fudge in response to consumer demand for a gourmet fudge without animal or dairy products in the recipe.

The idea for Vegan Fudge evolved when several consumers approached the Got Chocolates display at a Whole Foods Market farmer's market inquiring if the fudge was vegan. Seeing an opportunity, the CEO instructed his development team to expedite the creation of this new product. Within a week, the team had created a Gluten Free Vegan Fudge. They accomplished this by using the same quality natural ingredients as their regular fudge and replacing the cream with almond milk and the butter with coconut oil. The outcome is a smooth and creamy mixture.

After raising the capital to take our company public and most of 2008, we kept filing with the SEC the data they needed for us to be approved and issued a stock ticker.

In 2008, the SEC was in total turmoil with congress and other issues during the time Madoff had committed his ponzi crimes. With so many issues at the SEC with congress fighting about rules and regulations, each time we sent the comment list back to the SEC we ended up with dozens of new attorneys replacing other attorneys that left the agency who were reviewing our comment list and with each new attorney, we had to keep doing the comment list over and over with no resolution. I believe in one week alone I spent over $50,000 for attorneys and filing fees.

I finally called and spoke to the SEC in Washington, DC and he opened up to me and said, "LOOK, we see you're working hard to get your company public and doing the comment lists but to be honest, the SEC is not issuing any tickers at this time." He then suggesting we just pull our SEC registration and just file with FINRA to be a pink sheet company (Now known as OTC Markets).

Some bashers of GNGR keep posting that GNGR pulled the registration as if that was a bad thing. We pulled the SEC registration *(Before being public)* because it was going nowhere and re-filed with FINRA once the SEC registration was pulled.

We Filed with FINRA and December 2008 Gunther Grant was issued a ticker **(GNGR).**

Using more than $250,000 to become public and the legal, filing, compliance fees we paid out, there were some issues we still had to deal with after being issued our ticker. **NO ONE wanted to buy or invest in GNGR shares. BUT WHY NOT?** All the data that pointed to being able to raise capital once public **was a lie.**

We had big box (PROVEN) orders and even Whole Foods and SAMS Wal-Mart wanted our products. Most GNGR shareholders know we started with 5 BJ's locations selling our fudge and also had displays in stores. We also had teams setting up booths at BJ's, and Whole Foods in NY and Florida to meet people, tell them about our product and give free taste samples.

Richard E. managed and hired the teams, set them up, gave them inventory and handled payroll and we were paid for each fudge that went over the scanner at each store.

I was at dinner one evening with Marcie in Oakdale, NY where we lived and said to her, "You know I have people working for me on payroll I never even met?"

I saw a man I did not know with our *Got Chocolates* logo shirt at the grocery store and asked him where he got that shirt. He said he works for them and he did not even know who I was. That was a VERY WEIRD feeling but made me feel like "Wow! We are that big already!"

We even made contact with Hearst Publications in NY who issued us the rights to Betty Boop to sell Betty Boop chocolates at CVS and Walgreens drug stores for Valentines Day. Another estimated $25,000,000 deal!

ALL STOCK scams say they INTEND to get big orders or say they PLAN to go to the big box stores and say they will TRY and get licensed products, but they never do.

WE DID!

What I never understood is, the 99% will quickly invest in a pump and dump that says they MAY do the same that we DID! But when you have the proof you did and show how we made the plan a reality, investors still say "NO, it's too risky."

That, I never understood, and further proves investors want to invest in the DREAM lotto returns and not the REALITY returns that is a sure thing.

What I also found ODDLY interesting is, MOST of the 99% when they invest, know before investing the company will likely fail but they feel the need to get in with a few bucks anyway, and they are the FIRST to start bashing the company after they bought shares.

WHY? Because they can't brag about a long or short term WIN so they quickly post publicly the company is horrible and not going to succeed just for the fact it's the ONLY way they can show others they were right about the company when it does end up folding.

HOW CRAZY IS THAT? Proving you're right by posting negatives about a company that you invested in and how it's going to fail. WOW!

GNGR in various PR news promotions said we DID achieve those goals and was not just some bullshit _**intent.**_ We sent news releases saying its TRUE as a fact.

By saying we DID we now had to meet with the SEC to prove it and we did and GNGR was not in violation.

IT WAS ALL-TRUE!

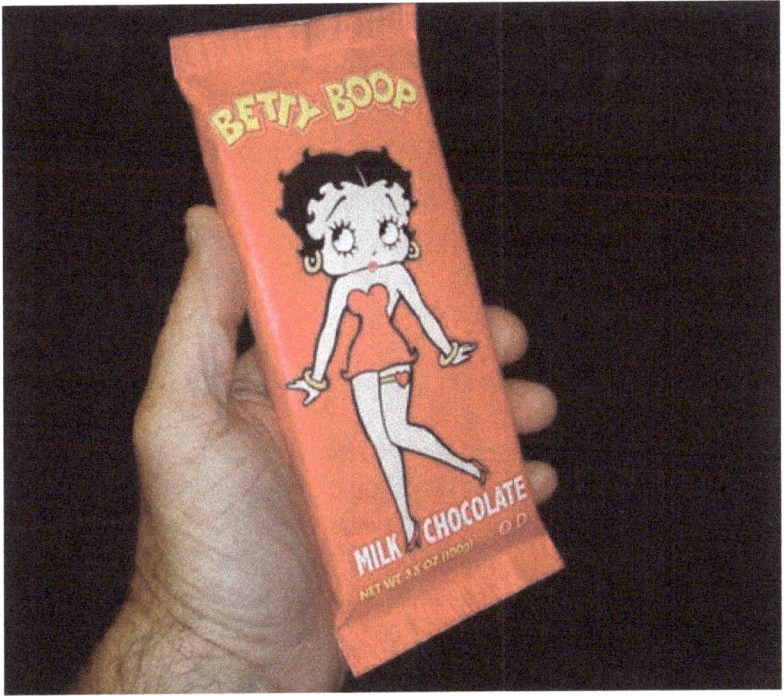

Betty Boop bars and deluxe gift assortment box with garter.

Getting orders was EASY because we were and still are THAT GOOD at designing and creating, but you can't cover a $14,000,000 order that requires $4,000,000 for fudge ingredients to make $10,000,000 profit without CAPITAL!

We tried to look for capital being public. We had the facility, the team and orders and the proof of sales. What more did we need? Banks said NOPE won't lend you the money even with a FIRM guaranteed purchase order for $14,000,000 for starters.

I started to look at investment groups for capital.

I heard that 12 professionals in NY City who each put in $1,000,000 to start an investment fund had $12,000,000 and they agreed to chat with me. I showed them BJ's checks, orders and sales and all the facts and proof that this is a sure thing. I needed $4,000,000 to make $14,000,000. I told them if they lend me $4,000,000 I'll pay them back $8,000,000 (GNGR would profit about $2,000,000) and issue them 100,000,000 shares in GNGR stock.

If they did that, GNGR would be doing at least $80,000,000 with just Wal-Mart and Sam's clubs in the northeast and GNGR shares would be FLYING at least $5 per share or higher. With only 8,505,450 shares in our float, our EPS would have been around $10 per share.

A few days later one of the investors called me and said they decided to invest all $12,000,000 into another company. I said how about $1,000,000 to GNGR so I can at least move to more BJ's locations and I'll still issue them 100,000,000 shares. They still said NO.

I said, "Might I ask where you are putting all $12,000,000 into?" He replied, "CRUMBS bakery at $3.00 per share." I said, "CRUMBS is Dead, they are finished." He got mad and said, "WHO THE HELL ARE YOU? You're just a little POS candy maker and CRUMBS is a huge well-known public company on the move!"

He got really offended when I told him he is going to lose all $12,000,000 and if he does $1,000,000 with me, he will make back his entire CRUMBS loss of $11,000,000 with my stock and even more as we expand.

He said, "CRUMBS is going to $20 per share," I said, "Really? How do you know that?" He said he couldn't tell me. He did say when they sell CRUMBS at $20 per share and they make $80,000,000, then they will invest in GNGR. I told him to kiss his $12,000,000 good bye. He cursed at me and hung up.

Move ahead. He was right! Crumbs stock did hit 20! Only it was 20 cents NOT 20 dollars.

If I recall, CRUMBS eventually put stickers on all the locations saying they are BANKRUPTING and everyone is fired and no one will be getting their paychecks (Something like that).

If they took my offer for 100,000,000 shares and we expanded our existing sales, we would have seen our share price rise quickly to about $.25 then to $5 or more. The investment group would have easily made $25,000,000 at only $.25 cents per share, twice the $12,000,000 they lost with Crumbs bakery.

Once the CRUMBS hit $.05, the investors 4,000,000 shares they paid $12,000,000 for, was now worth $200,000 with no bid. The stock tanked just as I said it would. The share price ended up at $.00001 with no bid. 4,000,000 shares the group paid $12,000,000 for are now worthless. ***NICE!***

I did get a call from the same investor after they lost the entire $12,000,000 who said they NOW want to invest with my company. I said, "REALLY what's your plan?" He said, "$100,000 for 90% of my company." I said, "SURE I'll think about it and call you back."

Crumbs sank to $.00001 per share and I never called him back.

Home > Investing > Quotes > Stocks > United States > CRMBQ > Overview

Switch Quote | **CRMBQ** U.S.: OTC

Crumbs Bake Shop Inc.

• OPEN

$**0.0000**

0.0000 0.00%

< Advanced Charting   1D ▼ $ %   VOL

Last Updated: May 9, 2023 9:30 a.m. EDT
· Delayed quote

The outcome was GNGR raised capital early on to expand what was working. We secured a larger facility, added new equipment and took the company public for far more than what I raised having invested over $150,000 in personal money as well.

Around 2011 it was obvious we did not do Wal-Mart. Sam's or Whole Foods due to no funding, and most of what GNGR raised took us public and expanded to handle the larger orders we were preparing for. We went through over $1,000,000 and used what sales we had to pay 3-6 employees. With NO funding options left, *GNGR ended up being a publicly traded candy store.*

We ended up doing favors for CASINOS using the WONKA themed bars. The Casinos paid for the rights to use the WONKA labels and we did sell some in the store to kids but it was not illegal to be a supplier to Casinos who paid for Wonka slot machines and the use of the Wonks bars to give to customers and contests. I even created a way to stop fraud with the prizes and contests that the media picked up on.

Marcie packing Wonka Bars at the 133 location.

Fraud in chocolate prizes curbed by Gunther Grant

By **Kacey Culliney**
02-Oct-2012 - Last updated on 03-Oct-2012 at 11:02 GMT

SHARE f 🐦 in ✉

Gunther Grant has developed a security feature for promotional prize tickets in chocolate bars used as giveaways in casinos to curb fraud among customers, it said.

Gunther Grant is no stranger to chocolate prize tickets...

Those orders helped but were just not enough to keep the overhead covered and when summer came, we had to pay rent for months with far less sales. The warm hot weather killed us while I still paid the overhead. The fudge kept selling, just not chocolates.

Even American Express took notice of Got Chocolates! They ran ads in major papers and magazines like the Wall Street Journal and Forbes Magazine for "FREE," promoting Got Chocolates.

How flexible payment made the sweets business a little sweeter.

GotChocolates.com founder Grant Newsteder relies on the American Express OPEN® Plum Card's flexible payment options to keep his company's finances deliciously nimble. The defer pay option gives Grant more control over his cash flow – so he can offer his clients adjustable payment schedules. As if the chocolate alone didn't make for happy customers. What will you do with everything, everywhere trade terms?

1.5% EARLY PAY DISCOUNT *or* UP TO 2 MONTHS DEFER PAY, INTEREST FREE

APPLY AT 866-973-PLUM *or* PLUMCARD.COM/CRAINS

OPEN

Calling all business owners.

Our factory store at 133 East Islip, with NO funding to be able to buy what we needed for the larger orders for Whole Foods, Sam's and Wal-Mart, we still continued to do BJ's store door sales.

We had 3 credit cards (Banks would not give us a line of credit). We had 2 CITIBANK cards and the AMEX PLUM CARD (Like in the American Express ad). And I spent $250,000 to go public.

We had a $35,000 credit line on each CITI Bank card and unlimited on the AMEX. What I did to keep the BJ's funded and pay people till we got paid was I used the credit cards to fund production, then pay it back when we got paid. One card we owed $8,000 and the other $9,000 at 8%.

We used the cards to fund production and chipped away at the debt. Even without Sam's or Whole Foods, we were holding ground and looking to go to more BJ's. I think we picked up another BJ's location in Farmingdale.

At the same time (2009) during the bank collapse issues with the financial markets and sub prime all messed up, I got a letter saying that our CREDIT cards credit lines have been reduced to $4,500 for each card, down from $35,000 and since we owed more than what the new lower credit line was, the letter said you ARE OVER YOUR LIMIT and are being switched from 8% to 29% interest and to pay the overage in full.

As soon as we paid the cards down to $4,000 balance under the $4,500, they said they are reducing our line from $4,500 to $1,500 forcing me to pay down the cards but we couldn't, we had to wait for the BJ's checks and I had to pay people and overhead.

Both cards went into default so they cancelled the cards and said pay the balance plus we had NO MORE credit line.

Visibly angry, I called the credit card companies and said, "What the hell. You are ruining my business!" She said, "DON'T CARE pay the balance in full."

I said I can't and she said THEN I would go to collections. I said maybe I'll file bankruptcy and she said DO what you have to DO! I said,

FUCK YOU! Then hung up.

And then when I went to get supplies for the BJ's fudge using the PLUM AMEX card, it was declined.

I called AMEX and she said they reduced the unlimited credit limit to $1,500. I said OK but the supplies were only $650 and I was declined. She said AMEX annual fee for the PLUM card is $1,500 so they charged my card the $1,500 annual fee so I was at my limit.

I said, "YOU are FUCKING charging me $1,500 for an annual fee on a card with only $1,500 credit limit?" She said YES. I said cancel the card, she said NO.

I said YES she said NOPE. I said, "STOP THIEF! Oh my God! Someone just stole my wallet and my AMEX card was in there! Cancel my card! It was stolen!" she said. "YEAH SURE IT WAS."

So they never cancelled the card and that went into default as well. SO, now I had NO credit lines right when BJ's sales were growing.

Damn it, now I have to start over yet AGAIN!

The first Chocolate Company I worked for when I came back from Idaho lent me $2,000 for a car who took $100 from my pay each week. I told him when I left to just take the year bonus he owned me to cover the loan.

I did not know he filed a suit against me for $2,000 from many years earlier. I guess because they did not know where I lived, he won the case and he added interest year after year that amounted to over $8,500 I did not even know about.

I'm sure the banks saw that judgment and that's why no one would give us a loan.

I never knew he did that until I checked my credit. I can't believe he did that knowing he owed me $2,500 bonus but probably said NO BONUSES that year so he could sue me.

Between the credit cards, the loan judgment and the house credit line loan issue, I had no choice but to file bankruptcy. Our own fucking lawyers were even in on the HOW TO SCREW GRANT plan!

I do not think there is ONE securities attorney out there who does not want to get a piece of some Pump and Dump scam money. They know they don't make millions being a lawyer so they have to help scammers by *fucking over clients!*

Our first attorney before we went public helped to write loan agreements with investors and help incorporate. We paid him $1,000's and $1,000's only to have HIM introduce me to scammers to set us up into a pump and dump after we were public.

He sent people to our store (Dangerous people) to make a deal to take over the vehicle. One group said they wanted control of the company but would keep me on as CEO but they need controlling interest because (He said) "what if we invest $1,000,000 and you drop dead"

Our own FUCKING ATTORNEY did that.

Then the second attorney tried to convince me to sell *his people* the public vehicle and when I said, NO I have plans, he said *YOU'RE A FUCKING IDIOT.*

With no credit lines, no funding and no money, I had to make a drastic choice and shut the 133 operation down.

At around early 2011, I closed up the 133 East Islip location and started to sell some of the equipment, candy cases, displays and put some things in storage.

While at home in Oakdale around 2012, the year the super storm Sandy hit the East Coast, I also thought about that and recall when the DOMINO sugar factory exploded in 2008 that caused a huge sugar shortage and my fudge needed sugar and we ended up producing less for each BJ's stores we were in. Both events affected our business.

My feeling was we were lucky to have closed up the 133 East Main Street factory and store because all businesses were disrupted as well as suppliers for materials and no power for weeks due to the storm.

SURE, we were out of money but what good would having money be paying rent and overhead with no sales money coming in due to the storm floods and no power plus all the damage to the 133 building.

Marcie and I stayed at home during the super storm Sandy when everyone in our neighborhood left town (we had no place to go) while Oakdale was pretty much under water with no power. Oddly enough, our house was the ONLY house that may have been slightly on a bump preventing any significant flooding while it looked like an ocean all around us, and I had a huge generator.

Some thieves came down the street at 2am in a 4x4 going house to house with flashlights looking to rob vacant homes. The police said they couldn't get there and to do what you need to do to protect your lives. People were being robbed and murdered at this time.

The truck kept getting closer and closer to our house and the thieves on foot with flashlights were headed our way. I knew they would be at our front door at any moment. I shut the generator off so the house was dark and prepared to welcome them.

I had various firearms and a high-powered professional competition sniper long rifle with scope and green laser. I set up position at our second floor open window and aimed the laser rifle at the truck driver's head (he was about 70 yards away) and I could see him panicking in the truck as the lasers reflection inside the truck bounced back and forth in his interior glass as he frantically looked to see where it was coming from.

HE honked the horn and they all ran in the truck and he took off probably looking for a fast exit out of the neighborhood and a clean pair of underpants. But good luck for them. Remington 35 cal. OUCH!

Our neighborhood street in Oakdale during storm Sandy.

212

FINALLY THE BREAK WE NEEDED THEN THINGS GOT WORSE

Around late 2012 while recovering from Sandy and the floods, I planned my next move. While at home, I was contacted by an individual who was a knowledgeable respected SEC attorney and, by all aspects, legit and had many dealings with the SEC.

Even our stock transfer agent confirmed he was a respected attorney with a good track record that gave us a positive feeling he will help. After declining many other lizard's offers, I decided SOMETHING had to be done to help expand our company and this attorney was well recommended. Or so I thought...

We had a low float of only 8,505,450 shares (Not even CLOSE for liquidity). We were offered a deal that would get our company $1,000,000 if we issued the attorney 100,000,000 restricted shares. Easy to do, just get a certificate for 100,000,000 from the transfer agent and send it to the attorney and we get $1,000,000 expansion capital, RIGHT? *Not so fast.*

But with no factory and equipment in storage, I took his offer. We would use the $1,000,000 to regroup, open a new location, set up the equipment and start again, SMARTER than before.

We issued Davies a 100,000,000 restricted share certificate that could not be tradable for at least 12 months under rule 144, but soon after we issued him the certificate, the stock was rallying up, and the shares were being added to the float. I was not sure how he was able to sell those shares but kept an eye on the situation and, over time, found out about the debt conversion rule after the SEC questioned my involvement with Davies and his debt dilution short selling scheme of our company shares.

Davies sent us money in small amounts-$10,000 one week then $20,000 the next and believing we'll get the total $1,000,000 we opened up a new location in Sayville, NY again adding power, equipment set up, health certifications with the idea to go back to ASI orders for casinos and AD specialty markets. The rent I believe was $2,300 a month with deposits and other costs.

I had already issued him the 100,000,000 shares so I figured at least we'll get the $1,000,000 and start over again. Not quite.

As the months passed, Davies ended up issuing GNGR $200,000, not at once but over a 6-month period.

I used the $200,000 to get the new location up and running, bought some new equipment and had a few helpers to wrap and pack chocolates. But, starting over, we had to start back at the beginning.

At this time, I also invented and created the VORTEX chocolate tempering machine that was revolutionary. I NEEDED it for myself only to find others wanted the machine as well.

It worked GREAT! There is a video of it on YouTube and I'll post a link to the video at the end of this guide. It made making chocolates fast and easy. I used part of Davies' $200,000 to have the Vortex built believing $800,000 more was on the way.

Davies soon called me and said he needs another 100,000,000-share certificate. I said, "What about the $800,000 you owe me?" He said he couldn't pay it because the initial 100,000,000 shares are gone. GONE? How can they be GONE? They were restricted.

He said just issue him another 100,000,000 shares and he will get us $1,000,000. When I said NO, he hung up and that was the last time we spoke.

When I made a video of the Vortex unit, I got amazing feedback and requests for them, but again, under funded. It seems everything I did required funding of some sort, like most businesses. With all I accomplished with proof and sales and all that is needed to show we can make GNGR a monster company, EVERYTHING, I mentioned early on in this guide, proves;

THE BEST IDEAS with no money are DOA

I had no reason not to trust this attorney based on others saying he's well known and compliant in the securities market. But I learned the hard way and never expected a reputable well-known attorney to end up committing fraud and felony crimes that landed him in hand cuffs and loss of his legal license.

The Vortex unit I designed was SUPER EASY to use, portable, cost efficient and easily processed difficult types of chocolates and coatings and was a workhorse in our factory in Sayville.

The 4 arches at the top were my own invention that allowed the vortex air (This did not need water like most kettles) to flow out and aim it to the center of the mixing bar to keep the inner chocolate in temper where it usually cools and hardens like most kettles. The VORTEX kicked ass! It was also lightweight and portable.

So no $800,000, what's my next move.

Davies ended up wanting many more certificates for 100,000,000 each, probably attempting to add the entire 4.5 billion authorized shares to the float (That is dilution). I declined, and as I said, we never heard from him again.

But how did he add those shares to the float when they were restricted? They legally could not be sold for a year but they were registered the same week we issued them. Turns out he committed fraud and created false debt on false documents and forged my signature to free up the shares using the debt conversion rule I mentioned in previous chapters. I did not issue him additional shares and ended our relationship with him before I found out about the fraud.

Our company was right back to where we were a few months earlier but with 108,505,450 in the float and a sinking share price. Without someone pumping the stock, there was little chance it will ever be seen or spoken about without a pump program in place.

After we were DUPED in 2012, that individual we gave 100,000,000 shares too, committed the same fraudulent activity to another company only this time he got caught and faced up to 20 years in jail. No help to us, we did not get the other $800,000 and we were out the 100,000,000 shares. Our float increased and our share price dropped.

My guess was he sold the 100,000,000 for an average price of $.10 cents raking in about $10,000,000 but I eventually found out it was shorted much more.

Many years later, I found that over 400,000,000 shares sold that same year (2012) and another 400,000,000 a few years later. This means he must have had brokers naked short sell GNGR and since we did not go out of business or sell out, those shorts are still open today.

If he had given us the $1,000,000, we would have issued him another 100,000,000 shares and opened a new modern facility for our business. This is rare for an OTC company to use funds to expand and grow the company since most just sell shares and walk away with the cash.

Paper is worth more than chocolate AND gold, remember that.

I now believe this attorney figured I was just the normal P&D CEO that will issue shares cheap, dilute the float and close up eventually.

By not giving us the $1,000,000, he figured he would squeeze us into issuing more and more shares cheap, eventually allowing us to get that $1,000,000 but only after he diluted a few billion shares to the float.

The reason these pumpers only give a fraction of what they promise is because they figure it's ONLY paper for the OTC company so why not just keep printing 100,000,000 certificates for $200,000 over and over like most Pumped OTC's do. Again we declined.

Many failed tickers and CEO's, in fact, do that because they know they will never make products or revenue so selling the certificates is the only way to make any money.

With no factory and no sales and in need of capital, I could have easily done the debt dilution and made myself $2,000,000 with Davies but I wanted to be legit and somehow make the company eventually work.

Many CEO's end up issuing shares that dilute the market and price and as the price declines with every 100,000,000 shares issued, the CEO is paid less and less. $200,000 for 100,000,000 shares, then $100,000 for 100,000,000 shares, then $20,000 for 100,000,000 shares, then $5,000 for 100,000,000 shares. The CEO may make $1 million and end up issuing billions of shares that end up at $.00001 or less. And, end up like most tickers that continue to happen to this day.

Eliminate the debt conversion rule and FRAUD would stop!

After the dilution, they sell the shares cheaper and cheaper and that is why the CEO does not make as much as people think when they dilute on a debt conversion pump and dump.

If we had depleted the entire 4.5 billion shares in TRANCHES, as they call them, we would have sold 45 blocks of 100,000,000 shares and we would have raised maybe $2,250,000 but probably less as they kill the share price and get more 100,000,000 certificates for less and less.

Knowing we are legit, I guess all I had to do was keep issuing 100,000,000 certificates, raise the $2,250,000, fill orders and then maybe reduce the shares down the following year and expand the business, increase the share value and expand the company products. Like what a real company does.

If I knew what I know now, I could have done that. I guess diluting and recovering to make the company work would have been OK since most companies dilute and fold the company.

In a way, it would have worked out because we would have grown and increased sales not dumped and diluted then closed up the company. So what I thought would have been dilution, would have helped, not hurt, our company. But would it also help the share price, probably not.

When the money from Davies never arrived, things again caused a downturn. I was paying rent in the new Sayville, NY location month to month (no lease) and the landlord ended up selling the *DAMN* building that, today, is some large deli food market. I had to vacate in 30 days.

Without the $800,000 owed to me, again back to square one with no factory or capital. I moved back home and put the equipment again in storage.

While at Sayville, I had just landed the 7-11 account where they said we could self-deliver direct and we picked up 5 locations. This was right when the landlord sold the building. With the $800,000 never being received, we had little money to move AGAIN!

I did try hard to hold that Sayville location together but we had to move out of the facility quickly.

Before leaving the Sayville location, I created the MINI fudge with mini spoon and 7-11 said I could go to each location and sell direct with corporate approval. We were ready to supply 100 locations in the NY area and self-deliver $250 per month per store ($25,000 per month) for starters.

I started with one 7-11, then other locations with the plan to move to a new factory and expand further. I soon found certain individuals had reasons to STOP GNGR from succeeding. Why would anyone want GNGR to fail or fold? Why would some individuals work so hard back in 2013/2014 to "try" to stop us soon after the Davies scam situation? Coincidence? I think not. And why are they continuing (unsuccessfully) to see GNGR's demise 11+ years later? *That will be exposed soon*.

This person on IHUB was so desperate to find the *EXACT* locations of our fudge in 7-11, not just 7-11 corporate approval, but also the actual stores. Someone who knew must have told him thinking it would convince him it's true but his motives were to have it REMOVED and he did just that.

Every 7-11 location we were in, took the fudge and threw it away and said not to bring any more to the stores. They said people called each store saying there were glass, mouse poop, and hair in the fudge.

This is back in 2013/2014 (10+ years ago) and he still is at it on IHUB bashing GNGR, but why? I don't care, I'm NUMB to these idiots. But it shows how in the food business ONE person can kill your company.

He tried to do that but failed because GNGR is still alive and well and making a new, bigger mark in the global marketplace with castings, not a food product. He's a hack lawyer that used to be a *Securities trader (UH OH)* so now we may know his motives and possibly was a short seller and OWES people lots of GNGR shares he shorted.

He still watches GNGR closely because on his website resume, he used to have numerous trading series licenses and what may have been a boiler room in his office and likely may have naked shorted GNGR with the dead crooked lawyer. If we prevail and expose the naked shorts, HE could be in serious trouble with the SEC and financially.

Here is his post back in 2014. He wanted EXACT locations. And soon after he got those locations, ALL products were taken off the shelves.

Wednesday, November 05, 2014 7:49:04 AM

Why don't you make me look foolish by listing 7-Eleven locations now selling GNGR fudge? You're the one talking up the subject. Substantiate what you've posted.
Note that the photo on the GG website doesn't say it was taken in a 7-Eleven. In fact, there's no text a all on that page:

My simple question is still unanswered: **Has ANYONE here seen GNGR fudge for sale in a major store lately?** If so, post the locations.

When he called and lied to (5) 7-11's to have the items removed from shelves, what if he did that to 100's of 7-11 stores in the NY area?

So why would our great company and great products be a threat to some hack attorney in NY who says he has no shares or interest in GNGR or any OTC companies as he so claims?

Maybe he needed to stop us fast so 7-11 does not even let GNGR go to 1,000 more stores that would have been difficult for him to stop.

I was going to form a new confection company LLC, with no link to GNGR, Grant or Got Chocolates so no one, not even my inside shareholders would have known but decided it's too risky.

When I fix this stock issue, some will have much bigger problems to deal with than trying to shut down GNGR. They may end up facing SEC violations, fines, financial ruin and even jail.

Or end up like the crook Davies and the death spiral scammer guy in upstate NY (Both deceased) and it was NOT from Covid.

2 down 2 more to go!

I am adding in some additional data and how things happened then we'll get back to the issue with NO FACTORY!

Being in the confection industry also presented a problem for my company that many don't realize exists when you go into business for yourself that has to rely on ***others*** to get your items into stores.

Here are a few examples from 2012 we had to deal with.

Around the same time we were in 7-11's, I called 1-800-FLOWERS to see if they wanted to add our fudge to their edible gift baskets and the buyer said OK, I sent samples to her with their logo on the label and she said to call back next Friday. When I called it was around noon and I'm guessing it was her lunch break. She said they LOVED THE FUDGE!

When I spoke to her she seemed rushed and I heard someone in her office say "THE FOOD TRUCK IS HERE." She said she had to go and I said, "Should I call back?" And in her rush to get to the food truck, she just said. "NO thanks we don't want the fudge" and hung up just because she didn't want to miss the ***fucking food truck.***

We also made contact with PUBLIX grocery store chain and the buyer told us to come to Lakeland Florida to meet him for an order. We flew to the head office in Lakeland and met the buyer and when we showed him our fudge and labeling, he said looks good, what's in it for HIM? I said what do you want and looked at Marcie in confusion. He said to me and I quote:

"So I'm about to give you a $5,000,000 fudge order and make you a millionaire and I'm not a millionaire so what's in it for me"?

A kickback payment? We left with NO ORDER.

221

About 3 months later, we saw fudge for sale in PUBLIX grocery store with the same box as mine with a similar label. It looked like SHIT and tasted worse. I found out that PUBLIX slime ball took my idea and had his relatives TRY and copy our product so he can make money on the side. The product flopped.

At a store here in Vegas, they put fudge in the reduced section. I bought one and spit it out! This is **NOT GNGR Fudge,** obviously.

When you make a SHIT product, it's still SHIT when it's in a nice box and that is why they ended up in a BIN in the "marked down" section of the stores. You may sell ONE to one person, but never again.

Our success was fewer locations but with constant repeat buyers because we made a superior product and that was KEY to being in the BIG box stores. That same, "Being the Best" is applied to what we are doing now globally! Read on.

That is why GNGR was on the move to being a major brand. If we sell to the same buyers over and over and we keep expanding, we end up selling to millions of buyers over and over and some did **NOT** want that to happen.

When I sold fudge to FAIRWAY stores in NY City, our sales kept growing and they LOVED our products. Here is my Aunt, (and me taking the photo) on line waiting to deliver 2 carts of a variety of fudge flavors and sizes from our Farmingdale location.

DELIVERING FAIRWAY

A week later, I went to the store and noticed ALL our fudge was sold and the store checked the computer and said only 60% sold but there was NO MORE on the shelves. I noticed on OUR shelves was a competitor's bags of cookies and my sign removed.

I looked around and saw that ALL our fudge was PUSHED back so it all fell behind the rack onto the dirty floor in a huge pile so he could use our space for his FUCKING cookies.

I was so pissed, I poked and slashed holes in the cookie bags with my knife and crushed all his cookies to crumbs so no one would buy them. This is what I had become, ***ONE OF THEM!***

People lying to get our products removed from shelves to harm the business or competitors destroying our winning product out of jealousy. Then there are the buyers who either hate winners or they need to feel superior by denying your success, same as the PUBLIX grocery store buyer and the mythological venture and angel investors.

Everyone hates winners!

The point to this is that most businesses like our confections, requires someone to buy the items before it gets to the shelves and after it's ON the shelves, you have to worry about asshole competitors or a scumbag (Ex securities trader) lawyer that wants to kill your accounts or ruin your business to cover their securities fraud.

A typical day at GNGR.

I kept pushing to expand but, in the back of my mind, I knew this wouldn't be easy with so many forces against the little guy. I was getting angry and, many times, almost gave up. So you win some, you lose some and I kept chugging along. And with each new day came new ideas and ways to market and sell our products.

I am sure if we did not go public, no one would have cared about 7-11 or want GNGR to fold while most of the aggressive constant attempts from others trying to stop me only came *after* GNGR became a publicly traded company.

And NOW I know why. Debt conversion short selling FRAUD!

The following document is about the attorney who we gave the shares to who forged my name and stole my identity to commit fraud and illegally create false debt so he can operate a debt diluted pump and dump scam. We can't even sue him since he is no longer alive.

The following data is taken from publicly available SEC records

FOR IMMEDIATE RELEASE

Suspended Attorney Indicted for Securities Fraud.

Defendant Forged Signatures and Backdated Documents as Part of a $3 Billion Pump-and-Dump Scheme

Today, before United States Magistrate Judge Vera M. Scanlon, suspended attorney XXXXX Davies was arraigned on a four-count indictment charging securities fraud, conspiracy to commit securities fraud, wire fraud, and aggravated identity theft in connection with a market manipulation scheme.

A federal grand jury in Brooklyn returned the indictment against Davies who was previously arrested on a complaint. Richard P. Donoghue, United States Attorney for the Eastern District of New York, William F. Sweeney, Jr., Assistant Director-in-Charge, Federal Bureau of Investigation, New York Field Office (FBI), and Edward Gallashaw, Assistant Postal Inspector-in-Charge of the New York Division of the U.S. Postal Inspection Service (USPIS), announced the indictment.

"As alleged in the indictment, Davies used both sophisticated means and some of the **oldest tricks** in the book, including *backdating documents and forging signatures*, to deceive the investing public and manipulate the price and ownership of a public company's stock," stated United States Attorney Donoghue.

"The defendant's scheme ultimately failed as a result of the outstanding investigative work by our prosecutors and our law enforcement partners, who are committed to protecting the integrity of public markets." Mr. Donoghue also expressed his gratitude to the New York Office of the United States Securities and Exchange Commission for its assistance during the investigation.

"Criminals take what isn't theirs and have no regard for victims they harm in the process," stated FBI Assistant Director-in-Charge Sweeney. "Mr. Davies allegedly pumped up the price of the stock for a public company because he controlled the information being made public.

He knew exactly when to sell to make the most money, leaving other investors in the lurch. Instead of enjoying the large sum of money he made, he now faces time in prison." "This is a classic case of greed overcoming honest business practices," stated USPIS Assistant Postal Inspector-in-Charge Gallashaw.

"Mr. Davies allegedly used his knowledge of the market to 'increase' the value of stock he knew was worth pennies, taking money from investors he knew would result in a loss. While Mr. Davies tried to cover his illegal tracks with bogus documents, he couldn't cover-up his crimes from Postal Inspectors and their law enforcement partners."

Davies, an attorney whose *law license was suspended*, controlled a publicly traded company, and manipulated the price of its stock in a pump-and-dump scheme. **Beginning in 2012, Davies exercised secret control over the company** and its predecessor companies through a series of nominal Chief Executive Officers.

As a part of his scheme, Davies accumulated a large number of shares in the company by *fraudulently converting corporate debt into stock* at no cost.

Debt-into-stock *(remember these words)*

Davies forged the signatures of purported board members and backdated documents. After accumulating large amounts of stock, Davies artificially increased the price of the stock through false and misleading press releases. Although the stock had historically traded for pennies, its price rose to $12.00 per share at the height of the pump, resulting in a market capitalization of over $3 billion.

Davies' coconspirators then dumped the stock at a profit, causing heavy losses to investors. The charges in the indictment are allegations, and the defendant is presumed innocent unless and until proven guilty. If convicted of wire fraud, the top count in the indictment, Davies faces a maximum sentence of 20 years' imprisonment. Before Davies could sell one share, the SEC cancelled the stock ticker.

End of report.

Debt-into-Stock conversion rule explained.

If a company has debt, debt investors can use true debt and convert shares to free trading on the debt conversion rule *legally* but that rule is mainly used in most pump and dump diluted schemes.

Even if your company has **no debt** (Like GNGR), crooks will forge the names of the CEO (Like Davies did to me and others) to add fake debt to any company they want to infect so they can debt dilute shares for money *illegally* and cause serous damage to the victim company and CEO (Like he did to me). BUT I did not run and fold or give into the scheme. I fought back and the next move will be made by me.

The DEBT conversion rule DESTROYS ALL companies, not just the pump and dump schemes that are in on the scam but hard working valid no debt companies like GNGR that had the debt added illegally.

HERE IS PROOF the debt conversion rule MUST ME ELIMINATED!

Davies would **NOT** have been able to **legally or illegally** put debt on ANY company financials and scam me, my company, GNGR shareholders and maybe many other victims. And 100's of others doing what Davies did and CONTINUE to do to 1,000's of OTC tickers every damn DAY would not be able to either. Get rid of the rule and:

THE FRAUD WOULD STOP!

When a crook **ILLEGALLY** puts debt onto a target victim company, they can't let the CEO know they are doing it so they create the fraud forged debt documents and file in court to have shares free trading and the data is never seen on the financials. The CEO does not even know the debt exists. Davies pulled the wool over my eyes but I did question the float increase and stopped his plan to dilute more.

You have to be a real STUPID CEO not to see the float increase and wonder and question HOW your attorney was able to sell the shares to the float without the mandatory 144 restriction-holding period of one year.

CEO's may not see the fraud debt forgery but they SURE can see the float increase. If you're not part of the scheme, you need to find out how those shares got to the float before you issue any more shares.

The crooks that file the fraud debt will hold back funds to get the CEO to issue more shares for more money (Dangle the carrot). If the CEO is not careful and continues to issue more shares, the CEO can be seen as a willing participant in the debt fraud scheme.

Davies knew full well that if I had continued to issue him additional 100,000,000 restricted stock certificates 4 or 40 more times as the CEO, and knowingly issuing more shares and seeing them added to the float, means the CEO must have known about the fraud debt just to enrich themselves.

Davies needed to get me to issue more shares to implicate myself in his fraud. When I saw the float, I was very concerned and when I questioned him about that, he vanished and ran to another ticker to do the same scam hoping that CEO would not question him and take the scheme bait.

He must have been sure I would say OK and issue him more shares knowing I needed the $800,000 and he also had to have known he could be in trouble with the crimes unless I did issue more shares so the authorities would go after the CEO, not him.

It looks like Davies did this forgery on me as his first illegal plot, and my guess is he was going to try and raise a lot more from GNGR and maybe also the other company he scammed in an attempt to cash out and vanish out of the country and avoid prosecution. That had to have been his plan because he knew he committed serious felony crimes that would catch up to him here in the USA, and be arrested.

Remember Davies was a LIZARD who did not get that $80,000,000 from selling 800,000,000 GNGR shares short for $.10. He may have only gotten $1,000,000 as the debt investors, brokers, market makers and others got the majority of the money.

Davies NEEDED me to issue him more shares so he can also make more on the 4 billion shares he would have diluted to the market from $.10 on down to $.0001. If he even averaged $.003 just for himself on 4 billion shares, his cut of the fraud would be $12,000,000 while the others split $200,000,000. $12,000,000 to Davies *IS* run away money, $1,000,000 was not enough so he had to scam another ticker when I ended our relationship with him.

My guess is he panicked and had to move FAST before the SEC nabbed him for what he did to GNGR, but he miscalculated and his actions caught up with him. I am sure when the brokers did not get the delivery of GNGR shares after they shorted them, they refused to short any more but they still have the existing shorts open that

MUST BE CLOSED!

The outcome is Davies caused serious harm to GNGR that I now have to fix when most would just say, shut it down, I stayed to fight!

Davies did not act alone. Market makers, brokers and others were also involved including that loser attorney over on IHUB who also had 5 different series trading licenses around the same time Davies was in full scam mode and may have had some hand in the scheme and may have to answer for it.

After Davies arrest, we were stuck with the stigma of being a debt diluted pump and dump like other P&D's did willingly. It was not until years later I found out he did not sell just the 100,000,000 shares we issued to him, but possibly 400,000,000 to 800,000,000 or more short.

When Davies made the shares drop in price with help from the brokers and market makers and with so many shorted shares, we may, in fact, have 20 times the true 108,000,000 float. Those shares are in the market and tradable even though not registered with the DTC. ***Our true float of 108,000,000 shares is considered very low.***

At the current price you can by the entire DTC float for ONLY! $108

Investors do not care or even understand what happened to Gunther Grant due to the criminal attorney's actions but one thing is for sure, his shorts remain open to this day and they will stay that way until I take serious decisive action to close them out.

No one cares about anything but the share price regardless of any reasons why it may have dropped in value. When it comes to retail Investors, they think there is some button that makes the share price rise. There is no button. Validity means squat, revenue and profits mean nothing to investors.

As long as the shorts remain open, any trades allow the shorts to trade and with so many shorts, the share price will never rally up. It will be that way unless I force them closed. That is what I am doing.

Davies and others are gone and GNGR is still alive and a valid public company that has a good structure with a low float. I managed to prevent the company from ending up destroyed like most companies with similar issues they had to face and I now have to force the shorts to be closed to reduce the fraud shares that could be 800,000,000 or more oversold.

I also found out, not long ago, that Davies also set up GNGR to be non-complaint with the issuing state (DE) that prevents me from correcting the issue with FINRA until the DE issue is cleared up.

Davies fraud set up only leaves open the ability to issue more shares on a pump and dump that requires no filings. I also found out some data was changed at the OTC with our company description that was not done by me. I remember seeing it and saying **DID I DO THAT?** When I did not. But I did question my sanity for a moment. Not to worry, I am SANE, unlike the Ex-Cop lizard that admitted he's insane. **HA!**

Here is a shorter detailed review of the timeline of events.

We met Davies in 2012. He said he would get us $1,000,000 for 100,000,000 restricted shares. I agreed and issued him the shares.

What I did not know is: To un-restrict the 100,000,000 shares so he can Pump and Dump them, he had to file fraud documents forging my name in court and at the SEC showing he paid off debt using the debt conversion rule to allow those shares to be free trading. Davies also forged my name to increase the authorized shares with the Secretary of State (SOS) of Delaware.

I guess he just figured he would get billions of shares from me for his scheme. He was an attorney not acting on my behalf and he knew GNGR needed debt so he can use the debt conversion rule and since **GNGR HAD NO DEBT,** is when he decided to illegally add some debt-ridden entity as if GNGR owned that entity creating debt for GNGR. An entity I did not own or even know about.

His actions gives more proof he knew, as an attorney, he was committing serious criminal acts and was likely **not** going to remain in the USA to answer those crimes. He also had to have set up GNGR and myself to prevent me from correcting his fraud so he changed our good standing status to not in good standing with the state of DE.

How did he do that? There is a fee for shares over a certain amount that is called "franchise tax on shares authorized" I always kept GNGR shares below a certain threshold so the fee is only $59.

What I did not know is: Since Davies also forged my name with the DE SOS and he increased the authorized shares so much higher than the threshold, GNGR was faced with a massive share increase franchise tax of $450,000.

WARNING! If you do take your company public with the state of DE, make SURE you know about the franchise (Par value per share) tax and threshold to avoid the $100,000+ franchise tax.

I had decided to issue a small affordable **cash dividend** to GNGR shareholders but it was not approved by FINRA. The reason was, since I did not know about the franchise tax issue, I filled out the dividend forms with FINRA saying GNGR is **in good standing with the state of DE.** In order to allow any corporate actions to be approved by FINRA, GNGR has to be in good standing with the registered state of DE.

Since Davies caused that massive $450,000 franchise tax issue that we did not know about, the data to FINRA came back from DE as GNGR is not in good standing and the dividend was denied. FINRA knew what Davies did and FINRA could have easily charged me with falsifying FINRA documents when I said GNGR is in good standing. But since they knew what Davies did, they just cancelled the dividend action and refunded me the money. **THANK YOU FINRA!**

GNGR is still a valid public ticker in good standing with FINRA but the state of incorporation (DE) also has to be in good standing to allow FINRA to approve corporate actions such as a Cash Dividend or any other corporate action.

In fact I can't even electively say I don't want the ticker active any more unless DE says I'm in good standing. Not that I want to get rid of the ticker. And I have BIGGER plans for GNGR, and they are COMING!

Now knowing what Davies did with the SOS (Secretary of State) of DE (Delaware), I now realize he also did that to STOP me (GNGR) from correcting his illegal mess that is possible with FINRA corporate actions that I can't achieve unless I pay the $450,000 to the State of DE to be in good standing.

He figured with NO other option, I would just cave to the pump and dump pressure and issue him billions of shares for a few bucks, then fold GNGR like all the other schemes on the OTC. ***Boy, was he wrong!***

I am talking to the SOS of DE to see if we can retract his fraud filings and reverse what he did and eliminate the franchise tax issue and be in good standing with FINRA. Davies is dead so I can't sue him or have him charged.

But Davies did not work alone. He had help, LOTS of help. Brokers and others he used in his plans to pump and dump and also sell naked shorted shares while telling others that he will be getting billions of shares from GNGR soon or so he thought. He also lied to the people helping him. Remember crooks screw everyone, even associates.

Davies is gone but others that helped him in his scheme are still alive and should be VERY WORRIED, as some that had a hand in Davies fraud will have to face the outcome of that fraud. That is why some who keep trying to STOP GNGR are working very hard to have that happen since 2012. Lizards and buyout attempts to cover the fraud.

Why would a few paid bashers and some hack lawyer that used to have many securities trading licenses keep posting publicly for over 11 years constant negativity when what they post is 100% incorrect?

Fear and stress.

They can't stop us, they tried but they can't. And why try and stop what they claim they have no interest in or even shares in? Not to mention any post on IHUB is maybe read by 10 low level retailers.

My guess is they are so worried they need to stay close to what's happening with GNGR and use IHUB to get information or some confidence that they may get away with what they did? ***WRONG***

You think they would have other things to do than sit all day on the GNGR chat room since 2012 ***every day*** waiting for some HINT they got away with their crimes knowing their main focus now is how to stay out of jail.

232

Some posts are mainly to try and get me, the CEO, emotionally drained so I just give up*. ME? HA! Never.* And like I said in the beginning of this guide*, I'M NUMB to those idiots and laugh*.

They post no valid issues and post nothing to do with the company or securities, its just insults to try and get the CEO to just say "FUCK IT, I QUIT" and sell the vehicle. But they may be very worried to the point they have to know every day what's happening and if they are getting closer to being arrested or end up in financial ruin.

Since they are mentally weak and worried, the syndrome they are expressing is the same as the fire arsonist who lights a building on fire then comes back to the crime scene to watch it. The reason they are active on social media is to stay close to the crimes they committed so they don't have to live with not knowing.

Remember how the lizards get when they don't get their way. It's because they don't make money. When lawyers who were securities traders say the same irrational stress rants, it's not because they want the public vehicle, its because they know they may end up in jail having already been part of a failed illegal scheme that ended up with huge open short positions. *SHORT SQUEEZE!*

The reason some are very worried like the Brokers and securities lawyers who helped pump naked shares, is none of them figured they were dealing with anything other than the status quo they believe never changes, Pump and dump, then fold.

Same as when 100's of lizards use the same reverse merger phrases... "Sell us the vehicle only," "$100,000,000," "we make billion$," "let me talk to my people," and then "you suck". By now those reading this can see this is the same play over and over. That is why when the status quo with GNGR did not go as planned, Davies and those involved knew very well that IF GNGR survives and actually breaks out and moves ahead, the status quo is compromised.

GNGR got screwed out of the $800,000 to get me to panic and issue more shares. A slime ball caused GNGR to lose our last account at 7-11's that left me, once again, with nothing but my wits and drive to never quit.

You can see why many victim CEO's under the same scenario will just walk away, not being able to take the pressure. The main problem is MOST pump and dump stocks have a CEO that is **IN ON THE SCHEME** and not just a victim of what I had to go through.

The proof is: GNGR is a global operational company, has a very low DTC float and no debt. Without debt and a low float, GNGR cannot be a pump and dump with *none of the 4 Ingredients!* That is why companies with the 4 ingredients to be a pump and dump, you can bet the CEO knows full well what's going to happen and the CEO is in on the scheme.

So now lets go back to 2014 after we lost the 7-11 account and I never got the $800,000 we were owed and we had no factory.

I was at home with no capital and no sales or income and had to figure a new way to move ahead. I did have lots of time to think.

With nothing to do but think before making decisions led me to believe, thinking FIRST before reacting is also KEY to moving ahead with fewer roadblocks. I realized that thinking of new plans before acting on them could be KEY to changes that better the company.

That is why I mention many times to not react or believe in the data you read about forming a company and getting funding.

If you think about what I wrote you may not take your last few bucks to open a store only to find you won't get investors or funding and end up failing.

MARCIE MOVES TO NEVADA 2014

Around 2013, Marcie's mom in Nevada had passed away and her dad was in desperate need of help. Marcie and I packed up her SUV with things she needed and our dog Cocoa and we left NY and drove cross country to Nevada and I flew back to NY to focus on the dire situation and what can be done to correct things that I needed to face alone.

GNGR raised initial capital to expand and lost $250,000 going public hoping to sell shares to get funding, our funding sources (Credit cards) gone, we're out 100,000,000 shares and no $800,000. No factory, most equipment sold, $1,200 cash in the bank, the house being sold at a loss and our company shares grossly and illegally shorted into the market that killed our share price and individuals who ruined the 7-11 sales.

My lawyers fucked GNGR over as did the brokers shorting GNGR and even the market makers were fined but no help to us. I can't sue dead people and now I'm sitting in a cold house alone in the winter hoping to sell it fast or just give it to the bank.

Can it GET ANY FUCKING WORSE!

I called the bank and asked them to just take the house but they were backlogged and you can't legally abandon a house and can be liable for squatters or damage so I had to legally stay in NY until I sold it or just gave it back to the bank. The bank said they are backlogged 2 years from all the homes abandoned by Hurricane Sandy and the sub prime market issues so they suggested I try and sell it.

NO ONE wanted a house close to the water after storm Sandy.

I made the best of it and made repairs wondering what to do for 2 years until I can legally vacate the house. I figured I'd fly back to Vegas, get a job and let GNGR lay dormant until I can figure things out another day? But what do I do when I relocate to Vegas? Struggle with GNGR or get a job?

I did not want to Start ANOTHER confection factory (Again) in Nevada and deal with more of the same shit, just in another state.

What about GNGR? The investors, people that trusted me to make things work out for them, and what about ME? I had no savings and never even took a paycheck since going public. I was all in and risked everything, even my own survival.

After we lost 7-11, I knew there would be no going back to confections. It all had to do with GNGR being under attack from the status quo after being a publicly traded company that was also a victim of Davies fraud while others, then and today, keep trying to shut down GNGR. So now it was a waiting game.

New Year's Eve was a few days away and I figured maybe reflect on my life and what I know I can do and more importantly, what not to do. Maybe the New Year will offer renewed focus in life. Or, so it happens in the movies, *It's a Wonderful Life* and *Miracle on 34th Street*. But the reality is what it was with no *wonderful miracles.*

Three feet of snow on the ground with nothing to do but think and wait for the winter to pass so I can sell the house.

Late December, I was bored so I decided to make some holiday fudge in one of the kettles I took home and sent some to Marcie in Vegas and kept some for my chocolate fix.

HERE IS WHEN THINGS GOT REALLY INTERESTING

I decided to try something new and very different, and with no reason or expectations, I took 10 of the 35 one-pound fudges I made and added a pure .999 silver 1/10th ounce coin to each fudge box and listed them for sale saying:

FREE 1/10th ounce .999 pure SILVER with each one-pound fudge.

I don't remember where I sold them, maybe Etsy?

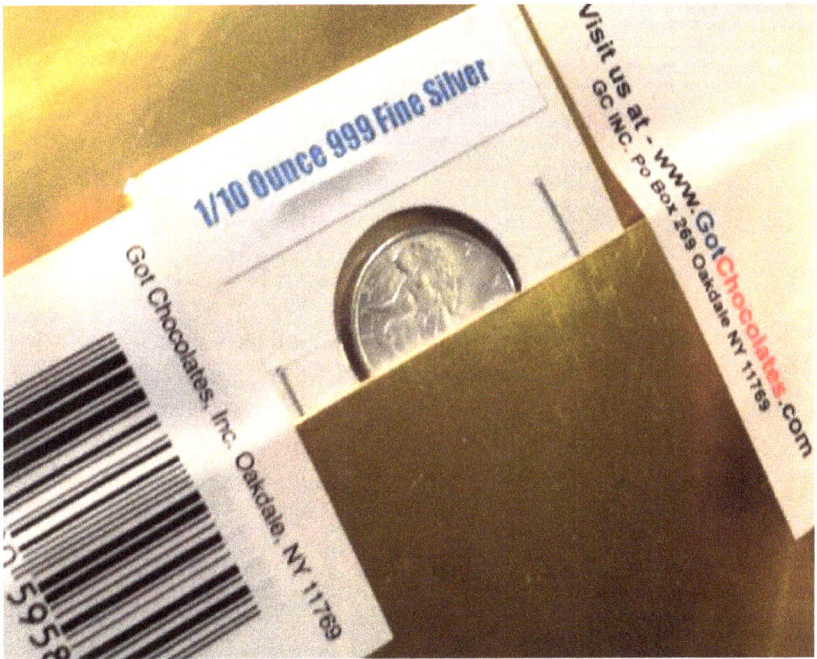

A customer ordered 10 one-pound fudges but asked me NOT to put the silver in them and to just give them all to him. He said he didn't really want the fudge so he used the purchase as a corporate gift write-off and said he bought them because of the silver he wanted for himself. I thought, "That's strange, he bought 10 fudges only for the silver."

I guess people like SILVER more than CHOCOLATES? Hmmmm

Since I had time and was bored, I got creative and tried something new to keep myself preoccupied. I had a kiln in the closet I bought 10 years ago to use to enamel on copper but never did. I took out the kiln and set it up in the kitchen. I went to an art camp when I was 13 and took metal jewelry classes where I sculpted clay and cast some sterling silver figures. Here are the ones I made in that class at age 13 that I still have today in my display cabinet.

Since I thought the kiln was only for enameling, I played around with some silver clay and enamel I had in a box for years. The chocolate factory was no more and I figured I had 2 years, more or less, in the house giving me time to liquidate and then move to Las Vegas and get a job. *I was just killing time waiting for the winter to pass.*

I started to tinker with silver clay and enamel I had bought years ago and created this crude sterling silver Woodstock pendant but it still looks kind of cool, or maybe not?

238

Most sleepless nights I was on Facebook researching how to network, but network WHAT? Being a broke CEO? I had $1,200 in the bank and a kiln. When poking around Facebook, I stumbled on a Facebook fan page for **Fruit bats** since I liked bats.

I looked at the pages and saw someone was selling bat earrings (Junk, cheap earrings) and it said **SOLD OUT.**

I thought maybe I can make an enamel bat pendant or ring (Like the Woodstock pendant) and see if they will sell them. I sent a message to the page owner and she said if I make a web page on my company website so people can buy pendants from me, she only wants a % of the sale and she will post the link to my bat pendant page to her Facebook fans. Simple enough, no costs and nothing to lose trying.

The next day I sculpted, in clay, the FIRST Gunther Grant Jewelry item.
Bootsana, the fruit bat sterling silver pendant.

Since I had no casting equipment, I sent the wax I made to Texas to have cast for $149. I told the bat lady it would be about $89, she gets a $20 donation, the silver cost is about $20 and I get $49 so the first bat cost more to make than what it would have sold for.

239

At age 13 at art camp, I used an old style centrifugal caster where you melt the silver and it spins but it was not very efficient.

I bought a $300 spin casting kit and some supplies, and it was horrible. On my first casting, the silver flew all over the kitchen so I lost that ounce of silver as it was in tiny pieces all over the floor. With $900 left after buying the USELESS casting unit, I searched and found a new technology vacuum casting unit that casts by a vacuum, not spinning. I bought a demo unit from a jewelry supplier in Farmingdale NY, which left me almost broke with $20.

I made the bat pendant web page with a Buy It Now PayPal button for $89 and showed images of the silver bat I had cast in Texas and info saying $20 will go to the bat rescue.

I launched the page at 10am and she posted it to her Facebook bat page with a link to my website. I waited for hours and all day and NOTHING, not one damn sale. The price was right; the bat pendant was kinda cool, new and unique, but no sales. Maybe $89 was too expensive or they hated the bat design? I risked my FOOD money and was preparing to scrap the silver bat to get groceries and my car was almost on empty.

With $20 in the bank, I went to McDonalds (Sad to say, it was a luxury I should have not spent money on) and a few bucks for gas. I came home and NOTHING, not one sale. I said to myself, this is not good. I have $3 in the bank so maybe I'll have a garage sale on the weekend (In the winter blizzard?). I just sat and watched and NOTHING, not even an emailed question.

Now I was worried.

As evening came, I drank what little scotch was left in the bottle and passed out on the couch. Tomorrow is a new day, I guess, but still with the same problems to deal with. At about 3am, it was pitch black except for the blizzard snow outside reflecting from the outside porch light. I kept hearing a ding noise over and over that woke me up. I was half asleep and thought, what the hell is that?

I went to the computer and thought something was resting on the keyboard making the error noise so I turned the screen power on to check my email (With one eye open).

HOLY SHIT! It was emails from PayPal! YOU MADE A SALE, and not just ONE! The page was full of orders, at least 20 so far. I had not realized that in Australia (Where her Facebook BAT page was based), it was night time when I was awake here and when I went to bed, they woke up and fans saw the link and started to order the bat pendants.

25 bat pendants the first day x $49 profit was $1,225 to me after silver cost and the $20 donation. I had back my $1,225 and also it's pre-paid so I get the money before I have to pay to have them made. And NO factory means no rent, no landlord and no OVERHEAD. I also had to learn REAL FAST how to cast. And I mean, like, in ONE DAY!

I was making over 50% NET profit and shipping most bat pendants to Australia. I could never do that with chocolates. The bat rescue said, "Make another bat! People want more." So I sculpted this flying bat pendant. GNGR's second design, and more lifelike than the first bat.

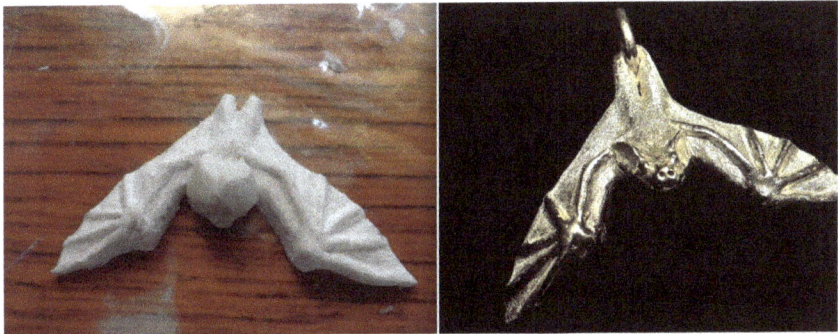

I sold 100 of them, that's $4,900 net profits plus $1,222 that took my bank account from $3 to $6,125. No costs, No overhead, No employees, No health permits and I get my money before I have to buy materials means pre-paid, no banks or credit cards to borrow from. Soon I started to make other wildlife, Owls, Foxes, Chimps and more. They all sold. I knew I was onto something big. I just did not realize how big it would end up. It literally happened over night.

241

A BIG THANK YOU!

Dear Gunther,

We're the Delphi Clan and yes, we know we're handsome! When The Fox Project took us we were tiny, cold and shabby, but here's us not long before we went back to live in the wild, which is the only place we want to be. There are many more like us who are unable help themselves but with your support, they will get a second chance. We think your silve fox pendant is gorgeous, and **thank you for your donation from the proceeds of sales!**

SAVE THE CHIMPS sterling silver pendants.

This was not normal. I was used to spending and not making any money, now I am making money and using the customer's money to fill orders. The bank account kept going UP, not down. And all this happened FAST.

I started to tell local garage sale friends when they get silver, BRING IT TO ME, I'll buy it all. I started to load up on silver inventory and the house was full of silver coins, bars, flatware and more. Silver was everywhere. Everyone knew I paid more for silver than the scrappers because I make more when it was converted to jewelry, not just bullion.

A garage sale guy said his rich friend wants a custom cigarette case made by hand. So I created a one-off creation for him for $3,500 and he was so happy, he paid $5,000 and said keep the change!

One day the floor had tears and a McDonalds wrapper on it and now there were buckets of silver and money! $5,000 for two days work! And I could ship worldwide and silver did not melt in transit like chocolate. And, it's hard to sell ONE person $5,000 or even $89 in chocolate but not with silver bats and other wildlife castings.

And when that *dick weed lawyer on IHUB* found out I cast jewelry, he posted, "AWWW Grant is making little trinkets for gumball machines." NOW I know *He must be very worried!*

TRINKETS, MY A$$...

For the Sea Turtle rescue, a pendant with silver eggs inside.

I had silver piled up all over the house. It was everywhere

Silver bars, ingots as well as gold and diamond rings.

I lost track of how much silver I had. It was all over the house.

Skulls and more wildlife, Whales, Rhinos, Owls and more!

I even take all the scraps and shavings and cast GNGR silver bars that are sold online to stackers. Nothing goes to waste and nothing has an expiration date unlike confections.

A $5,000 Hand fabricated sterling silver candle drip cylinder case with bats and skulls with lock and key mechanism I designed. Then he wanted one in solid 18K gold! *IT WAS SOO COOL I ACTUALLY ALMOST KEPT IT.* Then, I started to make political items.

After I made political items for the 2016 election, I did have to vacate the house and with over *$50,000* in cash on hand, I was NOT about to put that into a chocolate factory ever again.

After the election, I shipped all my casting equipment and supplies to Vegas and gave my car to a friend and flew to Nevada to be with Marcie and help with her dad and set up GNGR castings in Henderson, NV.

GRANT MOVES TO NEVADA 2017

In Henderson, NV, I turned the garage into a casting studio. I design all the art and create the molds; I pour the wax, cast and ship all over the world under one roof with *NO overhead.*

The boxes I used for the fudge are now used to ship our castings globally. I spoke with our BJ's rep and he wanted to know if I want to add some nice affordable pendants to the big box stores. I am working on that and also looking to obtain the BETTY BOOP license again, and 100's of other licenses.

With GNGR still in good shape, no issues or debt dilution or funny business, some still want to see GNGR out of business like that IHUB asshole ex-securities trader lawyer and NOW maybe you all know why. With open shorts, some are VERY worried.

NOW! No one can stop GNGR and the shorts will soon be exposed.

SIGNET JEWELERS AND OTHERS NEVER LEARN

While I worked on perfecting the castings and jewelry, I made contact with SIGNET and figured maybe I could get some of my designs into their stores. Signet was a public company ticker (SIG)

I emailed the Board of Directors about a plan to partner with GNGR and let GNGR supply Signet's companies with items to sell under the Gunther Grant designer name, or they can use their own name or brand.

Signet owns **KAY and JARED** jewelers to name a few. When I emailed the USA offices and also communicated with a few executives, my plan and offer was simple, let GNGR make items they can resell in their mall stores and online and GNGR will also give them 250,000,000 publicly trading shares of GNGR stock.

I could not have been more professional and generous with a company (Signet) that makes MONEY from items that I would provide to them. To cut to the chase, a Signet executive (David) declined my generous offer that would have added $10's of millions of new revenue, maybe $100's of millions, because what I offered was proven sales with items no one else has or even can figure out how to make.

This would have put GNGR in the $5 per share range since our DTC share float was still very low, except for the naked shorts.

I mentioned to the SIGNET executive while I was here in Nevada that GNGR can be an affiliate or supplier to SIGNET and with no discussion, he just said NO without even taking time to discuss or look at my very unique line of jewelry. I told him I would send samples and he said SIGNET is not interested, without even looking at what I was able to do or offer.

Some professional! Not likely, and a poor excuse for an executive.

Why would a retailer who buys items from different vendors not even look at our various lines of designs and MAYBE salvage their *soon to be* destroyed share price? Who knows what is in the minds of *unqualified executives*. Who cares!

REMEMBER, I am so aware of the market and how this shit works, I can EASILY look at data and know when the markets will change (Good or Bad) and SIGNET was next.

I mentioned to this executive "David" that 250,000,000 shares at even $.10 is $25,000,000 "FOR FREE" to Signet. He again replied NO DEAL and I replied, "OK but if you do NOT take my offer, you could KISS your stock price goodbye when your $140 shares DROP BELOW $25." He got really mad and told me SIGNET'S going to $200 per share.

I said, "NO IT'S NOT, GUARANTEED under $25!"

All communications with SIGNET stopped and my emails were blocked. I did post on their FACEBOOK page to warn others about the drop below $25 I knew was coming. Facebook fans told me to take a hike and who am I to say that rubbish. But SIGNET and that executive had much bigger problems headed down the pipe. A different USA executive got wind of my posts and did not block me and did communicate with me, but I was careful he might be trying to get info from me to sue.

But like CRUMBS and countless others, that deal was DOA.

SIGNET (Kay, Jared) and Kingold and other jewelry companies had their share of problems that made headlines. Problems **THEY created themselves.** Those companies committed crimes and their shareholders and customers became the victims.

Most of the horrible things SIGNET did that cost them $100's of millions in damages, not to mention the money lost in shareholder value, **happened AFTER** I made contact with them. If they made ME CEO, none of their issues would have happened and SIGNET stock would be around $500+ per share today.

GNGR had issues but they were NOT created internally and GNGR is now making a HUGE comeback, while as for the others? Just **Google search any of them.**

Signet Jewelers in $240 million settlement over sexual harassment, loan portfolio

By Jonathan Stempel   3 MIN READ   f   🐦

NEW YORK (Reuters) - Signet Jewelers Ltd has reached a $240 million settlement of a shareholder lawsuit accusing the company of concealing sexual harassment allegations against senior executives and losses in its customer financing credit portfolio.

The preliminary settlement of the proposed class action was filed on Thursday with the federal court in Manhattan, and requires approval by Chief Judge Colleen McMahon.

2022

RETAIL

Signet Jewelers reaches $175 million settlement of gender bias lawsuit

PUBLISHED THU, JUN 9 2022 3:07 PM EDT

Note: All these articles are available to the public with a simple Google search.

Signet hit with $11M penalty for deceptive credit practices

Jewelry giant accused of swapping real stones for fakes

By Lisa Fickenscher   June 4, 2016 | 2:33am

MORE ON:
JEWELRY

How the wealthy are still buying jewelry during the pandemic

This may be the season of happily ever after, but Signet Jewelers is living a nightmare.

The owner of Jared, Kay Jewelers and Zales has been under fire since a report last month accusing the company of swapping real stones for fakes when customers brought their jewelry in for repairs.

The scandal involving Nasdaq-listed Kingold Jewelry, one of China's largest jewellery makers, has raised eyebrows in China's business community as company officials and bankers feel the heat from the fallout.

The company was alleged to have used 83 tonnes of fake gold bars, or gilded copper, as collateral to secure 20 billion yuan (US$2.83 billion) of loans from onshore lenders, Caixin reported on June 29, describing it as one of the largest gold loan fraud cases China has ever seen.

Also, a lot of the jewelry from China is TOXIC and made with cancer causing cadmium. Google toxic jewelry from China, it will make you CRINGE! FYI, GNGR is made in the USA using only USA sourced silver!

Warning over cheap Chinese-made jewellery

AP and AAP | The West Australian
Wed, 30 June 2010 9:08PM

US regulators have found high levels of the toxic metal cadmium in trinkets distributed free to children at some doctor and dentist offices over the past five years.

The news follows the country's Consumer Product Safety Commission recall of nearly 70,000 charm bracelets and rings.

It is the fourth time this year that the federal government has ordered that cheap Chinese-made jewellery be pulled from shelves because of cadmium, a known carcinogen.

CRMBQ
Crumbs Bake Shop, Inc.

$0.000 +0.00
OTC Markets · USD

| YTD | 1Y | 2Y | 5Y | 10Y | **ALL** |

13
10
7
3.353

2010 2013 2016 2019 2022

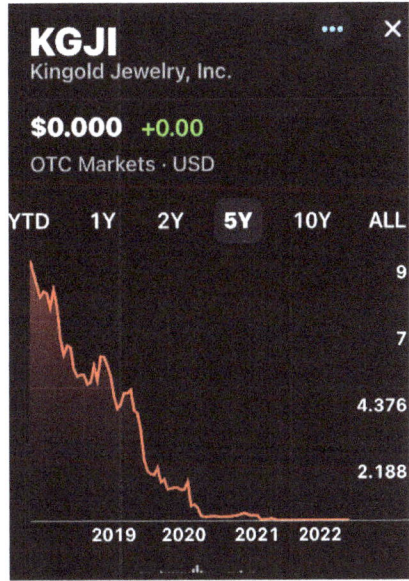

KGJI
Kingold Jewelry, Inc.

$0.000 +0.00
OTC Markets · USD

| YTD | 1Y | 2Y | **5Y** | 10Y | ALL |

9
7
4.376
2.188

2019 2020 2021 2022

Two companies both similar to what GNGR was and is, **_Confections then Jewelry_**. CRUMBS and KINGOLD, both **self destroyed** their companies as did the executives at SIGNET.

The data is pretty simple and straightforward.

GNGR shares started at $.10 (10 cents) that is now under a penny thanks to crooks who shorted GNGR that will **_soon be reversed._**

GNGR share price as of May 2023 is still higher than these two tickers that were once over $10.00 per share that did the damage to themselves.

GNGR also has a very low float and only has to get the share price back to $.10 to where we started while the others will likely NEVER go back to $10.00+ per share. And SIGNET looks to be stuck at -65% as well. **_And GNGR was never a high priced stock to begin with!_**

But that may soon change!

The money LOST to those tickers and investors who took positions in them that I proposed offers to when those stocks were high that are now at major losses could have made GNGR a monster global company and also provide significant returns in the 10's of millions in profits to those investors. As I wrote earlier, they are NOT that smart.

257

GNGR is valid, performing, expanding and not screwing over investors like those NASDAQ and OTC listed or delisted losers did and to themselves.

If Signet, Crumbs and other investors took our offer back before they crashed AND BURNED, Those companies and all who invested in GNGR, and myself, would have been sitting on GNGR shares worth MORE than KGJI and CRUMBS high prices combined.

There is a difference between being a crooked company and being a company (GNGR) that became a victim of crooks.

I did some research into the SIGNET stock data and a man in NY who owns a very large hedge fund owned 1,000,000 shares of Signet. I called his office to speak to him (Like that was going to happen) but his attorney did take my call. I told him about GNGR, our new plan and that it's working and we are in need of expansion capital to supply and obtain licensees for sports and characters to sell a new exciting expanding product line globally. Since he invested in SIGNET (Jewelry), he may have interest in GNGR (Jewelry), LOGICAL!

The attorney got back to me and said his BOSS owns 1,000,000 shares in SIGNET that he paid $140 per share so he had $140,000,000 invested in SIGNET *(OUCH!) because I know what was coming.*

My offer was simple, valid and was not in the idea stage but already *Operational and achieving global sales and is WORKING!*

I told the attorney to have his boss sell 5,000 shares of his 1,000,000 SIGNET shares for $700,000 and invest that with GNGR and GNGR will issue him 100,000,000 GNGR shares.

When we expand and move up to a higher trading platform, those shares, even at $.05 cents per share, he would make back 8x his money and at even $.25, would make $25,000,000!

The attorney came back and said his BOSS declined the offer and said the following, JUST LIKE CRUMBS! He said, "When SIGNET goes to $200 per share, he will take your offer." I again said NO! SIGNET is not going to $200, it's going to DROP below $25!

I knew that as a FACT! <u>Don't ask how I know, I won't tell you!</u> So when I say GNGR will recover and could go to $1 or $5 or higher, you better put GNGR on your stocks to watch list.

Further proving, I DO KNOW IT ALL and, to be honest, I bet the attorney never even told his investor boss about my offer. More lackeys that want to pretend to be the boss.

I told the attorney that his BOSS is about to lose on SIGNET that will be worthy of the 1922 crash so keep him away from tall buildings he can jump from. And I was not joking.

The attorney asked me about my education. I told him I have Dyslexia (159 IQ) so I only obtained my GED and went right into the work force. THE REAL WORLD!

He said his BOSS has business degrees from Wharton and Harvard and is one of the richest men in the USA (which was true), I said, "YES, I KNOW but money does make you smart and that rich people always lose money even though they remain rich. If you don't listen to me and my SHITTY GED, how can you be so sure that $200 per share is a sure thing when you may have been told that by someone else with the same GED as me who is NOT as smart or maybe is a crook?"

I told the attorney to tell his BOSS!

"Rich or super rich," losing $100,000,000+ is GOING to be painful.

He said, "This is going no place, good luck with your little OTC Company." So again, I kept hammering away with my growth all on MY OWN! And just like CRUMBS, my shitty GED was no match for his Wharton Harvard degrees.

But I knew otherwise. YES, It's a FACT!

The SIGNET stock kept dropping and when it *hit $22*, my target price of under $25 per share *(Down from $140),* I sent an email to the executives at Signet under a new email that was not blocked and said, "*Hi David! It's me, Grant from Gunther Grant, TOLD YA!*"

I was blocked again but the other USA executive emailed me and said HOW DID YOU KNOW it would drop below $25?

I said, "Below $25?" Wait until it drops below **$8 (That I also knew would happen).** I also created another email to send to the other executive David when the share price went below $8 and I was again blocked. **Total denial!**

I also posted on SIGNET'S Facebook page it will soon fall below $8 and THEN they all said I was a fucking lunatic and it WILL NOT HAPPEN!

And since I know IT ALL!

The stock hit $7.74 per share down from $140 (-95%) "OUCH"

And today, it's still down over 50% (+-). I also called the NY investor and the call was not taken. I did send an email saying, "**TELL YOUR BOSS!** Mr. GED wants to congratulate Mr. Wharton Harvard on his SIGNET loss of **$133,000,000** and even today his investment is only worth around $50,000,000, a fucking **$83,000,000 loss."**

Rich or super rich, that has to STING!

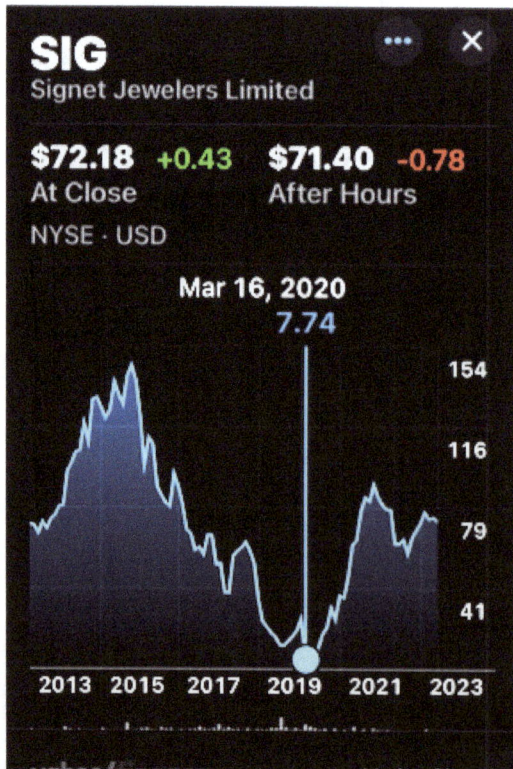

Maybe I should be CEO of SIGNET? At least I know, for *a FACT,* I can get the stock back to $200 then onto $500 per share like they all thought it would.

They failed and I know what to do.

And I know how to get Amazon to $800+ per share.

And I know how to get GNGR to $5 or more per share.

YES, I know it all. I just have to do a few course corrections that crooks left in their wake with my company and then it will be smooth sailing!

For shits and giggles, I sent the SIGNET executive another email on June 22, 2023 and I am still blocked. All too funny... high-level professionals in complete denial that refuse to listen to a REAL industry professional. *With only a GED, HA!*

Who knows, who cares!

Message blocked

Your message to david.bouf███@signetjewelers.com has been blocked. See technical details below for more informa

LEARN MORE

⚠ This link will take you to a third-party site

Have to at least laugh at that.

So how do I, or anyone reading this, get back so much lost time or the time wasted trying and never achieving their goals or had major obstacles in their path? How can changes be made, after so much lost time, to correct? Take a step back for the better.

GNGR "UPGRADED" TO A GARAGE

Since GNGR relies on selling products to generate revenue, I never had to consider dumping shares on a scheme to make money. A simple change that made GNGR a global brand with a realistic goal to sell a minimum of 200,000 items for $99 from my ever-expanding jewelry line over the next few years is well within our reach and has already started.

My goal is to eventually bring our share price to $.75 based on REAL and proven sales, expansion and licensed items for the global markets, and be an SEC reporting company and bypass the OTC all together FAR away from the schemers and the retailers who rarely pay more than one penny for shares.

Just like the **WSJ pyramid chart** shown further ahead in this guide.

GNGR "is" the needle in the haystack. Remember that.

A low estimate on GNGR's target share price at a quarter ($.25) puts my net worth on 789,000,000 shares at $197,250,000, I can then sell 45,000,000 of the 89,000,000 free trading shares direct to the market easily for $.20 per share for $9,000,000.

I would take $5,000,000 of that and issue it back to GNGR to expand the operations while also negating any need for funding or loans.

I would put the remaining $4,000,000 into a money market account for me personally and to cover capital gains tax.

With the necessary and less compliant requirements to up list to NASDAQ GM or CM (The lower tiers on NASDAQ), we can file to be off the gray markets and listed where higher share prices and higher caliber investors look for **needles in the haystack**. It is also where major corporations look for acquisitions of companies on the move

The NASDAQ Stock Market has three distinctive tiers: The NASDAQ Global Select Market, The NASDAQ GM and The NASDAQ CM. Applicants must satisfy certain financial, liquidity and corporate governance requirements to be approved for listing on any of these market tiers. Schemes always avoid required transparency.

The initial financial and liquidity requirements for the NASDAQ Global Select Market are more stringent than those for the NASDAQ Global Market and likewise, the initial listing requirements for the NASDAQ Global Market are more stringent than those for the NASDAQ Capital Market.

NASDAQ may <u>deny applications</u>, or apply additional conditions, if necessary, to protect investors and the public interest.

- Standard 1: Earnings
- Standard 2: Capitalization with cash flow
- Standard 3: Capitalization with revenue
- Standard 4: Assets with equity

Pump and Dumps, in most cases, can't pass the 4 requirements to be listed on any NASDAQ tier and 15c211 has NO protections like the 3 NASDAQ tiers do. GNGR will focus on the CM tier at first.

Pump and dump tickers do NOT want to file anything with the purpose of protecting investors from those very same tickers...

I am sure (Hope) those reading this know that by now.

Once I make the move with GNGR, a new $4,000,000 state of the art facility, mass marketing, and with $1,000,000 to inventory silver and gold, could guarantee global sales to $10,000,000++ annually the first year after we expand.

The **TRUE DTC** float would also increase from 108,000,000 to only 153,000,000 and is considered a VERY low float for a public company that is **ALREADY** making global sales. **With NO DEBT!**

After the expansion and increased market share, there is no reason to doubt our shares could rise up to $.75 per share (My conservative target price) where I would then sell off my remaining 45,000,000 of the 89,000,000 free trading shares for $.50 per share taking in personally another $22,500,000.

I would issue another $10,000,000 to the company for marketing, expansion and have our brand dominate this industry that **has already started.**

As CEO, I am also allowed to cash in 5% of my personal restricted 700,000,000 shares every 2 years and being public for 15 years, I have built up the ability to sell 35% (245,000,000) shares. At even a broker discount to $.25 so they keep up with the marketing of GNGR, this allows me to cash out $61,250,000.

Even if I added all those shares to the float, GNGR would still have a very low float of about 400,000,000, tons of cash, a global operation expansion to get even more sales, and no debt. And of course, by then we'll be out of the garage with a much higher and healthier share price as the shorts are knocked out of the market.

Just FYI, Amazon has 9 billion shares in the float.

If we even make it to 20% of Signets greatly reduced share price *(with no swapping diamonds or sexual harassment issues),* GNGR could settle in at $12 per share. At $12 per share, my holdings would be worth $8.4 billion and put me into the FORBES list of richest people.

As I stated in this guide, SHARES equals Wealth. Remember that!

And everyone who bought in at $.10 or phase two shares for even less will be saying, *GIVE THAT CEO A CIGAR! But I don't smoke.*

Buy me a COLD BEER!

BUT FIRST, before I make my drastic positive HISTORIC move, I have to clear out the open shorts to reduce the naked shares in trade that can affect any spike in price by having more shares trading than what is in the actual registered float. That is being done WHILE I expand the business. *GOOGLE "Gunther Grant Jewelry" and click images.*

In this stock pump game, there are winners (The schemers) and losers (The investors). I just choose to be a winner and also make inventors winners while at the same time making GNGR a monster company.

I don't need to scam people out of $20,000,000 like those pump and dumps do. Even if I was *not public,* I could make millions selling products worldwide that I am selling now so being a private or public company, *I WIN!*

And being public, if I really wanted $20,000,000, I'll just sell my 89,000,000 free trading shares for $.22 cents that will also benefit the company further and also increase shareholder value. The fact is, MORE money can be made for the CEO, the company and investors, like GNGR can offer while pump and dumps screw shareholders.

Does the CEO sell out the failed company to a pump and dump or does the CEO actually struggle, work and make changes to make the company a success? I choose work! And I'm making GNGR a success!

This life issue with time and age shows the drastic contrasts showing that change can be good and also, with hard work you can end up with a GED at retirement age with $10's or $100's of millions and maybe even Billion$, not just a pension or some lame 401K that could be wiped out by those managing your money, *that is going to happen, remember that.*

With the way things are working now with no stress or saboteurs, I also still remember what struggle is *(By now I am sure you can agree to that)* and often help those who I see struggling, as much as I am able to do. I lent a friend $1,200 when I only had $1,400 in the bank and never heard from him again.

Here in NV, I went to 7-11 to get some snacks *(Obviously not MY Fudge)* and walked out with $14 in change and gave it to a homeless man sitting there with his dog. He was not crazy and was well spoken, just down on his luck, I guess. He took the money and got up and went into 7-11 to buy a $5.99 pizza, water and items for his dog.

When it is time to hire people that requires no technical skills, I will pay $50 per hour plus bonus. My only requirements are... if they can do what they are told, can think on their own, and **NOT** have an education above a GED like me.

And if I find him, I'll hire that homeless guy, get him a place to stay until he gets back on his feet, and get him back some dignity.

Those pump and dump lizards are probably the worst tippers and would walk over some innocent down-on-his luck homeless man and his dog if it means putting another $14 martini in their pie hole.

Lizards **never** make it to any list of wealthy people or even end up being able to say they succeeded as they end up spending it all and the IRS seizing their assets only to end up PRAYING someone buys **THEM** a pizza! If they do find a scheme to work for, they once again end up saying to victim investors "**HEY BRO,**" buy some shares.

Many struggling to succeed will beat the so-called horse to death and rather than focus to make things better by change, they end up trapped in a cycle of WHY is this not working, and never change.

When I started Got Chocolates in Farmingdale, NY, we went to buy a living room set. The kid there was the salesman and the only car there was a white Honda Civic. As I moved from store to store, then ended up a publicly traded company, every time we drove down that highway for over 10 years, we saw that same white Honda parked at that store in the same parking spot. That bothered me, but not sure why.

If you're a success, you never have to say you will never give up.

Never giving up means you are still looking for success.

If doing the same thing keeps you from never giving up, give up!

Just don't give up and quit.

Give up and make changes and fight till you win.

As for GNGR confections, IT WAS working, it was the (Myth) capital that was needed that did not exist. Most companies can be great and a success if there is money to make it work. The problem is, money is not so easy to get, even when you are told it will be, or read it on some investment website.

With no money the BEST ideas will not work so the answer is…

Make the BEST ideas work with NO money. I proved it's possible.

There is not ONE Fortune 500 Company that does not need to make minimum sales to remain operational (like GNGR can). When you read about large companies facing financial troubles, the first thing they do is fire employees and sell off assets.

Does that make GNGR, with no overhead and no financing needed while being able to expand global sales, a better company than all Fortune 500 companies? It sure looks that way. Actually, YES!

I know what you're thinking!

HOW can this guy actually believe and tell others GNGR is structured better than all Fortune 500 companies when GNGR is in a garage and not even close to what those companies achieved? The answer is:

Many of them started in the garage! Only GNGR is doing it better.

GNGR did **NOT** start in a garage, we moved back a few steps to the garage for specific reasons. But, by no means are we in the startup or exploratory stages of business like most that started in the garage. We moved to the garage as an already established global selling brand to get rid of those pesky costs like Rent and Overhead. And our footprint for production is so small at under **200 Sq Ft**; I don't even think there is a place for rent that is as small.

So why pay for what we don't need?

People post GNGR is nothing but a garage operation implying that is a bad thing, when the fact is, the end product that is shipped all around the world is real and tangible and *is* what matters.

When a pump and dump website posts just images of what does not exist except a P.O. Box, it may be EXCITING, but the 99% seem to LOVE the deceit. Not sure why but they do...

When I'm mocked for working in a 200 sq. foot 1/2 garage, I take it as a compliment from the same idiots who invest in a scheme located in a 6 inch P.O. Box. I often wonder, "How do they fit those gold mines and marijuana fields in that tiny little 6" PO Box?"

GNGR, a garage-based business with no overhead that designs and manufactures castings that sell all over the world and makes profits with actual items you can buy with accurate TRUE data on the website. But in the minds of 99% naive retail lotto investors, that has no merit and cannot offer the same GOLD MINE $.0001 to $8 possibilities (or can we?). **Wait and see...**

Investors believe a scheme P&D company will get real big real fast if they buy shares. That seems to work with investors who, in reality, love to lose their money real fast and end up missing real opportunities and ALWAYS end up with mounting financial losses.

And *EVERY ONE* of the 99% ends up saying they wish they had bought shares in a garage-based company before the stock took off, and the millions they see others made who did buy into those garage-based companies, you would think they would change their investment strategy? Never.

You think by now investors would realize NO company can sell shares on an idea and the following year become a $500,000,000 profitable business, and again the money spent on those shares *does NOT* go to the company *(Read page 7 again!)*.

Just for the record, I don't want or need anyone's pity and I am under no stress to get people to agree with me about my operations or get people to admit I am right about what was written in this guide. I know I'm right and that's good enough for me. And it's all proven.

Penny stock investors condemn those who are valid and hard working, even from a garage, because they keep getting sucked into the dream schemes talk of unlimited wealth and riches fast, and many are just too scared and cheap and rely on what the pump and dumps offer, *cheap dreams of quick millions overnight.*

Pump and dumps don't start in garages.

Pump and dumps are always the billion-dollar idea soon to be overnight success that started with some exciting marketing. They don't even need a garage or a location because they only exist on a website, not in reality.

The only garage pump and dumps have, is where they park the Rolls Royce and Ferrari they bought with investors money. TA DA!

So what happened to other garage based companies investors passed on that they accused of being scams the same way they accuse the new and improved GNGR of being that also is in a garage?

A few SMALL garage based company's retail investors passed on.

And of course Gunther Grant. Nice garage!

Penny stock Investors need to look at data and change how they invest to succeed at investing the same way a struggling business has to make changes to succeed in business.

A pump and dump stock will always fail and investors who keep investing in them end up with the same fate. GUARANTEED!

My advice about business is, think about the MONEY needs before you think about business and how to make things work for less costs and overhead and do not, for **ONE SECOND,** think your BIG idea can easily be funded from a business plan or from investors. **IT WON'T!**

And investors who buy into scheme stocks need to also remember those companies not only have **no money (Read page 7 again)** but they always seem to want to start at the TOP (On paper, not reality).

Every operation I had, my focus was not on retail store sales but moving to wholesale as fast as possible. In most cases, like potholders, it won't work but for GNGR, it did work. It was the funding and other issues that caused me to stop and start over again.

I never gave up and quit, I gave up and fought back by switching plans along the way having realized that the real business world is far different than what you learn in school or are told or when you research it on the internet.

That is why this guide is so brutally honest and tells it like it is.

A real operational global profitable business (GNGR) vs. a pump and dumps billion dollar delusions of grandeur, are worlds apart. One is a physical reality; one is an impossibility that is based on what does not exist physically. A photo of a gold mine does not mean it exists.

Pump and dumps **MUST SELL** shares to make money! And they use the pretty picture on the website to find sucker investors. As long as there are suckers, there will always be a pretty picture to show them.

As long as the 99% don't change how they invest, a pump and dump scheme also does not have to change to a valid business.

If I don't sell ONE SHARE, GNGR will survive and expand from actual global product sales that most public companies will never achieve. To succeed in business you have to change the way you operate a business. Same with the 99%, to succeed in investing the 99% have to also change the way they invest.

GNGR's change from a struggling company to changing the stock market status quo and Investors changing the way they invest are all part of the process to achieve positive results.

CHANGES and DRASTIC DECISIONS MUST BE MADE

WRIGLEY'S chewing gum started out as soap that people did not like so they created GUM and said FREE gum with each wrapper of soap redeemed. People loved the GUM more than the soap and the company switched to GUM. The rest is history.

WRIGLEY'S also offered silver-plated items when you saved wrappers. I sort of did the same, offering free silver with each Fudge purchase that quickly changed us from confections to silver and gold jewelry.

Like AMAZON, Avon used to sell books and gave away free perfume if you bought a book. People wanted the perfume, not the books and the rest is history. Even the electronics giant, NOKIA, initially made toilet paper and then rubber boots. Changes must be made.

I also made changes with the help of our enemies when they **TRIED and FAILED to destroy GNGR.** What they did not realize is; they picked the wrong Company and the wrong CEO. When those schemers, short sellers, hack securities lawyers and crooks' plans backfired, they helped make GNGR A BETTER, STRONGER COMPANY!

NO, they will not be compensated except for securities violations.

Our last hope of taking our products to the masses, starting with (5) 7-11's, with the plan to sell to all locations in the tri state area that was eliminated by those that wanted GNGR to fold, was actually a blessing in disguise. After they publicly posted cheers of GNGR's loss of the 7-11 account when they called each location saying they found mice poop in our fudge, they never expected **GNGR to capitalize on that**.

Mice and poop in STERING SILVER may not be so bad after all.

HOW'S this for a **FUCK YOU** to those that *tried* to SHUT GNGR DOWN!

Saboteur's used mice poop in the fudge lies, to get our fudge removed from 7-11 stores and now Gunther Grants very popular mice and poop are helping us get closer to millions in sales.

People LOVE mice and emoji poop jewelry. In fudge? Not so much.

HA! Saboteur's actions ended up helping GNGR's global success.

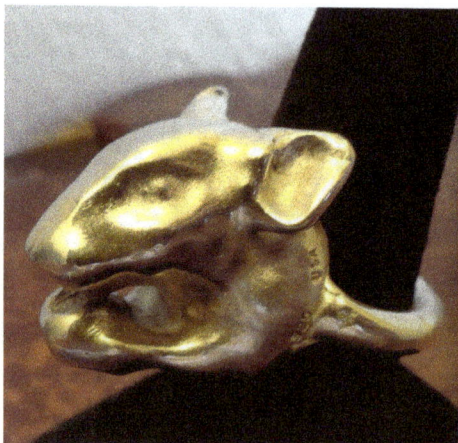

To anyone even thinking about changing to become a public company and believe that they will get funding and end up a profitable company and blossom to success...

IT WILL BLOSSOM! But it will blossom into *poison ivy* and by then, the Russian and the Ex-Cop lizards will not even be able to afford *Calamine Lotion!*

Lizards, begging to take over GNGR, say GNGR is worthless yet industry professionals say the opposite about GNGR and why the lizards KICK and CRY when they can't get our Public Vehicle.

A professional who evaluates tickers looked at GNGR and said, *GNGR's aged 2008 ticker* being direct to public, not a reverse merger, with a low float and no dilution or ticker changes with no questionable activity is worth between $1,000,000 and $2,000,000 as it sits now.

He said, any pump and dump scheme using our aged great company structure would allow them to reverse into a new Artificial Intelligence or MUSHROOM (intent) operation scam and easily sell 100,000,000 shares initially on a low float for $1 per share. The scheme can claim they have been in business since 2008 because that is when GNGR's ticker was activated. The older the ticker, the more value it has because it looks like they have been in business that long and well established. *Artificial Intelligence, since 2008!*

They would make $100,000,000, add debt and increase the authorized and dump another 1,000,000,000 fast for $.20 to make another $200,000,000 and then another 10 billion shares for $.001, and then fold the ticker. That's $310,000,000 from a P.O. Box with no operations other than a fancy website and images of fake data and the HOT NEW Drug Mushroom or AI scheme that will attract the 99%.

And without the GNGR vehicle they can't make it happen.

That explains why the Russian and Ex-Cop keep cursing and crying all the time, without GNGR's vehicle, they make $0.

ME! I'm not cursing and crying to 100's of Lizards to buy my vehicle so why are THEY all cursing and crying when I don't sell it? Now you know.

Make changes for the better, if you can, and avoid Lizards.

273

Now when I say GNGR is doing great, anyone would say I'm just another scammer pumping the stock. ***That is physically impossible!***

You can't pump what does not exist (low float and no debt) and without the 4 ingredients needed, GNGR cannot debt dilute.

What really changed for GNGR and who did this to our company?

In 2024, lizards and brokers manipulated GNGR down to $.000001 to try and get angry shareholders to pressure me to sell the vehicle. Investors believe that ANY offer is better than the current situation. The problem is GNGR shareholders on any buyout or merger will **NOT** have any shares in the new entity. As long as I hold out and stick to the plan, GNGR shareholders at least have a chance.

At $.000001 Let's see someone buy our ENTIRE 108,000,000 float for only $108 and watch what happens. They probably will be sold more naked shares.

While I regroup and move ahead with changes to our operational business, I am also working behind the scenes on the details of what needs to be done to benefit the public part of our operation and to close out the shorts **(Short squeeze).**

After creating the Cigar Band Rings that took GNGR from a hand crafted line (the wildlife castings) to be able to use the same ring design and just change the theme and see if we can sell more rings of different designs to more people, would it work or just be a novelty?

I initially thought it would work on a small scale locally like craft shows and never be able to compete with the major jewelry companies on a global scale.

BOY, WAS I WRONG, and that's coming from someone who says they are right all the time? HA!

And I did it all alone in the garage and look at GNGR now. This first CIGAR band ring was made in 2021 less than 3 years ago and now 100's of designs are sold globally, **and this is just the beginning.**

No more factories, I cast in a large converted garage with a supply shipping area; a jeweler's bench area, a polishing area and vacuum casting area and the graphics and office is in one of the spare bedrooms. GNGR now has the BEST company structure! No partners, no need for funding (All orders are pre-paid), no overhead and no credit cards needed. **NOW American Express** and others want to issue me high value credit cards? **Really! FUCK THEM!**

My most popular sterling silver rings sell for $89 and $99 (with enamel). Each week new custom orders are placed and I design new styles to add to the line. The goal is to have 1,500 different licensed designs by mid-2025 that easily sell only 100 of each annually. The plan is to add 10 more new designs each week adding to the 1,500, 520 more designs to end up with 3,000 styles to choose from by 2026.

Selling only 100 rings of each of 1,500 designs for $89 is $13,350,000 (Then onto 350,000+ by 2026) and that is just rings. I do so much more and adding new designs every day. **Made in a USA Garage!**

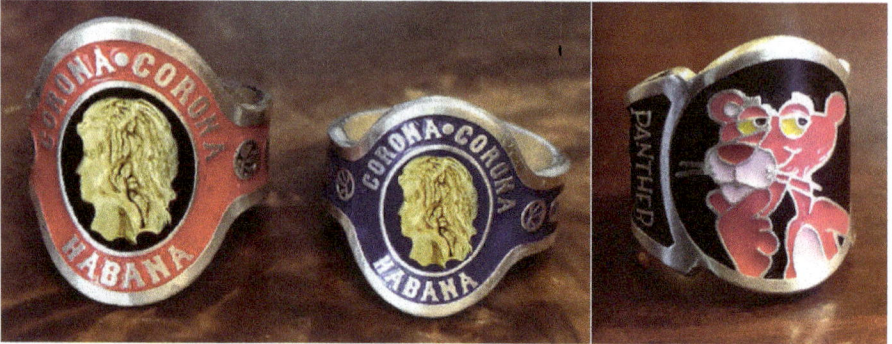

Sterling silver and 18k Gold cigar band rings...

Wildlife Foundation collectible jewelry

Change can be very very GOOD!

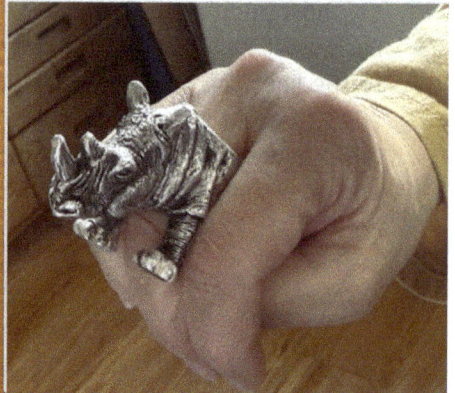

Corporate, Political, Custom and many new designs selling globally.

Getting lists of licensees for Hello Kitty, Peanuts, Mario Bros, Smurfs and much more to come. Custom orders and *repeat* business is happening every week. School rings is NEXT!

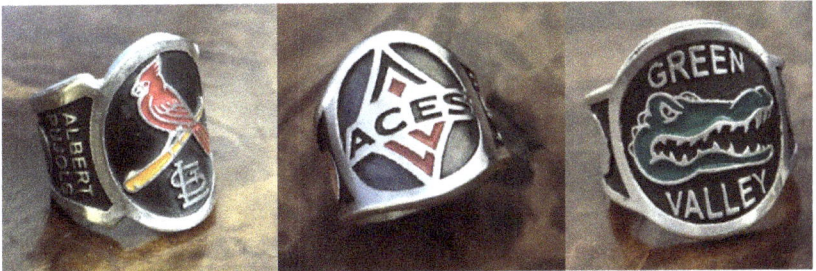

We may end up selling 1,000,000+ rings and pendants globally for $89! -
High quality, sterling silver, collectable and affordable to ALL!

Applying for the license for the GNGR NFL rings NO ONE ELSE HAS!

Now that the castings are all set up and global sales are a common event as well as more and more designs hitting the market, here are some benefits to changes to show why change is GOOD!

If you hate chocolate, you don't buy any.

If you hate Hello Kitty, you don't buy it but you may buy a Snoopy ring. If you hate snoopy, you may by a Batman ring and so on.

I guess if you have time, Google the OTC's 12,000+ tickers and click image and see what you find.

If you Google *"Gunther Grant Jewelry"* Click images is all you need to see we are here to stay and expand further into our already global brand.

The Wall Street Journal says it perfectly! NOT ME, the WSJ said it!

Every so often a stock breaks out and when it does, returns can be far ***greater than many Fortune 500 companies*** based not on hype but from a company with ***revenue and a product line*** and ends up the one ***rare needle in the haystack.***

GNGR is the needle in the haystack!

Investing in a "SURE THING" will result in limited returns that are not enough to support retirement lifestyle unless you have many millions to invest so the limited returns or interest i just enough to survive. Risky stocks like OTC penny stocks are highly risky but are ONLY risky i you are investing on hype from a company with no revenue and no product line. These risk stocks rarely if ever actually do what they claim. Every so often one of these risky stocks doe break out and when it does the returns can be far greater than many fortune 500 companie gains. The question is to know which OTC company will be that one rare needle in a haystac and when will it break out which depends on what the companies plans are, and when they ar introduced to investors.|

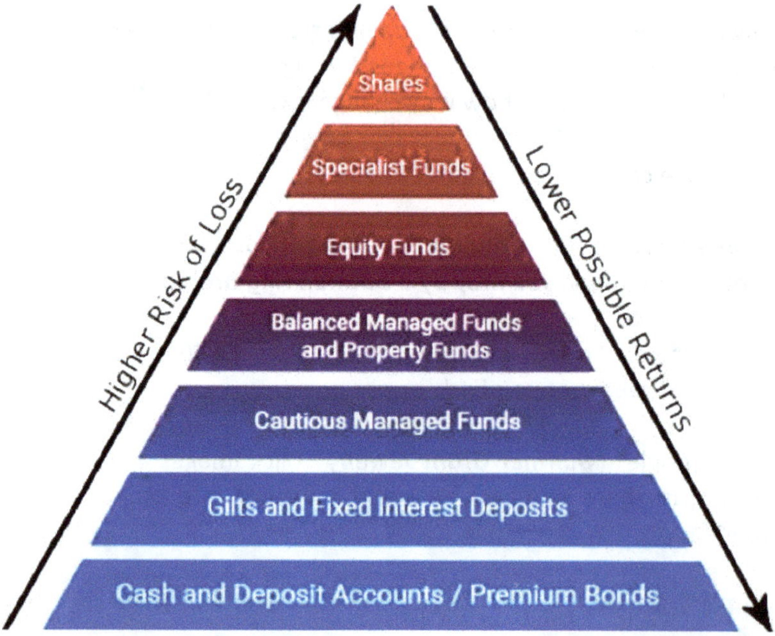

Shares
Specialist Funds
Equity Funds
Balanced Managed Funds and Property Funds
Cautious Managed Funds
Gilts and Fixed Interest Deposits
Cash and Deposit Accounts / Premium Bonds
Higher Risk of Loss
Lower Possible Returns

THE CLOCK IS TICKING

Most entrepreneurs will not risk change believing the plan they have will eventually work and any change will be the kiss of death when in fact, it could be the breath of life. *And the clock is ticking!*

You may have the BIG idea at age 9 or 90. You may think you have time but not as much as people think. *Better HURRY!*

Let's assume we all live to 100.

When you are born, the first 10 years are pretty much useless. You're either in diapers, being potty trained, learning to walk, jumping in puddles in the rain and still believe in Santa.

Then you have to get through grade school, Jr. high and high school that consist of pretty much being grounded or hanging out with friends on weekends. You may go to college (I did not) and spend 2, 4, 6 or more years getting an education or if you hit the pavement like I did, you spend the same years learning about life the REAL-world way.

Now you're maybe 25 years old and have either graduated or found what you think may be your future success with or without an education. Either way, 25 of those 100 years are GONE so you only have 75 left to get to 100. Don't be so sure.

Now let's figure no one wants to or even can work at age 100 and most will not want to struggle later on in life and you still want to be able to enjoy things and not just be pushed around in a wheelchair while drooling. So, we can figure people want to stop struggling at least by 65, maybe 70?

That narrows the time we have to make our mark and succeed between 25 and 65 that is only 40 years, not 100.

And, at age 25, you don't just jump into success. It takes maybe another 10 years to be able to say I'm going to be OK (at a job, being an entrepreneur or in some career). That narrows the time you need to make your mark from 35 to 65, is only 30 years.

Since we all need sleep and relaxation time, we can figure 12 hours a day is needed for tasks that have **NOTHING** to do with success or achieving a goal, (Sleeping, eating, watching TV, exercising) means the 30 years needed to achieve success is reduced by half.

That makes our true useful time to achieve our goals just 15 years. And that does not deduct for weekend time off **OR FALURE** along the way.

15 years is all the useful time we get. That means if you struggle for 7 years to make something happen (Entrepreneur or a solid career) it's HALF your working lifespan. If you bust your ass for 7 years and it's not working and you keep struggling another 7 years, TIMES UP.

I am 61 years old as of July 2023 (while I wrote this guide) I did not go to school for 6 years. I spent my years out in the real world learning while I also gave a career a chance when I worked for other confection companies that proved you can't rely on **ANYONE but yourself.**

I took my company public after I went on my own in business with NO partners. It was 2008, I was age 47 and Gunther Grant was issued a ticker. Since I'm 61 years old, I have 4 more years to make my mark as a success at 65 (even though I will work well beyond 65 year of age).

If you go to school and get a Masters degree and become a well paid professional earning (If you're VERY lucky) $100,000 annually and net $75,000 and you work from age 35 to 65 (30 years) and **save every penny**, $75,000 x 30 years is $2,250,000 when you retire and that is assuming you get a $100,000 a year job right out of college and save all the money.

No rent or food or a car just, living 30 years in your parent's basement, you will be able to save that much, **but not likely.**

I never went to school and never earned $100,000 for 30 years. What I did was roll the dice but I did not gamble because I was at least smart enough to know what I know and learned.

From age 35 to 61, I never saved and kept struggling and pushing ahead. BUT, between age 61 and 65, while very few MAY have $2,250,000, that is **highly unlikely**, the last 4 years from 61 to 65 is the end product of all you read about.

It could make my age 65 nest egg between $20,000,000 and YES possibly $8 billion or more because of the sales I am expanding on and the public shares I own in my public company.

Regardless of the stock or its price. I will still draw from sales of the products I make (That most sub penny stock CEO's cannot do) and I will end up with at least $2,000,000 at 65. The shares are a bonus and also the share's performance is long over due with my shareholders.

Shares make wealth and ***sales also make wealth***. Pump and dump stocks rely only on selling shares to make money but that's getting harder to do and private companies only rely on sales to make wealth.

GNGR HAS BOTH! So it's WIN WIN for my shareholders and me.

Since I never gave into the scheme or diluted the shares in my company I also maintained full control of GNGR. With only 108,000,000 shares in the float, I still own and control over 95% of the issued shares. My personal holdings are just over 700,000,000 restricted shares and 89,000,000 free trading shares.

With the plan to correct the illegal stock manipulation that was done to GNGR by the crooks and brokers, my focus is to have our low float shares rise back to even our starting point of $.10 cents per share and then move up higher. As mentioned, to move shares back to only 10 cents or even to $5 per share is much easier than to move a $2 share to $3,400 like Amazon.

Most of those OTC (Pink sheet) pump and dump company's CEO's know they have the same short life span to make something a success and when they're company failed, they know they have to make a move as well because their clock is also ticking. Most of them just sell out their investors and end up converting what was once their dream idea into some scam questionable pump and dump just to walk away with a few bucks by screwing over investors.

The short time we have to make money later on in life also shows why the schemer's and lizards get so angry and curse. Because their life's struggle is to keep finding some legit public company to infect and turn into some scheme so they can live for the moment and never think about their future or even care who gets hurt in the process.

GNGR MOVING FORWARD

Expand on what *IS working* and offer more designs every day to more buyers worldwide, simple and easy to do, for me at least.

And I'm DOING IT! Competitors are pissed, but I don't care!

A few months ago I launched the MAKE YOUR OWN RING option that allows anyone to make custom rings of whatever they want for one low price and no minimums. Here are just a few examples of some of the many custom ring orders we continuously receive.

We had the Bat, the Ball and the Glove when in confections yet no one wanted to play so now I'll go it alone like a winning game of solitaire. *Win alone or lose as a team? I choose to WIN alone.*

Many past and new lizards that keep contacting GNGR, call and just wait for me to stop talking so they can just say *"HOW MUCH FOR JUST THE PUBLIC VEHICLE"* when there is far more money in this from sales and share value than any reverse pump and dump.

I posses the knowhow and proven products that made Nestles and Hershey's look like amateurs. NOW I have castings that also make many other jewelry companies look like amateurs and it shows in their closed operations and self-inflicted falling share price. Then there are the jealous competitors and those that invested in them that lost most or all of their money.

I knew what I was doing in confections, and I know what I'm doing now with castings. Its knowing how all this works to any business.

This is work and also art and is incredibly exciting and fun to do.

Every new design I create from idea to art to finished product is so exciting, they find new homes on happy customers fingers worldwide.

And this change will allow me to not only regroup but also the castings grew faster than I planned and GNGR is now a trademarked global brand.

Here are just a few of the 1,000's of feedbacks for Gunther Grant. I show this to prove a point. Anyone reading this, I challenge anyone to find any penny stock ticker that has 1,000's (Not just 3) reviews from customers. HELL, someone find me a ticker that actually sells products that anyone can buy.

➕ I can't say enough good things here. Totally amazing custom rings. Seller takes your ideas and makes them into reality. Terrific communication, speedy shipping and one extremely happy customer. A++ Thank you for the beautiful rings. Will do business again.

Formula INDY ring set of (3) pre cast sale! USA (#256024132087)

➕ An AMAZING interaction. The seller/artist could not not have been better.

Gunther Grant sterling silver HUGE mouse ring Heavy USA (#266077509434)

➕ Excellent hand crafted-to-fit custom made quality jewelry piece! A true master at his craft! Thrilled with my purchase! Will buy from again! Thank you! 5 Star seller / artesian!

Sterling Silver Pink Floyd tribute ring USA! (PF2) (#264960536850)

➕ Another fantastic ring. Sized perfectly to my ring size. Amazing artistry. So talented. Very highly recommended. A++++++++++++++++++++++

2023 Wonka Bar limited edition sterling silver ring. USA (#255880880002)

➕ Absolutly beautiful! Beautiful craftsmanship. This is a ring of substance, not some cheap trinket mass produced overseas. My grandsons will fight over after I'm gone. Excellent communication and wonderful experience. This seller puts on a clinic in customer service!

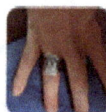

Mason past master 32 ring sterling silver 7-16 USA (#266393498313)

➕ Wow! I purchased the Grateful Dead ring in antiqued finish! I am totally impressed. I have #47 ring. Thanks for the nice note about being sorry for delay due tooth issue, but there is no need to be sorry as it arrived early. Mind you I am not the biggest Grateful Dead follower, but your ring design just drew me in and after some debate with myself I had to purchase, and I am so very glad I did. You sir are a craftsman. I highly recommend your work. Thanks! A Dead Fan in Ohio.

Grateful Dead skull BIG sterling silver ring Made in USA! (#266837556402)

➕ Second buy from this seller. He does excellent custom work. I highly recommend this seller!!!

sterling silver ring USA (#256335415402)

➕ Absolutely fantastic!!!!!!!! The workmanship is outstanding. It was well worth the price. The craftmanship and service are second to none.

INDYCAR series champion sterling silver ring. sizes 7-16 USA (#266207847482)

➕ Excellent seller. This is my 3rd purchase and I could not be happier. He is very easy to work with and creates amazing custom pieces.

Creature black lagoon sterling silver ring sizes 7-16 USA (#266030429145)

This change HAD to happen to keep GNGR alive.

There was NO other option except giving up.

Let's compare the differences between Confections and Castings.

<u>CHOCOLATES **vs.** CASTINGS</u>

Chocolates - 133 East Main Street NY cost me as much as $10,000 per month between rent, overhead, labor, insurance, health permits and other costs. 7 years cost me *$840,000 in overhead.*

Castings – no loans, no rent, no employees, no health permits, no funding needed. So far 7 years in NV has cost *$0 in overhead.*

$0 vs. $840,000, you see why change is good!

Chocolates - To make $14 million, I needed $4 million to finance production and was impossible to get.

Castings - To make $14 million, castings are all pre-paid, no funding needed.

Chocolates – If you don't like chocolate, you don't buy any.

NO SALE

Castings – If you don't like one design, buy another of our designs.

SOLD

Chocolates - To cover production we needed a funding source, then have to wait to be paid by those we wholesale to.

Castings – Again all orders pre-paid. No funding source needed.

Chocolates – Too costly to ship a fudge ($14 to ship a $12 fudge) and impossible to ship overseas

Castings – Affordable to ship a ring ($7 to ship a $96 item) and we are already shipping globally with ease.

The best part!

To make $2.5 million annually @ $7.00 net, we have to sell **357,000** of the same fudge with lots of overhead and funding.

To make $2.5 million annually @ $60.00 net, we have to sell **41,000** of many different design rings with no overhead and no funding needed.

Confection orders have to be shipped and delivered at the same time so we would have to store it as we make it. Confections can be risky with heat, aging or expiration and lots of storage.

Castings *are now* being shipped globally as they are sold individually pre-paid and never go bad or have expiration dates. NO storage.

Also to mention, when we made the confections and fudge, we did not have time on our side being a food product. After the year end Octoberfest event where we sold $20,000 in products in 2 days, we ended up with inventory that would not last until the next holiday and it had to be thrown away and cannot be reused to make new products.

That's MONEY in the garbage, plus a month's $10,000 labor and overhead paid out when it was made. And also paying $10,000 a month during the warm spring and summer months when no one buys chocolate. Winter profits covered the slow summer months.

We did manage until the credit card lines were taken away.

Just to note. The last Octoberfest event before I closed up the 133 New York location, the promoter decided to let another fudge person attend the show (His cousin) who he must have said Grant makes $20,000 so he let his cousin in the show instead of us. That October was a huge storm and flooded the event, wiping out all vendors inventory with zero sales. SO we dogged that bullet.

It was biblical I think...

To make the same $20,000, I only have to make 225 rings. With NO overhead and alone out of a garage in about 3 days, rain or shine, hot or cold, and all orders pre-paid, so the sale is *"PAID then MADE."*

We can also inventory silver bullion that is still worth the cash paid with no expiration date and can be resold, if needed.

You can't store raw chocolate because it would end up going bad and if you needed to sell it, no one would buy it. Confections had a loss of capital component while castings has a ZERO loss component.

Confections loss HIGH: Overhead, dead inventory expired or outdated.

Jewelry loss NONE: No overhead, Inventory is cash, no overhead, no waste.

So many factors, so many decisions, but you can see the major difference. *ANYWAY!*

With the change to castings, you can see this is the way to go and get GNGR back on track and also generate far more revenue and profits EASIER with less operational issues, costs and risks than with confections. NOT to mention the fudge *saboteurs.*

I also calculated that the space I use to cast has the smallest space (Footprint) with the greatest profits of most other business.

So how can I improve further on what is proven to be working already?

I even went FURTHER to make sure we have guaranteed success with NO possible way to fail by making sure:

Our sales are HORRIBLE. YES, HORRIBLE!

CRAPPY SALES CAN BE A HUGE SUCCESS

I decided to work my business backwards. I got rid of what cost me about $10,000 every month when we had our store and factory and when combined with no working capital and a public company under the status quo attack, I had to make changes fast.

Since it is SO EASY to have crappy sales, why not focus on what is easy? Crappy sales and make that a success. That is what I did.

I also worked my numbers backwards. Most people will say they want to make a product like potholders and sell 1,000,000 of them to make $1 on each to make $1,000,000, correct? Seems simple yet proven WRONG like the lady who mortgaged her house to get them into Sam's Club, and they did not sell.

When I created the first ring for the cigar club "Brothers of the Leaf", I ended up making and selling 50 rings at $89 each. That generated about $4,500 in sales and for a public company or even some small home-based craft that is crappy sales correct?

To make $1,000,000 on one design ring at $89, I have to sell 11,235 rings of the same design. That is not easy to do as proven by the **Brothers of the Leaf** ring. For one reason, they only have 200 members so it would be impossible to sell 11,235 rings to only 200 people.

Selling only 50 rings of more designs (at only $89 each) adds up to more than just trying to sell 11,235 of just one design. Fewer sales to more buyers' means LESS sales of each design to be a HUGE SUCCESS combined. Here are examples of our plan moving ahead.

Brothers of the Leaf - 50 rings @$89 is $4,450.

1,000 different designs - 50 rings of each is $4,450,000.

2,000 different designs - 50 rings of each is $8,900,000

SPORTS licensing -10,000 of each of 32 teams is $28,480,000

We know there are millions of fans for each of the 32 football teams. That's **a fact.** And, we know each team has a stadium that holds on average 50,000 fans.

I used CRAPPY sales figures that represent only 10% of the seats in each stadium as a means to gauge what will sell nationally to all fans, not just those who attend home games.

10% of 50,000 stadium seats is only 5,000 rings **per team** worldwide. If we use the die-hard fan base of only 3,000,000 per team, that's only 5,000 rings sold to 3,000,000 fans of each team.

1% of 3,000,000 is 30,000 rings, 5,000 rings are $1/6^{th}$ of a percent.

Selling 5,000 rings per team to fans is so low, it is 100% guaranteed CRAPPY sales. Plus, having them sold in team stores to boot!

5,000 rings @$89 is $445,000. Times 32 teams is **$14,240,000.**

30,000 fans (<1%) jump the sales figure to **$83,440,000.**

This same data passes on to **baseball, hockey, basketball, soccer, F1 INDY and all sports** (For starters).

And the process is the same. To make 1,000 rings all the same or 1,000 all different; there is no difference in the production process. Pull the molds from the files, make as many as needed, cast and ship. **DONE!**

I am working on more designs for licensing well-known brands and other clubs (Car, tennis, Motorcycle as well as Military rings and civic clubs like Masons), to name only a few. 100 clubs buying just 50 rings each is the same 5,000 of one football team. It all adds up!

1000's of different designs, 50 crappy sales of each ring design = HUGE SUCCESS! I LOVE CRAPPY SALES! If you didn't before reading this, I bet you do now. Sell less of more designs and it all adds UP!

Some say, how can GNGR make that many rings and keep up with orders? Leave that to me. I know what I am doing**. Order one and find out! HA!**

With the dramatic change to our company and plans moving ahead, the LIZARDS keep asking who is on our board of directors and how many employees do I have. They figure if they can get to my board of directors or inside investors, they can convince them to OUST ME!

So I send them this data.

Here is a list of our staff and titles.

CEO: Grant Newsteder

Manager: Website sales and marketing, Grant Newsteder

Manager: Customer service, Custom orders, Grant Newsteder

Manager: Graphic arts and sculpting, Grant Newsteder

Manager: Laser technician, and molds, Grant Newsteder

Manager: Metal casting division, Grant Newsteder

Manager: Sizing, numbering and catalog castings, Grant Newsteder

Manager: Final finishing, Antiquing or Enamel, Grant Newsteder

Manager: Inspection of finished casting, Grant Newsteder

Manager: Order and shipping department, Grant Newsteder

Manager: Drinking a cold beer after a long day, Grant Newsteder

Manager: returns & complaints: *NO ONE! We are 100% PERFECT!*

COMPANY OVERVIEW

No rent or overhead.

LOANS AND DEBT: NONE unless some crook decides AGAIN to forge my name and add HUGE debt so they can short GNGR illegally, then ends up DEAD! *2 down 2 more to go!*

GOING CONCERNS FOR GNGR:

None, we can't fail, we cannot lose. If we don't sell even ONE RING, it does not matter since we have NO overhead, NO debt, NO loans and NO bullshit intent that pump and dump scams use.

We are an operational global performing business that is growing FAST!

Samples of SPORTS rings with Fanatics logo cast in the mold. USA!

I added this data to the book to show just how easy this could be. I sent this proposal to **Justin Sun** the buyer of the $6.5 million dollar banana art with a **LEGIT PLAN THAT WOULD WORK!**

I cast the tangible Gunther Grant banana ring numbered edition 1 to 50,000. Justin adds in the NFT block chain on his end combined with my tangible editions.

We EASILY sell out the 50,000 NFT plus tangible asset for $2,000 each (that comes to $100,000,000) I also issue to Justin, 50,000,000 FREE TRADING shares in GNGR stock.

We split the $100,000,000 ($50,000,000 each). I use my share to reduce the float and force a short squeeze and move our ticker (GNGR) to the NYSE and not just **INTEND TO.**

Our shares, soon after moving to just $1 to maybe even $5 or higher, would give **Justin Sun** $250,000,000 in additional wealth based on the shares he can sell. **Yes, it can be that easy IF he responds to my offer.**

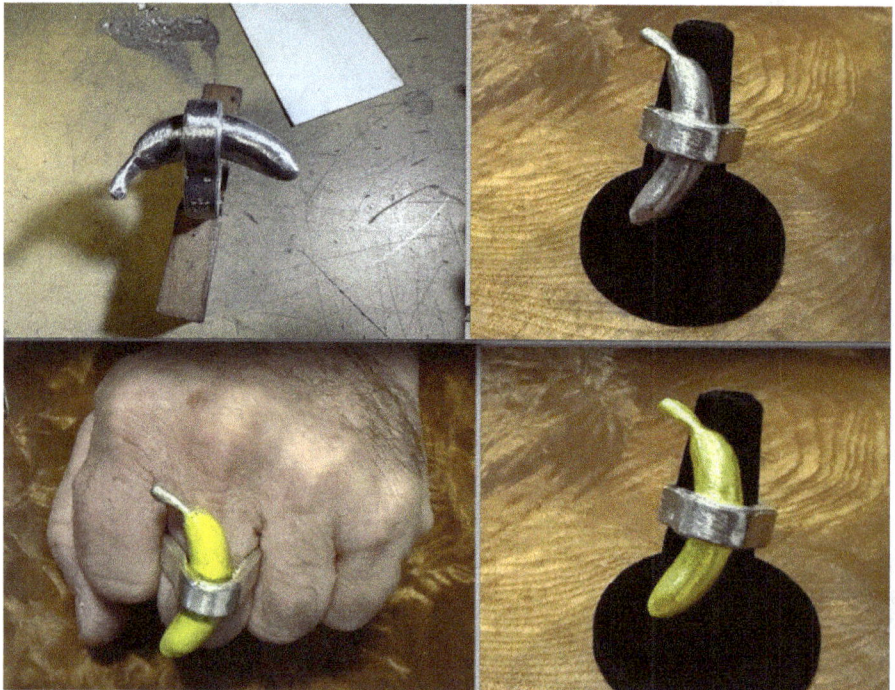

THE END GAME HAS JUST BEGUN

Now after all you read about, the status quo and why proven data over words and intent is imperative when making any business or investment decisions must be looked at under a microscope.

Do not invest without looking at proof, not just some fancy website or some mystery person saying you should invest fast before it's too late.

And, do not believe ANYONE who says they can make you a huge success and get you funding if it involves **paying them upfront fees**. It only takes about 2 minutes to see if a public company or financing lender is real or a scam. Most are not real.

Starting a business or taking your company public, my advice is to not spend money on things you do not need and stay in the garage as long as possible to keep costs down. If you are embarrassed or humiliated remember that many Fortune 500 companies started out the same way, so you would be in great company.

And those who do try and humiliate you, are others who are jealous or paid to hurt you, ignore them, they are idiots!

In most cases, individuals who make fun of or harass you are just too chicken shit to even get off the couch and get into the garage and make something work while the field lizards that search for a ticker to infect, are lazy and desperate and will never be fair or honest.

Everyone wants the end game to befit themselves with some taking others to the end or leaving them behind. That is based on the CEO and if their end game is to help or screw others in the process.

My share price is the **ONLY factor** that people associate GNGR with being a scam because most investors only use the share price to make that assumption, if you go public and you are not a schemer you will likely fall the same fate as I did. **But it can be corrected.**

I understand investor's frustrations. I am also frustrated but I am doing something about it and not quitting or selling out GNGR to some lizard. I am still here making GNGR a better company and have a plan to take others to the end game with me and not leave them behind.

Now it's me against the world and I also have the responsibility to my *(Pre-public)* investors as well as myself *(excluding the dirty ex cop)*. I have done the best I can to protect shareholders single handedly from pump and dump lizard predators and toxic funding scams and the time is now to move ahead smarter and knowing there are *far more* in the world that want to see GNGR and me personally fail than succeed.

It may seem to many that whatever *I did* went to HELL over the years and figure if it keeps happening, it must be my fault. **Not true.**

Whenever I entered *other's environments* that had control over the operations decisions or the company finances whose motives differed from the game plan or they failed to make changes to compete or expand, that is when things went south. In most cases those who failed to make changes ended up folding the business.

And let's not forget about partners and others I was in business with that if it were my fault, why did they end up folding or closing the businesses *after I left?* And yet here I am today, STILL operational.

Then there are the lawyers who work with the pump and dump schemes to put clients in harms way while others are banned from filing securities documents. Many lost their law license and many are facing charges while others have mysteriously died. All those you read about never made it to their end game because they failed or died before getting there.

I DID NOT DO THAT!

The outcome to all this is GNGR is alive and well after a major change to the business plan and a change in direction that let me expand what is working into a global brand while avoiding the detour signs as we head toward our end game and **WIN!**

I DID THAT

I guess it is my fault for TRUSTING PEOPLE. But, we are still here while most of them are not, and I don't trust many anymore.

Being a LEGIT valid company means we are in a very small group of the 12,500 listed public OTC tickers *not* considered a pump and dump.

That is a very exclusive club to be in.

GNGR has been public since 2008, and as a company many years before that and no one cared if we made fudge or confections. It was only **after being public** that lizards, brokers and crooked lawyers only objective was to get GNGR to sell the ticker or force me to close the business to hide their stock fraud that will soon be exposed.

Most people I have been associated with chose to destroy themselves out of greed, spite or just plain being bad at business, or was just a schemer trying to make some end game cash by screwing others. Some who **tried (and failed)** to STOP GNGR after we became publicly traded are still trapped in living purgatory with no end game plan other than to stay out of jail or out of the morgue.

I give them a D- for effort and an F for the outcome.

The pump and dumps that have a $500,000,000 website plan that was never an operational company to begin with, capitalize on the initial stages of the game knowing full well the INTENT end game success is not part of the plan because the actual plan never gets off the website and into reality.

They end the game mid-play and move to another game before the previous one ends in disaster. That is why they focus on making a quick scheme dime in a week vs. an honest $1 over 5 years.

I decided our end game will be epic but it takes time and also proves that a change IS part of the end game process. Change to your company, your investment strategy and if you become a public company, a change to the status quo.

IF Amazon (just books), Wrigley's (just soap), Coke-a-Cola (just coke) even ME (Gunther Grant) and 1,000's of other companies that succeeded did not make changes, they would have all vanished.

Billionaires lose millions on bad decisions the same way a 99% investor loses $500 on a bad decision. Being rich doesn't mean you are smart and being smart does not make you rich. Hard work, be open to change, watch your back, trust no one and take risks for the better is what is key to making a small success into a global brand.

The wealthy investors I wrote about that lost all their capital or a good chunk of it, also need to change and diversify their investments and as they say: DO NOT bury your eggs in one basket like those that invested in Signet jewelry, Kingold jewelry, CRUMBS bakery and many other brands that failed or suffered irreparable damage.

If things are not working, look closer at the markets; don't fall for the greed factor or those who ask you for money to secure capital. Look at the data, not what others tell you or a fake website that has NOTHING to do with an end game other than to take your money and vanish.

NO MORE will I rely on anyone but my customers to better my future. Since I am taking care of my customers, they are taking care of GNGR, plain and simple.

If I wanted to be a scam, I would have continued to dump shares to the crook attorney so he can dump 4 billion to the float and he would make $12,000,000 and I would make $2,000,000, then close down the company and ticker. And this guide would never have been written.

The end game is not hard to do if you're not lazy and stay focused and stay sharp. The benefit to change and a well-planned end game is, the company and shares can be worth far more than any pump and dump scam that sells shares cheap then vanish.

I created our successful cigar band rings just 3 years ago and after the change that started back in NY with a half bottle of scotch, $3 in the bank and a crazy idea to put a silver coin in the fudge, there was no turning back to confections, especially with saboteurs in our midst.

I am not worried about what ANYONE thinks about my garage and me. I am not wasting money on a physical location just to impress investors. *I am focused 100% on impressing my CUSTOMERS!*

Impress the customers because that is ***ALL that matters.*** If happy customers don't care or even know you operate out of a garage, why worry about what ***non-customers*** think? **RIGHT!**

I forged ahead having been hammered as a kid and as an adult, even before starting out in business and somehow, I made it here.

There is still time for many, yet time is not infinite. That is a fact and many are using that precious time to hope and pray their private or public company succeeds or the stocks they buy makes them rich.

If your end game ends up with a small house paid off with $50,000 saved and collect Social Security (If it's still available when you retire) your end game may not be so bad after all. You do not need lots of money to win the end game even if you just worked a regular job and never owned a business. Just don't live above your means.

Winning can be easy but playing the game can be hard and take decades. If you play chess for hours it's the one move that wins the game but it also takes the previous hours to see and react and plan ahead to avoid failure. *Yes I am a great chess player.*

That is why many CEOs give into the schemes; they are desperate and have no other options but mostly because they *gave up.*

With $3 when the final blow hit GNGR with confections and before casting our first bat pendant, I was about to just give up and just accept GNGR was finished. When I went from $3 to $6,000 after that first silver bat was cast, I knew something positive was on the horizon and also that this could benefit those who invested in my company.

If I took one of those scheme deals offered, GNGR would be no more and that means anyone who owns shares would end up with nothing. The lizards, lawyers and most brokers believed I was so desperate I will give into the status quo because of the damage they did to GNGR believing it is uncorrectable. *BOY, WERE THEY WRONG!*

They offer a few bucks they know can help the CEO and never look at what that CEO accomplished or what the company *IS actually doing*. They don't like legitimacy, they just want to dump billions of scam shares to suckers and move on. Like locusts they come, eat and leave.

I had many calls over the years that say *they LOVE the great things GNGR is doing* and they want to invest (For a fee, I'm sure). Or they are a lizard or brokers in disguise. Over 100 times getting these calls, I say to them *"So what is it you think GNGR does that is so great?"* Then they say, "HOLD ON, what is your website?" They say that because they lie and don't know what we do, yet they say they LOVE what GNGR is doing.

I usually just hang up because it's just another lizard, another toxic death spiral or another scammer trying to get hold of our ticker or a lying investor to get me to pre-pay $5,000 to get non-existent capital.

The end game is what you make it. Rich or even below middle class comfortable, it's better than ending up in jail or the morgue.

If your car is not a Rolls Royce but a BUICK, and it gets you to the store for groceries or to the post office to send items you sold to customers you made in the garage, that makes you better than most who believe that is beneath them. Those who condemn you for that are IDIOTS!

Making changes and avoiding the status quo will be key when starting a business, going public or when investing in public stocks. And remember, stock schemers, crooked lawyers, liars and lizards are more common than you will ever realize.

Stay sharp. The more convincing or honest others may seem could just be a scammer that is better at conning you than others.

NO ONE, no matter how convincing, can get your money or your company unless you give it to them. Remember that because... It's easier to make a dishonest dime than an honest dollar.

If some who read this take at least some of the advice to limit losses and also prevent the panic decisions you will regret, you have just made a huge jump into a better end game situation.

Regulations and rules change almost daily, you have to keep up on them and USE them to your advantage. You don't need an education to become a billionaire and you don't need to panic if you are aware, ahead of time, how to correct the status quo in your favor.

This guide shows past data about what I said would happen. It also is relevant moving ahead to existing schemes and those not yet even in play and what will happen.

The status quo is the same then, now and in the future.

Other than the NEEDLE In the haystack, if it's too good to be true, it's almost always a scam, and if you are the needle in the haystack (Like I am) achieving success will not be easy with all the schemers that want nothing more than to take your money and your legitimacy.

When it comes to truly understanding why this happens, people have to know that an armed street crook that goes to jail for 10 years for robbing $1000 from McDonalds could have just worked there and made $400,000 over the same 10 years they spend in jail. CRAZY!

Same with stock schemes who refuse to make things work over time that can generate more wealth than a fast buck on some stock scam.

Lizards can never keep making money on the same pump and dump long term so they keep introducing NEW HOT stocks to the 99%.

And the 99% investors who also refuse to take a position in a long-term sure thing continue to spend $100 over and over believing that one ticker will blossom to $1,000,000 in a month.

Crooks, scammers and greed rarely ever work in the long run. That is why the FAST dime in a day from scammers ends up costing the 99% investors $300,000,000 each trading day!

If anyone reading this guide applies what they have read not only to the stock markets or investing but also when seeking capital or starting a business or if you already have an existing operational business: Focus first on what is **predictable** before making costly decisions that make those decisions **preventable.**

Always look ahead but also look behind over your shoulder because someone who does not have your best interests in mind is always watching you and they are right on your heels.

Always remember that at any time at any place there will always be someone to take your cash legally or illegally. A pickpocket on vacation or a FORBES 500 listed billionaire.

TRUST NO ONE, Sad to say.

I may also write a few follow up books and guides on this and many other subjects that are to educate, not entertain.

My initial goal of this guide was to bring to light how this works and why it doesn't **and against great odds, how to correct it and make it work.**

This guide does NOT end here for you or me!

Anyone with questions can email me from the **Contact Us** page from the GUGR website. I will post questions and answers on the SECURITIES page link. Or, if you are a financial or market professional that wants to read my SHORT SQUEEZE plan or anyone interested in seeing what we do can just visit us at:

www.GUGR.com

If this guide saves even ONE SOUL, it's all worth it.

Grant Newsteder

Me, at the Long Island train station (2015), headed to NY City to testify before the SEC Legal Committee to defend our company from the criminal lawyers activity to show we had no part of his fraud, and the SEC letter with the outcome of the investigation.

UNITED STATES
SECURITIES AND EXCHANGE COMMISSION
NEW YORK REGIONAL OFFICE
200 VESEY STREET
ROOM 400
NEW YORK, NEW YORK 10281-1022

WRITER'S DIRECT DIAL LINE
MICHAEL D. PALEY, ESQ.
(212) 336-0145
PaleyM@sec.gov

March 25, 2016

By Email
Gunther Grant, Inc.
Attn: Mr. Grant Newsteder
133 East Main St.
East Islip, NY 11730

Re: **In the Matter of Gunther Grant, Inc (NY-8825)**

Dear Mr. Newsteder:

We have concluded the investigation as to Gunther Grant, Inc. Based on the information we have as of this date, we do not intend to recommend an enforcement action by the Commission against Gunther Grant, Inc. We are providing this notice under the guidelines set out in the final paragraph of Securities Act Release No. 5310.

Sincerely,

Michael D. Paley
Assistant Regional Director

305

This book is not a solicitation to buy or sell any securities. All data about the market, competitors and companies depicted are based on personal contact, emails and publicly available data.

The ideas and opinions of the author are based on true and historical facts as well as personal direct experiences mentioned in this book. This book is to bring to light, issues and events and facts as to how the market works in general and what needs to be done to correct it.

As laws and regulations change, so, too, will the data in this book be either correct or obsolete depending on changes to current or past laws and regulations prior to publishing or in the past events mentioned in this book. This book could have easily been 2500 pages long with even more data, experiences and events and a follow up book(s) may be needed to further bring to light *how it works and why it doesn't and how to correct it.*

www.ingramcontent.com/pod-product-compliance
Lightning Source LLC
Chambersburg PA
CBHW061137220326
41599CB00025B/4263

9 798998 624407